Scotland:
An Archaeological Guide
from earliest times
to the twelfth century A.D.

Euan W. MacKie

Euan MacKie, after a stimulating general introduction, describes the major archaeological monuments and sites by geographical zones so that visitors will find a succession of sites of many kinds in each area, described in the order they are encountered on the ground. Of particular interest are the information on antiquities which have not received much attention in the standard works on Scotland—such as the Early Christian remains and the Pictish stones—and the new theories about the astronomical function of some prehistoric standing stones.

The Guide is designed to help the appreciation of Scotland's pre-history and early history as a continuous story and also to show how the study of the Roman and later sites—whose origin and function are known from written records—may help towards a better understanding of prehistoric sites.

Euan MacKie is Assistant Keeper (Archaeological and Anthro
at the Hunterian Mu
of Glasgow. After a s
in Central America,
mainly into the Iron
Scotland, and more
aeological implications of Professor Thom s
astronomical theories about the stone circles.

Scotland : An Archaeological Guide

Archaeological Guides
General Editor: GLYN DANIEL

Persia   Sylvia A. Matheson
Southern Italy   Margaret Guido
Central Italy   R. F. Paget
Southern England   James Dyer
Wales   Christopher Houlder

Scotland:
An Archaeological Guide

from earliest times to the 12th century A.D.

Euan W. MacKie

NOYES PRESS
Noyes Building
Park Ridge, New Jersey 07656, USA

Copyright © 1975 by Euan W. MacKie
Library of Congress Catalog Card Number: 74-32286
ISBN: 0-8155-5034-0
Printed in Great Britain

Published in the United States by
NOYES PRESS
Noyes Building
Park Ridge, New Jersey 07656

for Rona

Beneath this mound to the north is Cumhall's grandson,
whose sword was hard; the white-toothed son of the
daughter of Dearg, he uttered no rude word in wrath.

Beneath this mound to the south is Duibhne's grandson,
whose skin was like blossom; to none did he refuse
his store, not mild was his hand in battle.

Beneath this mound to the east is Osgar, good in fame
and deed; Clan Morna, though good men, he held of no
account.

Beneath this mound to the west is the lad whom women
loved; Rónán's son, thanked by poets, is beneath this
mound to the west.

Beneath this mound beside me is Conan, who won all
love, beneath this mound beside me.

Book of the Dean of Lismore,
ed. Neil Ross, Edinburgh, 1939

Acknowledgements

For preparing the line drawings and for taking most of the photographs for this book I am greatly indebted to Mr Nicholas H. Hawley and for typing the manuscript to Mrs E. Mackenzie. Plates 38 and 42-48 are Crown copyright and are reproduced with the kind permission of the Department of the Environment. Plate 21 is reproduced through the kindness of Mr Douglas Hague. (Plates 19, 20 and 49 are the author's photographs.) I thank Mr Andrew Selkirk, editor of *Current Archaeology*, and Dr John Corcoran for permission to use the block for pl. 41. Many of the site plans are based on originals published by the Royal Commission on the Ancient and Historical Monuments of Scotland and I am grateful to the Commission for permission to use these. I thank the Society of Antiquaries of Scotland for permission to re-draw the plans used in Figs. 12, 17, 20 and 21, the Glasgow Archaeological Society for permission to reproduce the material used in Fig. 19, Miss Audrey Henshall for permission to use her plans as a basis for Figs. 34 and 40, Professor A. Thom for the use of his own plans in Figs. 8, 9, 25 and 27 and Professor Anne S. Robertson for allowing me to use her map of Roman Scotland as a basis for Fig. 3. Dr A. E. Roy kindly let me use his unpublished plan of the Machrie Moor stone circles in Fig. 16 and I thank the Iona Trust for permission to incorporate copyright plans in Fig. 23, and also the Department of the Environment for allowing me to use published plans in Figs. 5 and 36.

I am very grateful to Mr Alastair Mack for much useful information about the present location of Pictish stones, to Mr W. Senior for telling me about the anvil carving at Ring of Brodgar and to Mr Ian Fisher for information about the present arrangement of the Iona antiquities. Mr Eric Talbot was kind enough to read and advise on the sections dealing with post-Roman sites. However any mistakes or controversial interpretations are the responsibility of the author who will welcome any comments about the book.

Contents

2. South-west Scotland

3. South-east Scotland

4. Central Scotland

5. Western Scotland and the Western Islands

6. North-east Scotland

7. Northern Scotland

8. The Orkney Isles

9. The Shetland Isles

Illustrations

13

LINE ILLUSTRATIONS

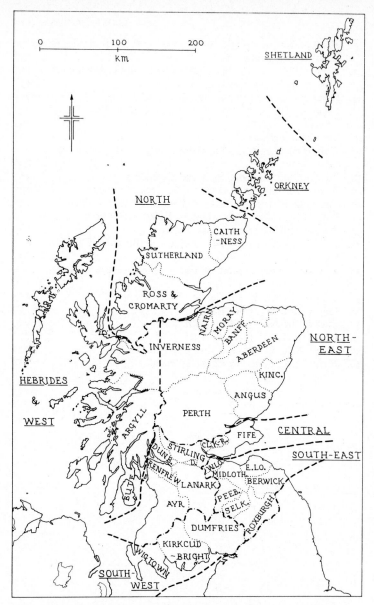

Fig. 1. Map of Scotland showing the counties and major archaeological zones described: the latter correspond to the chapters and are named in the same way. Scale 1:470,000.

1 · Introduction

1. ARRANGEMENT AND SCOPE

This guide is arranged by geographical zones, Scotland being divided for this purpose into eight regions (Fig. 1). These are the South-west, South-east, Central, Western (including the Hebridean), North-east and Northern zones and the Orkney and Shetland islands. A chapter is devoted to each zone and subdivisions within these are mostly by counties. The basic subdivision within counties is the route or area and in these the archaeological sites are described in the order they are encountered. Some roads extend through several counties and in these cases indications are given of where the description of the route continues. Throughout the guide the symbol * means that the author has visited the site and + indicates that the site is under the guardianship of the Department of the Environment.

The guide describes a selection of the most important and best-preserved structures dating from the 4th millennium B.C. down to the onset of feudalism in Scotland in the 12th century A.D. Because of this wide range only a limited number of each type are described in a given area. The work is thus aimed not at those with specialised archaeological interests—who will inevitably feel that many excellent sites have been left out—but rather at those who wish to see representative examples of the physical remains of the entire pre-Medieval history of the country. There are already a number of guide-books dealing with prehistoric Scotland (p. 286) but by contrast the Roman, Early Christian and Early Medieval monuments are less well known through such books. Yet of course the prehistory and history of Scotland were a continuous story and their appreciation as a whole demands a comparable, wide-ranging interest from the archaeologically inclined tourist.

There is another, more specific reason for regarding the post-Roman remains with special interest. Whatever may be said to the contrary by the more extreme advocates of the exclusiveness and independence of archaeological evidence, the simple fact is that the interpretation of prehistoric archaeological remains can only be done by analogy with living or historically recorded societies and their material cultures. The study of Roman and post-Roman remains, their origin and evolution, may thus shed much light on the mute monuments of earlier times simply because their origins, function and history are in many cases known from historical records. Our understanding of the way in which the Christian churches appeared and evolved, for example (p. 36 below) could have relevance for the problem of the origin and function of the Neolithic chambered tombs. Similarly the situation which produced the Norman mottes and early stone castles could help our understanding of the hillforts, brochs and duns of the Iron Age. An additional point is that the post-Roman populations were genetically and culturally related by descent to those of prehistoric times so that analogies drawn between the two eras should be on fairly firm ground. This is not the case with primitive peoples in other parts of the world—with whom analogies are sometimes drawn by archaeologists—whose nature, origins and evolution have had no direct connection with Britain at any time save in the most remote past.

Maps and distances

The location of the sites in this book is defined in terms of the grid system on the Ordnance Survey's maps, each site being given its six-figure grid reference. Short verbal descriptions of their situations are also supplied. Ideally sites away from the main roads should be sought with the aid of the Ordnance Survey's 1 inch to 1 mile maps (scale 1 : 63,360) but since there are some 74 of these covering Scotland this may not always be practicable. The eight quarter-inch maps in the same series (scale 1 : 250,000) are excellent and grid references can be plotted on these quite accurately: with them and the aid of the verbal descriptions most of the sites should be found easily.

The Ordnance Survey has also produced some excellent archaeological maps, the one of the Antonine wall (scale 1 : 25,000) being particularly useful to users of this book (there is also one of Hadrian's Wall). There are also maps of Dark Age and Monastic Britain (1 : 1,000,000 and 1 : 625,000 respectively) but it should be remembered that these depict all available information and not just that which is visible on the ground. The 1 inch to 10 mile map of Ancient Britain (North Sheet) (scale 1 : 625,000) is particularly useful and many of the sites mentioned here are marked on it. A map of Roman Britain is available (scale 1 : 1,000,000). Bartholomew are producing a series of useful maps showing ancient monuments and those for South-east and South-west Scotland are published. Many of the sites described in this book are marked on them. The Highlands and Islands Development Board has produced a comprehensive guide to travel services in highland Scotland (*Getting around the highlands and islands*) which is well worth the 20p it cost in 1974.

A better understanding of why early settlements were located where they were can sometimes be obtained by consulting a geological map. The Geological Survey has a useful map of the solid geology of Scotland at a scale 1 inch to 10 miles (1 : 625,000) which can be recommended.

Throughout the text distances and measurements are given in the metric system: conversion tables are on p. 285 and these include one for megalithic yards.

It is advisable to carry a compass on the expeditions.

Place-names

The Gaelic and Norse place-names of Scotland preserve a vast amount of information about the early settlements and about the nature of many ancient sites. The Ordnance Survey has published an excellent booklet containing lists of the commonest place-names encountered on the Ordnance Survey maps, with a guide to pronunciation, which all interested in the past should carry with them on archaeological explorations.

Private property

Unless the monuments are under the guardianship of the Department of the Environment they are likely to be on private land. There is a minor difference between the laws of trespass of Scotland and England, the former being marginally more lenient, but it is not enough to make any practical difference. In any case the advantages to present and future archaeological tourists in keeping on good terms with farmers and landowners are obvious and it is always advisable to ask permission to visit sites which are on farmland or enclosed ground. It goes almost without saying that great care should be taken to avoid damaging the ancient buildings which constitute the rapidly vanishing primary evidence of man's past.

2. APPRECIATING THE MONUMENTS

Appreciation and understanding of the physical relics of the past—

particularly the large buildings—can be enhanced in several ways. In the first place it is of course essential to have some knowledge of the age in which the structures were made, and to that end most of this chapter is devoted to a brief account of some of the major developments in Scotland between 4000 B.C. and A.D. 1200. Secondly it should be realised that when one is looking at non-domestic structures (in which category fall most of the sites described in this book) one is probably looking at relics of the activities of specialised groups or classes within the ancient population. Normally archaeologists tend to assume that the pottery and other artefacts found represent the material culture of the population as a whole, and in some cases this is true. However, the existence of massive or sophisticated, non-domestic wooden, stone and earthen structures—like brochs, wheelhouses, hillforts, henge monuments, barrows, cairns, churches, castles and sculptured stones—is as likely, if not more so, to indicate the activities of specialised and skilled groups of people. The same almost certainly applies to the products of craftsmen in metal and sometimes to pottery too. Obvious examples from proto-historical and historical times are legion. The Christian churches—from the earliest wooden chapels to the great Gothic cathedrals—were built for religious orders intrusive in the 5th and 6th centuries and again in Early Medieval times. All major fortifications in such periods were built at the behest of powerful ruling groups, either to defend a territory against invasion or to hold down a newly subjected population. Equally significant is the fact that the steady increase in the architectural sophistication of churches and defence works, and in the art of decorative sculpture, was due to professional builders, architects and craftsmen who perfected and handed on their skills under the patronage of wealthy individuals or groups. It is difficult to believe that things were fundamentally different in prehistoric times.

In summary, a stratified society—containing specialised classes following full-time non-agricultural pursuits—is much more likely to produce monumental structures and complex technologies than a simple, homogeneous, rural, peasant population. It seems to me that, in viewing the archaeological remains of Scotland, it is only rarely likely that one is looking at the creations of the mass of the rural population.

One further thought is relevant when looking at prehistoric and early historic structures and this is that they must be judged in terms of the technology of the age which produced them and not against the products of later ages. This may seem obvious but in fact it is difficult to look at ancient structures—prehistoric ones in particular—without subconsciously judging them as 'crude' or 'primitive' against the far more sophisticated architecture of the Roman and historical periods. Yet the chambered cairns, for example, certainly represent the largest free-standing buildings that Early Neolithic technology could produce; and when the building material was particularly good—as in Orkney and Caithness—the Neolithic architects became positively inspired. Such huge, hollow cairns must have excited as much wonder and admiration among the Neolithic rural population of the time as the great Romanesque and Gothic cathedrals and abbeys did among the Medieval peasantry or the Apollo spacecraft do among today's man-in-the-street. The best of structures of each kind in each age—Maes Howe and the stalled cairns (p. 235), the broch of Mousa (p. 272), the Ruthwell cross (p. 42), Melrose Abbey (p. 83) represent the summit of technological and artistic achievement in their time and should be judged as such.

It may be that massive structures of earth, wood or stone have always performed a psychological service for recently settled societies by symbolising through their size and permanence both a secure social order and the durability of the faiths and institutions which raised them. By altering the landscape with a tumulus, a broch or a cathedral—raised with a huge communal effort—men put down roots, emphasise the integration of their society and forge visible links with the past for future generations.

3. AN OUTLINE OF SCOTLAND'S PAST

This summary of Scotland's prehistory and early history is inevitably geared to the material remains. Most of it therefore is likely to be an account of the activities of special groups within ancient societies, particularly those which constructed massive buildings. Descriptions of artefacts and archaeological cultures and of the general historical background are omitted save where they are directly relevant to the problem of the structures themselves. The interested reader is referred to the bibliography (p. 286) for more general and comprehensive accounts of Scotland's past. A simplified chronological chart is included (Fig. 2).

Chronology and dating systems

The earliest historically dated event in Scotland is the first arrival of the Roman army at about A.D. 80 (p. 29 below). The occurrence thereafter of fragments of well-dated Roman artefacts on native sites throughout Scotland provides an extremely valuable fixed chronological horizon from which it is possible to work forwards and backwards to a limited extent. Some structures and objects of the period A.D. 300–1000 can be approximately dated with the aid of the few texts and by their links with firmer chronologies elsewhere, but not until the 12th century is the chronology of Scotland's ancient monuments on firm ground. Similarly approximate dates for the period from about 700 B.C. to the Roman invasions can sometimes be given to artefacts through their distant, indirect and tenuous connections with the historical chronologies of Greece and Rome, but what these dates mean for the structures with which the objects concerned are found is not always clear.

Radiocarbon (C-14) dating is now the mainstay of the prehistoric archaeologist's chronological system and is proving of great help in the 1st millennium A.D. also. Essentially the technique determines the time of death of a living organism—a fragment of a tree, a bone, shell or a heap of grain—and thereafter the meaning of this date for the structure or layer with which the organism was associated has to be estimated. For example a C-14 date for a fragment of a burnt wooden roof beam will give a date for the construction of that roof (or, more precisely, the cutting of that beam) and not for its burning.

Recently the inherent accuracy of C-14 dating has been tested in Arizona by using fragments of long sequences of tree-rings whose age is known to within a few years back to about 5300 B.C. Thus the C-14 date of a piece of this wood can be compared directly with its real age. In this way it has been discovered that C-14 dates before about 500 B.C. are too young by an amount which increases with age; in the 5th millennium B.C. the discrepancy amounts to eight hundred years. An approximate comparison between radiocarbon dates and real year dates is given in the chronological chart (Fig. 2). By the same means C-14 dates can be converted fairly easily into calendar dates and it is clearly important to distinguish which type of chronology is being used. Throughout this book dates in real calendar years are given as B.C. or A.D. while radiocarbon dates, or dates based on them, are given as b.c. or a.d. Thus the beginning of the Neolithic period in Scotland can be dated either at about 3500 b.c. or about 4200 B.C., radiocarbon dates for that era being about seven hundred years too young.

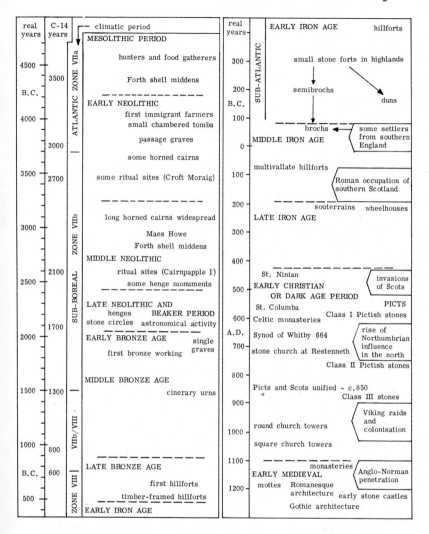

real years	C-14 years	climatic period	

MESOLITHIC PERIOD

ATLANTIC ZONE VIIa

4500 — 3500 — 3000
B.C.

hunters and food gatherers

Forth shell middens

EARLY NEOLITHIC

4000 —

first immigrant farmers
small chambered tombs

passage graves

some horned cairns

3500 — 2700

some ritual sites (Croft Moraig)

ZONE VIIb

3000 —

long horned cairns widespread

Maes Howe

Forth shell middens

MIDDLE NEOLITHIC

2500 — 2100

SUB-BOREAL

ritual sites (Cairnpapple I)
some henge monuments

LATE NEOLITHIC AND
  henges   BEAKER PERIOD
stone circles astronomical activity

1700

2000 —

EARLY BRONZE AGE   single
first bronze working graves

MIDDLE BRONZE AGE

1500 — 1300

cinerary urns

VIIb/VIII

1000 — 800

LATE BRONZE AGE

B.C. 600

VIIb/VIII

ZONE VIII

first hillforts

500 —

timber-framed hillforts

EARLY IRON AGE

EARLY IRON AGE   hillforts

SUB-ATLANTIC

real years

300 — 200 — 100
B.C.

small stone forts in highlands

semibrochs

duns

0

brochs

some settlers
from southern
England

MIDDLE IRON AGE

100 —

multivallate hillforts

Roman occupation of
southern Scotland

200 —

souterrains   wheelhouses

LATE IRON AGE

300 — 400 —

500 —

St. Ninian

EARLY CHRISTIAN
OR DARK AGE PERIOD

invasions
of Scots

PICTS

600 —

St. Columba

Celtic monasteries

Class I Pictish stones

A.D.

700 —

Synod of Whitby 664

stone church at Restenneth

rise of
Northumbrian
influence
in the north

Class II Pictish stones

800 —

900 —

Picts and Scots unified - c.850

Class III stones

1000 —

round church towers

Viking raids
and
colonisation

square church towers

1100 —

monasteries

EARLY MEDIEVAL

Anglo-Norman
penetration

1200 —

mottes   Romanesque
architecture   early stone castles

Gothic architecture

Fig. 2. Chronological chart of Scottish prehistory and early history from 4500 B.C. to the 13th century A.D. Straight horizontal lines represent the boundaries between periods.

Earliest times: the Mesolithic period

The ice sheets of the Pleistocene period finally retreated from Scotland during the 9th millennium b.c. and left the country open for colonisation by man. The earliest inhabitants seem to have arrived at about 6000 b.c. (in Fife) but, as these Mesolithic people were nomadic hunters and fishers, they left few obvious traces. The great shell middens on the coasts of Argyll and the Firth of Forth (p. 100), and occasional dense concentrations of flints as at Dryburgh (p. 90), are the clearest traces but the large numbers of shells and flints do not necessarily indicate a large population. It has been estimated that there were perhaps only about fifty people in Scotland at that time!

The natural environment, particularly the level of the ocean, also changed during the Mesolithic and later periods. Raised beaches and dry sea beds can be clearly seen in places like Kintyre and the Forth valley (pp. 132 and 114). The climate, also, altered several times and it must always be remembered that six thousand years ago the lower parts of Scotland were covered with dense forests. These have slowly been removed by man and nature and replaced by the peat bogs and bare moorland which are such a striking feature of the country now.

The Early Neolithic period (about 4200–2300 B.C.)

The first immigrant, stone-using farmers arrived in the British Isles by sea from the continent soon after about 4200 B.C. bringing with them grain, domestic sheep and cattle. The major change in economy which thus took place—from nomadic food gathering to settled farming—probably had two important results. The first was that the regular and expandable food supply provided by farming resulted in a steady increase in population which has gone on ever since. The second was that even the Early Neolithic farming economy was efficient enough to produce a surplus of food which was occasionally used to support many people working on large building projects for many months. The chambered cairns of this period are the oldest large stone structures in Britain and the earliest of them may have been built not long after the Neolithic colonists arrived (p. 128). Two types of chambered cairns have been distinguished: round ones with round central chambers—known as 'passage graves'—and long, often horned cairns with a long gallery-like chamber running in from one end. However, in recent years it has become clear that many of these long, horned cairns contain small round passage graves within them, that there was in fact a development and enlargement of these massive stone buildings as in the later churches (p. 36). The fact that burials are consistently found in these chambered cairns has understandably led to the assumption that they were built as collective tombs and, when the Neolithic period was thought to have lasted only two or three centuries, it seemed possible that they were communal graves for whole communities. Now that the period is known to have lasted perhaps two thousand years it seems unlikely that more than a select few people were entitled to such burial and possible that the cairns may have served also as the focus of religious ritual over many generations. The widespread conversion of groups of small round cairns into single, massive, long horned cairns could suggest some organised religious change. (Chapters 7 and 8.)

The Late Neolithic and Early Bronze Ages
(about 2300–1600 B.C.)

By the middle of the Neolithic period or even earlier, undoubted ritual or ceremonial circular sites were being built, as at Cairnpapple Hill in West Lothian (p. 102) and Croft Moraig in Perthshire (p. 181). These were used for a long time and adapted and modified and they lead straight into the great age of circular ceremonial sites, the contemporaneous Late Neolithic and Early Bronze periods. Most of the henge monuments and stone circles belong to this time; some of the henge sites in southern England, like Durrington Walls, are very large and contained elaborate wooden 'palaces'; the associated Grooved ware pottery indicates that the origins of these henges lie further back in Neolithic times, perhaps in the 'causewayed camps' of southern England. Grooved ware itself is found in Scotland, particularly in Orkney, and confirms that there were close links between the users of the ceremonial sites of England and Scotland. Other henges contain stone circles and at two of these —Stonehenge and Cairnpapple Hill (p. 102)—sherds of Beaker pottery were associated with the construction of the circle. Beakers were brought to Britain soon after 2300 B.C. by a new round-headed race from the continent who had the earliest bronze tools and who buried their dead crouched in individual short graves, often under round cairns.

These Beaker invaders may well have founded new dynasties of rulers: linear cemeteries—lines of Early Bronze Age barrows which could be the graves of important families—are frequent in the Stonehenge area and one has been identified in Scotland, in the Kilmartin valley (p. 151). Cup-and-ring marks are occasionally found pecked on to the stone slabs of these cist graves and also on a few standing stones (Pl. 19). Both the cup-and-ring marks and the stone circles have recently been shown to have been planned with geometrical precision and using standard units of length, a clear demonstration that the specialist classes of priests and wise men, implied by the ritual sites, were indeed in existence at this time.

Even more striking evidence of this is provided by the fact that large numbers of stone circles and standing stones have proved to be sited in positions from which celestial bodies—the sun, the moon and some bright stars—could have been seen about four thousand years ago rising or setting behind some conspicuous feature on the horizon at astronomically important times. A few standing stones mark important solstice observatories (pp. 132 and 154) and one has been shown to be such an observatory from independent evidence (p. 154). These stone circles and standing stones provide a very striking illustration of the principle of judging prehistoric sites by the capabilities of their time, put forward in the first section of this chapter. Their crudity is superficial: behind them evidently lies an achievement—in practical astronomy, geometry and surveying—which is truly remarkable for a non-literate society.

The Middle Bronze Age (about 1600–1000 B.C.)

Few major monuments have survived from this period; the archaeological evidence consists mainly of cremation burials in urns and hoards of bronze weapons and implements. However, there is no reason to suppose that the change in burial rite indicates any interruption of the cultural sequence; at Cairnpapple Hill for example (p. 102) these cinerary urns (which are mostly found in flat graves) were put into a huge cairn, showing clearly a continuity of traditions —and perhaps of a ruling family—with the preceding Early Bronze Age cairn and Beaker burials. The development of the bronze industry—the work of specialist craftsmen doubtless patronised by the chiefs and their courts—continues uninterruptedly through this period.

The Late Bronze and Early Iron Ages (about 800–100 B.C.)

Soon after about 1000 B.C. the bronze industry in Scotland exhibits innovations and improvements both in technique and in the design of its products—the appearance of the leaf-shaped slashing sword and the socketed axe for example—which follow on a smaller scale similar changes in England and on the continent. Probably in the 8th century B.C. began major social changes witnessed by the appearance of the first stone-walled hillforts: there may be a little evidence that new settlers were arriving in Scotland from the continent but the hillforts themselves should be clearer signs of a conflict between natives and intruders. The earliest known Scottish forts have timber frameworks within their rubble cores; this device was almost certainly introduced from the continent and it suggests that the hillforts were built by intrusive chieftains accompanied by professional fort-builders. This particular type of wall was very vulnerable to fire when built entirely of stone, as the many vitrified examples show.

The early date at which some of these timber-framed forts were built means that bronze was the main metal in use when they appeared. The gradual transition to using iron thus seems less significant than it did. Also at the end of the Bronze Age there occurred a deterioration in the climate—to cooler and wetter conditions—which may well have played some part in producing the unsettled conditions witnessed by the hillforts.

Some sites were fortified over a long period and these show how different kinds of defences were in use at different periods. In southern Scotland the sequence is often (1) wooden palisaded site; (2) stone-walled fort (not timber-framed); (3) hillfort with multiple ramparts, introduced to provide defence in depth (probably against the sling). Such changes are often accompanied by an increase in size of the defended area—most notably at Traprain Law (p. 95)—suggesting an increasing population. Further north however a different development is often seen in which the size of the defended area is reduced; a timber-framed hillfort is often succeeded by a smaller one, sometimes a tiny drystone dun (Dun Skeig, p. 131; Dun Lagaidh, p. 214). This reduction in fort size in the highland zone probably led, mainly after 100 B.C., to the invention and widespread adoption of duns and brochs (below).

The Late Iron Age (about 100 B.C.–A.D. 400)

By the 1st century B.C. fort-building traditions in Scotland had evolved in the way described and many varied tiny stone fortlets were being built in the highland-island zone (Atlantic Scotland). Towards the middle of that century there are fairly clear signs in the archaeological record of the arrival of people—few in number but doubtless influential—from southern England where disruption of the indigenous population is known to have occurred from about 100 B.C. onwards, first because of settlements by the Belgae and later because of the Roman invasions. It is just at this time that the earliest brochs seem to appear in the Western Isles and it is quite possible that the arrival of southerners stimulated the development of this remarkable tower fort from the local semibrochs which, it seems, had developed there some time previously.

The brochs are of considerable interest; not only do they represent the summit of prehistoric drystone architectural achievement, but they also seem to be the only really elaborate ancient buildings which were invented and developed entirely in Scotland. Unlike most of the other mighty stone monuments of earlier and later epochs— chambered cairns, timber-framed hillforts and cathedrals for example—they have no really similar comparable structures in other countries. The nuraghi of Sardinia do have a very similar outward appearance to that of the brochs, and are similarly built of drystone masonry; they may also have served the same sort of purpose. However, architecturally they are quite different, being essentially cones of masonry which are solid except for several superimposed central corbelled chambers connected by a stair. They went out of use several centuries before the first brochs were built.

The ingenious, light, hollow wall which allowed the brochs to be built to tower-like proportions must represent the most advanced architecture of its time. To a peasant farmer, accustomed to wooden huts and perhaps to forts with stone walls 5 or 6 m high, the first sight of a stone tower perhaps 13 m or more high must have been awe-inspiring. It seems very probable, since the least sophisticated brochs are in the Western Isles, that the towers were developed there and indeed their supposed prototype forts, the semibrochs, are thickly clustered in Skye and scattered in adjacent regions. Professional broch-designers and builders probably built the towers for other communities in the far north and improved them as they went. The pottery and artefacts found in them vary considerably from region to region showing that the rural population in the broch zone was heterogeneous even though the spread of the towers may be the sign of the spread of a new ruling group (perhaps the new southerners mentioned earlier).

The specialised type of stone dwelling known as the wheelhouse quite possibly developed out of the broch. The only site where a large number of stone dwellings of various ages can be seen is Jarlshof in Shetland (p. 261) and there the post-broch wheelhouses can be seen undergoing a steady development from a form quite similar to the interior of a broch (p. 266).

On the mainland the only domestic structures dating from the end of the Iron Age and the beginning of the proto-historical period are the souterrains of Angus (p. 185). Their origin is not clear and they do not closely resemble the Orkney souterrains of about the same period which seem to be refuges (p. 238). A local development in Angus seems quite probable and the pottery and finds from the souterrains agree with this. Probably the sunken passages were storage chambers and cattle byres.

The absence of a properly excavated, major hillfort in the region which was to become Pictland is a severe handicap to understanding the smaller sites. These inevitably give a fragmented picture of a society which was presumably hierarchical and tribal and whose power centres were in the hillforts.

The Roman invasions (A.D. 80–210)

The appearance of the Roman army in southern Scotland at about A.D. 80 marks an entirely new chapter in Scotland's early history and the siting and design of the Roman field monuments reflect this. These were the works of the highly skilled, professional army of a great urban civilisation penetrating into what appeared to it to be the northernmost limits of the barbarian world. The Roman sites can be understood only in military terms (Fig. 3): each fort is linked to the system of roads along which the legions and supplies went. The forts are planted confidently on flat ground overlooked by hills, in situations which contrast completely with those of the native strongholds. The design of the forts' defences and the tactical skill of the garrisons —developed in long series of continental wars—as well as formidable long-range field artillery (the *ballista* and the *catapulta*), must have made all but overwhelming mass attacks on them by the local tribes doomed and suicidal affairs.

Essentially there were three episodes in the Roman penetration of Scotland. In about A.D. 80 Governor Agricola occupied southern Scotland and built a chain of forts across the Forth–Clyde valley as well as many along the main eastern and western roads into the country (see Dere Street, p. 75). Newstead and Birrens (pp. 82 and 48) are examples of these last. Agricola also advanced north, fought and defeated the native tribes at the famous battle of Mons Graupius

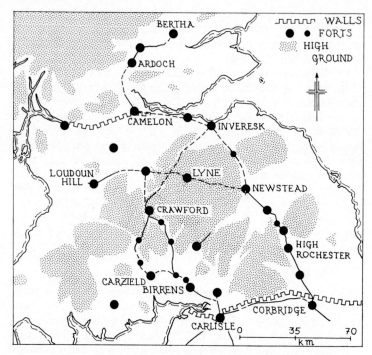

Fig. 3. Map of S Scotland under Roman occupation in the second half of the 2nd century A.D. (Antonine period) showing Roman forts and roads. Scale 1:230,000.

(p. 179) and built a series of forts running through Stirlingshire and Perthshire north-east along the edge of the Highlands. This was obviously to inhibit further forays out of the mountains by their Caledonian inhabitants.

Agricola was recalled by the Emperor Domitian in 84 or 85, before he could reap the benefits of Mons Graupius and conquer the Highlands, as he almost certainly could have done. It was one of those pivotal points in history when a different decision by Domitian might have altered the whole future of Britain. Had Agricola been allowed to complete his campaign Britain might have been rendered secure and held with very few troops, with incalculable consequences for the later history of the Empire and of the British Isles themselves.

The army withdrew from Scotland in about A.D. 100, obviously because its situation had been made increasingly difficult through Agricola's work being unfinished. It returned again in about A.D. 140 under Governor Lollius Urbicus, who, according to a Roman text, 'after driving back the barbarians, built another wall, this time of turf' (Hadrian's Wall had been built previously in about A.D. 122). Presumably he was unable to repeat Agricola's success and win a really decisive battle against the highlanders. The Antonine wall stretches for 58 km from Old Kilpatrick on the Clyde to Bridgeness on the Forth, and was defended by garrisons in adjacent forts of which Rough Castle is the best-preserved example (p. 117). However, the frontier was strategically vulnerable—it could be outflanked at both ends—and was breached in about A.D. 156 and again in about 180 when the invading tribes inflicted a serious defeat on the Roman army. The Antonine frontier must have been abandoned by 196 when the army in Britain was taken to Gaul by Governor Albinus in his unsuccessful attempt to become Emperor.

The third phase of Roman activity took place early in the 3rd century when Septimius Severus (who defeated Albinus) thoroughly rebuilt Hadrian's Wall and made repeated forays into Scotland to impress on the tribes the futility of standing against the Imperial army. The fort of Cramond (p. 99) on the south bank of the Firth of Forth was one of his bases for these operations but otherwise the Severan structures were mostly temporary marching camps which show up only on air photographs. After his day Scotland was left to her own devices.

The five known peoples of early Scotland

By the middle of the 1st millennium A.D. Scotland was inhabited by four distinct peoples, all probably speaking different languages and two of them relatively recent arrivals.

The *Picts* inhabited the north-east part of the country, beyond the Firth of Forth. The name—Picti or 'painted people'—was used by the Romans from about A.D. 300 onwards to describe the various tribes north of the Forth–Clyde line and we also know from the Romans that in the 2nd century these tribes were independent. However, by the 6th century Pictland was united under a single king, Bridei or Brude, and remained a nation until the conquest by the Scots at about A.D. 850. The archaeological evidence, though sparse for the Pictish period proper (about A.D. 300–850), is increasingly suggesting that the majority of the Picts were descended from the Iron Age, or even the Late Bronze Age tribes of the same area. The language spoken by the Picts seems to include some non-Indo-European elements but mainly to be a P-Celtic tongue with Gallo-Brittonic features.

The *Scots* were Q-Celtic (Gaelic)-speaking peoples from Ireland who began to settle in force in Argyllshire in the 5th century, thus forming the kingdom of Dalriada with its capital at Dunadd (p. 147) at the expense of the Picts. Ultimately, in about A.D. 850, Kenneth MacAlpin their king somehow overthrew the Picts and became the first king of all Scotland except the Norse regions (below). Modern Scottish Gaelic is descended from the dialects of the first Scots colonists.

The *Angles* were settlers from northern Germany and the Low Countries who established themselves in north-eastern England from about the 6th century onwards. They gradually expanded their power, overrunning several small British kingdoms in the process, until in the 7th century they had created the powerful kingdom of Northumbria, the great rival of the Picts. Northumbrian territory eventually included south-east Scotland up to the river Forth and occasionally beyond it. The characteristic Northumbrian decorated stone sculpture is found further north as the influence of this kingdom, and of the Roman Church supported by it, expanded.

The *Britons* were peoples speaking P-Celtic dialects (of which Welsh is a modern survival) who, early in the 1st millennium A.D., seem to have inhabited the whole of England, Wales and southern Scotland up to the frontier with the tribes later to be known as Picts. With the Anglo-Saxon, Anglian and Scottish colonisations their territory and power contracted until little was left. In the middle of the 1st millennium A.D. the British kingdom of Strathclyde included south-west Scotland up to and beyond the river Clyde and had its fortress capital on Dumbarton rock (Pl. 8).

From the end of the 8th century onwards the Vikings were sailing from Norway and raiding all round the British Isles. During the 9th century many *Norse settlers* established themselves permanently in Atlantic Scotland and came to dominate the western and northern islands, Caithness and Sutherland, Kintyre and the southern part of south-west Scotland. The power of the King of Norway in Scotland was not finally crushed until the battle of Largs in 1263.

It is possible that the various 'invasions' of Scotland described sometimes involved relatively small numbers of chiefs with their warriors and followers and that the *aboriginal population* often continued to exist under the new rulers. This is certainly suggested when the archaeological evidence is at all clear, as on the island of Tiree in the Iron Age (p. 159). Quite possibly the majority of the people of Scotland were descendants of the first Neolithic immigrants and perhaps a few in the remoter islands were survivors from the earlier Mesolithic Age. If this was the case the Beaker invaders, the Late Bronze Age fort-builders and the Late Iron Age refugees from the south would simply have formed new ruling groups as the Anglo-Normans did in Early Medieval times. Scotland's eventual unity was at first political, not genetic or cultural.

The Pictish stones

There are few archaeological remains which can be said to be definitely Pictish, but the symbol stones are a remarkable exception. They are divided into two classes, the first having only Pictish symbols and the second having in addition Christian crosses and symbolism. (The Class III stones have Christian symbols without the Pictish and presumably fall between the end of the Pictish kingdom in about A.D. 850 and the influx of feudalism in the 12th century.)

The Class I stones are boulders or undressed monoliths and the symbols and animals (Fig. 4) are *incised* on them. If, as seems likely, the Picts were the direct descendants of the Late Bronze and Iron Age populations of the same areas, the symbols should represent some prehistoric mythology or system of clan totems. Their meaning is not at all clear, however. The date of the Class I stones has caused dispute, though it is agreed that they lasted till the appearance of the Class II stones soon after A.D. 700. The Iron Age origins of some of the symbols seems clear so the Class I stones might go back to Iron Age times (the mirror symbol, for example, resembles the Iron Age Celtic bronze mirror). On the other hand, there are numerous Dark Age analogies for the Pictish animals which suggest a 6th- and 7th century-date for the stones.

The Class II stones are regular, dressed cross-slabs elaborately carved in relief in the pecking technique with the cross and Northumbrian interlace ornament as well as with Pictish symbols and scenes. The link with Northumbria forged by King Nechton in A.D. 710 doubtless brought north to Pictland craftsmen from whom the Pictish sculptors learned new ideas and techniques. The Class II stones are remarkable too for the wealth of detail they portray about the clothes, weapons, armour, horse-riding equipment and priestly activities of the period.

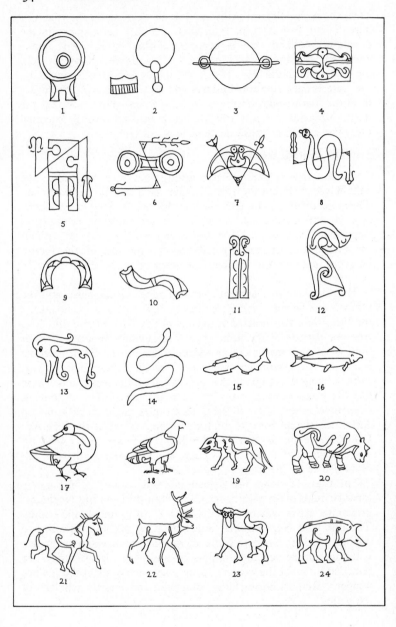

The spread of Christianity

The spread of the Christian religion through Britain must be re-garded as the great civilising process of post-Roman times and it also resulted in the appearance of some fine buildings and sculptured stones. Christianity had been originally introduced to England of course under the Romans by the 4th century but it was lost again in the 5th century by the progressive pagan Anglo-Saxon settlement of eastern England. However, the Christian Church evidently remained well established in Wales, north-west England and Ireland and it was probably this North English Church—already, it has been argued, organised with dioceses controlled by bishops—which began to send missionaries to Scotland in the 5th century, the first and most famous of whom was St. Ninian at Whithorn (p. 57). This is where the earliest Christian stone memorials and buildings are found but the effect seems to have been limited to Galloway. Iona, founded by the Irish St. Columba, followed in the 6th century and smaller monastic settlements of his Celtic Church gradually spread throughout Scotland during the 7th century. Columba is credited with the conversion of the Picts late in the 6th century.

There was a conflict over the dating of Easter in the 7th century between the Irish and North British Celtic Church and the Roman Church, now re-established in Saxon England and centred on Canterbury. This culminated in the Synod of Whitby in 664 at which the Roman rules prevailed.

The Romanisation of the Pictish Celtic Church, early in the 8th century, occurred after King Nechton had embraced the Roman faith and formed a political alliance with Northumbria. He had a stone church built for him in the southern fashion by Northumbrian masons and it is possible that a fragment of it is preserved in the tower at Restenneth Priory in Angus (p. 189). The Class II Pictish stones are the most striking archaeological evidence of these changes and they all probably date from after about A.D. 710 (above). We see again how decisions by rulers, and the resulting importation

---

Fig. 4. Common symbols found on Pictish stones: 1, disc and notched rectangle; 2, mirror and combs; 3, triple disc and cross bar; 4, rectangle; 5, notched rectangle and Z-rod; 6, double disc and Z-rod; 7, crescent and V-rod; 8, serpent and Z-rod; 9, arch or horseshoe; 10, S-shape; 11, notched rectangle or 'tuning fork'; 12, flower; 13, beast or 'elephant'; 14, serpent; 15, fish; 16, fish; 17, goose; 18, eagle; 19, wolf; 20, bull; 21, horse; 22, stag; 23, cow; 24, boar.

of craftsmen, have profound effects on the archaeological record. However the decision seems to have been reversed at the end of the 9th century and the Celtic Church again had free rein in the north. At the same time after 794 the increasing number of Viking raids resulted in the destruction of many monasteries, and during the 9th century contact between the Irish and Scottish Celtic Churches must have been tenuous.

The unification of the Pictish and Scottish kingdoms under Kenneth MacAlpin occurred at about 850 and thereafter there seems to have been an attempt to re-establish the Columban Church. Some Irish clergy returned to Scotland and the Irish round towers in Abernethy and Brechin bear witness to this, being devices invented in Ireland in the 9th century as protection against Viking raids. The other early free-standing towers—at Dunning, Muthill, Dunblane, St. Andrews and Restenneth—are square and illustrate the northward penetration a little later of Saxon and Norman architecture and the increasing dominance of the Roman Church.

The beginnings of feudal Scotland

Feudalism was of course brought by force into England—by William the Conqueror in 1066—but by invitation into Scotland. David I, first as ruler of Strathclyde (1107-24) and then as king (1124-63), introduced Anglo-Norman aristocratic families into Scotland in large numbers and the many Norman mottes—earthen mounds crowned with a timber tower—mark where they settled with their armed followers and craftsmen. Stone castles were later built on some, as at Duffus in Morayshire (p. 201) and at Castle Urquhart on Loch Ness. David also firmly established or restored bishoprics in many places including Glasgow, Galloway, Moray and Dunkeld. At the same time he brought into Scotland members of the reformed monastic orders of England and France who built the splendid abbeys and priories in the central and southern parts of the country. Here we have another illustration of the historical reasons for the appearance and spread of spectacular new forms of military and religious architecture. The great 12th- and 13th-century cathedrals and abbey churches represent again the summit of architectural and engineering achievement for their age.

The evolution of the church buildings

The development of Christian churches in Scotland provides an instructive demonstration of the processes governing the evolution

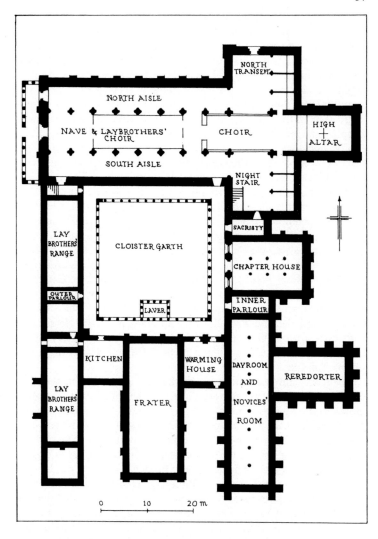

Fig. 5. Generalised plan of a Cistercian monastery, based on Dundrennan, showing the location of various rooms and ranges. Because of the presence of lay brothers in the community, the arrangements inside the church are more complex than with other orders. Scale 1:800.

of ceremonial buildings. In its early missionary days the Celtic Church in Scotland did not have the need nor the resources to import skilled masons to build large churches. The earliest chapels were of wood (Ardwall island, p. 53) and the type of small rectangular stone building which followed them was in use for centuries: similar small chapels can still be seen today serving small highland communities. Small cruciform cathedrals eventually appear in diocesan seats in the 12th century; probably, as at Whithorn, they were simply enlarged versions of the old rectangular buildings.

The first major development came to Scotland later in the 12th century as a result of the penetration north of Romanesque architectural ideas (and masons), ultimately from France. The most important innovation was the round stone arch (directly descended in France from the Roman arch—hence the name) with which an aisled nave could be created. The side walls were changed to massive round drum pillars—to which arches took the weight of the walls above—and aisles were added outside these to increase the total width of the building (Pl. 9). The whole nave roof—usually of wood and tile but occasionally stone-vaulted as at Durham Cathedral —was simultaneously raised on a further series of arches over the main pillars which reached up to the top of the aisle roof—the triforium—and then on a windowed wall above this, the clerestorey. Buttresses against the aisle walls ensured stability and the clerestorey and large gable windows allowed plenty of light into the high, imposing building.

Medieval church architecture reached its zenith late in the 12th century in France (13th century in Britain) with the pointed-arched, Gothic style. Finely carved, fluted stone facings were added to pillars and arches and the whole three-storeyed structure was refined and improved. Flying buttresses allowed a high, stone vault to be built on to the nave but these are rare in Scotland. Melrose Abbey is a good late example but the confidence of the French architects in achieving great height—so well seen at Bourges, Chartres and Amiens— is not apparent here since the triforium has been omitted to give the church a slightly squat appearance. The high Gothic cathedral, evolved before the principles of stress and load-bearing were understood mathematically, is truly the wonder of the Medieval Age.

The monasteries

In the 12th and 13th centuries many of the religious orders of Western Europe—particularly in France—underwent reformation, or rejuvenation. New orders grew up around the leadership of inspired monks, who had broken away from their over-worldly brotherhoods in order to return to the strict and Spartan rules of the 6th century St. Benedict. Under the Canmore kings, and particularly under David I (1124–53), many of these reformed monastic orders were introduced into Scotland, given grants of land and began to build their monasteries. The splendid architectural remains of the abbeys and priories so built bear witness to this influx of civilised and skilled foreigners into Scotland. Indeed, before the founding of the first universities in the 15th century the monasteries were the repositories of much of Medieval learning as well as being a civilising influence on the population. The monks pioneered systematic methods of agriculture, stock-breeding and fishing as well as supporting many other arts and crafts, and often members of leading Medieval families joined the orders.

The monks spent most of their lives within the bounds of the monastery and the design of the buildings reflects the needs of their self-sufficient communities (Fig. 5). The great abbey churches are visually the most impressive parts of the ruins but the cloister garth— a square, open space surrounded by a roofed, arcaded walk—was the centre of monastic life. It usually abuts the south side of the nave of the church to catch the sun and here the monks walked, read and copied manuscripts. Sometimes there is a wall press for books. On the east side of the cloister is a series of communal rooms including the chapter house (where a chapter of the Rule of the order was read to the monks each day) and the calefactory or warming house, the only place where a fire was permitted outside the kitchens. On the first floor would be the monks' sleeping quarters, or dorter, from which the night stair led down to the church for nocturnal services.

In orders like the Cistercians which included many lay brothers the west wing would be given over to their day rooms and dorter. The south range usually contains the frater or dining-room on the first floor with the kitchens and cellars below. This wing was adjacent to the drainage channel as also was the reredorter, or latrine block, usually attached to the dorter. Such highly organised, learned, moral and hygienic communities had not been living in Scotland since the Romans left and the contrast of the splendid stone buildings of these monasteries, and of the cloistered life within them, with the rural villages of 12th-century Scotland must have been striking indeed.

4. MUSEUMS TO VISIT

Most museums in Scotland are open to the public at regular hours and are listed in several publications of which the most convenient is probably the ABC Travel Guide's *Museums and Galleries in Great Britain and Ireland* (published annually) which alone gives the opening hours. The selection given here has been chosen with an archaeological emphasis. The museums marked with a + are under the care of the Department of the Environment and their opening hours are all the same: from April to September 09.30 to 19.00 and, on Sundays, 14.00 to 19.00: from October to March 09.30 to 16.00 on weekdays and 14.00 to 16.00 on Sundays.

South-west Scotland (Chapter 2): The Dumfries Burgh museum, the Observatory, Dumfries (weekdays 10·00–13.00: 14.00–17.00. Sundays, in April–September only 14.00–17.00): The Whithorn Priory Museum+.

South-east Scotland (Chapter 3): The National Museum of Antiquities, Queen Street, Edinburgh, has the largest collection of Scottish archaeological material of all periods (weekdays 10.00–17.00, also 18.00–20.00 during the Festival, Sundays 14.00–17.00): the Royal Scottish Museum in Chambers Street has much foreign archaeological material (weekdays 10.00–17.00, Sundays 14.00–17.00): the Huntly House Museum in Canongate has the finds from the Roman fort at Cramond (weekdays 10.00–17.00, 10.00–18.00 from June to September): Jedburgh Abbey Museum+: Melrose Abbey Museum+.

Central Scotland (Chapter 4): The Hunterian Museum in the University of Glasgow has good archaeological collections, especially of Roman material from the Antonine wall (including most of the carved stones) and Iron Age finds from the Hebrides (weekdays 09.00–17.00, Saturdays 09.00–12.00): the Glasgow Art Gallery and Museum in Kelvingrove also has some Scottish archaeological material (weekdays 10.00–17.00, Sundays 14.00–17.00): in Stirling there is the Smith Art Gallery and Museum in Albert Place (weekdays 10.00–17.00): in Montrose the museum in Panmure Place (weekdays 10.00–13.00, 14.30–16.30): the cathedral museum+ in St. Andrews, the St. Vigeans Museum,+ with many Pictish stones, north-west of St. Andrews: the Kirkcaldy, Fife, museum and art gallery in Station Road (weekdays 11.00–17.00, Sundays 14.00 17.00): the Dunfermline Museum, Viewfield (weekdays 11.00–

13.00, 14.00–19.00, but closed on Tuesdays and closing at 17.00 on Saturdays, Sundays 14.00–17.00): the Arbroath Abbey museum⁺.

Western Scotland (Chapter 5): In Rothesay the Buteshire Natural History Society museum in Stuart Street (April–October, weekdays 10.30–12.30, 14.30–16.30, also 14.30–16.30 on Sundays from June to September, November–March 14.30–16.30): The Campbeltown museum in Hall Street (weekdays 10.15–18.00 except Wednesdays, 10.15–13.00; open till 21.00 in summer).

North-east Scotland (Chapter 6): The Perth Art Gallery and Museum in George Street (weekdays 10.00–13.00, 14.00–17.00, Wednesdays and Fridays also 18.00–20.00, Sundays 14.00–16.00): The Dundee Central Museum in Albert Square (weekdays 10.00–17.30): the Meigle museum⁺ (Pictish stones) near Coupar Angus, (closed on Sundays): in Forfar, the Meffan Institute in the High Street (with a possible Celtic stone head) (weekdays 09.30–19.00, Saturdays 09.30–18.00): the Aberdeen University museums in Marischal College, Queen Street (Mondays–Fridays 09.00–17.00, also 18.00–21.30 on Wednesdays, Saturdays 09.00–12.00 and 14.30–17.30, Sundays 14.30–17.30): the Inverurie museum, Aberdeenshire (in the public library building: weekdays 09.30–12.00, 15.00–17.00): the Elgin museum in the High Street (weekdays 10.00–12.30, 14.00–17.00, except Tuesdays, 10.00–13.00): the Falconer Museum in the centre of Forres (weekdays only, summer 10.00–17.00, winter 10.00–15.00).

Northern Scotland (Chapter 7): The public library and museum, Inverness (weekdays 09.00–17.00, Wednesdays 09.00–13.00, 14.15–17.00): the museum in Dunrobin Castle, Sutherland (by application, if still open): the Thurso museum, in the public library (weekdays 10.00–13.00, 14.00–17.00).

The Orkney Isles (Chapter 8): The Antiquarian Museum, Tankerness house, Kirkwall (temporarily closed).

The Shetland Isles (Chapter 9): The County Museum, Lower Hillhead, Lerwick (weekdays 10.00–17.00).

2 · South-west Scotland

(Dumfries and Galloway)

These attractive counties run along the northern shore of the Solway Firth and contain many sites of great archaeological interest. The region is particularly important for its Early Christian relics, being the part of Scotland first reached by Christian missionaries, namely St. Ninian in the 5th century. The countryside south of the rather bleak inland hills and moors is open and well wooded, with many rivers running south to the Firth in pleasant, tree-filled valleys. The clear light of the region has long been an attraction to painters and artists. The main roads are not excessively crowded with traffic even in the high holiday seasons—unlike the northern Highlands—and on the minor roads one can quickly find solitude.

1. DUMFRIES-SHIRE

South-east of Dumfries

Travelling N from Carlisle one crosses the border at Gretna and enters Dumfries-shire. Turning W to Galloway take the A75 to Annan to see one of the most important Early Christian monuments in Scotland, the *Ruthwell cross**+ (Pl. 1) (NY/101682), which is not in the village of that name but in the church 1 km north of it. Take the B724 at Annan (or at Collin if going E); the key is obtained at a cottage on that road, at the by-road which leads north to the church.

Until 1640 the cross seems to have been intact and standing somewhere near the church but in that year it suffered partial destruction at the order of the General Assembly of the Church of Scotland at Aberdeen. However, the local minister managed to deface only one panel of the sculpture and had the cross broken in two pieces which were carefully buried in a trench in the clay floor of the church. Later, further fragments were detached but fortunately rediscovered in the 18th century. The main fragments of the cross were unearthed

Plate 1.
Ruthwell cross,
Dumfries-shire:
the S (rear) face.

when the floor of the church was paved over in about 1780 and by 1823 they had been reassembled and the cross set up again in the grounds of the manse. At present the cross is complete except for the transverse arms of the head. Modern transverse arms have been fitted to the shaft but the top arm is genuine.

The cross is an extremely fine example of Anglian sculpture, closely similar to the Bewcastle cross in Cumberland, and is usually thought to have been carved and set up some time between about A.D. 680 and 750, most probably in the first half of the 8th century. The ornamentation of the two principal faces consists of a series of rectangular panels with sculpted scenes in them, the flat borders being covered with Latin inscriptions. The sides of the shaft are covered with interlaced designs of foliage and birds, again with flat borders but with runic inscriptions on them.

On the main (north) face, the top arm of the cross shows St. John the Evangelist with his eagle: the damaged inscriptions on the margin probably read: IN PRINCIPIO ERAT VERBUM, 'In the beginning was the word'. On the lower arm of the cross, below the modern transverse arms, is a panel with two unidentified figures. The large panel below that contains the cloaked figure of John the Baptist holding the lamb; the figure has been damaged by a break in the shaft across it. The inscription on the margins of this panel are mostly defaced but (A)DORAMUS, 'Let us adore', is clear on the left side. Half of the right side is modern restoration.

The main central panel, 1·1 m high, shows Christ in Glory, the feet resting on two animals which look like pigs. This is one of the finest effigies of Christ of this period, the proportions being those of classical sculpture. There is a clear trace of a moustache but no obvious sign of a beard. The Latin inscription around the margins is awkwardly arranged for the modern reader. It starts at the top with a cross followed by JHS XPS; then JUDEX . AEQUITATIS.(top right margin); BESTIAE . ET . DRACONES . COGNOUERVNT . IN . DE . (left margin, top to bottom); the rest of the last word continues (DE) SERTO . SALVATOREM . MUNDI . (bottom half right margin). The full translation reads: 'Jesus Christ judge of equity. Beasts and dragons knew in the desert the Saviour of the world.'

The panel below the Christ shows the two early hermit saints of Egypt, Paul and Anthony. The inscription reads: SCS . PAULUS (top margin); ET A . . . (NTONIUS EREMITAE) (right margin, nearly all broken off); FREGER(UN)T. PANEM IN DESERTO. 'Saints Paul and Anthony, hermits, broke bread in the desert.' The basal panel shows the flight into Egypt with a finely carved ass (with a large ear) and a veiled Mary and Child seated on a blanket upon it. The object in the top left corner is a tree, not Joseph. The top margin bears the inscription: MARIA . ET IO . . . . The basal panel has been defaced.

On the back of the cross we see, in descending order again, a well-cut eagle on the topmost arm which grasps a bough. The lower arm shows an archer with drawn bow and arrow fitted. Neither of these figures has any obvious Christian symbolism. The next panel down shows the Visitation of Mary, part of the figures of which have been replaced with modern stone (the original plain stone under the feet suggests that the sculptor miscalculated the length of the figures). The marginal inscription is illegible.

The main panel shows Christ with Mary Magdalene washing his feet. The figure of Mary is only shown to the waist and is not kneeling as can appear at first sight: the curved object is her hair. The arm and hand are strikingly crude. The surrounding Latin inscription runs along the top margin (defaced), down the right, then down the left and finally along the bottom. It reads, separated out into words: A ... (TULLIT ALABA) ... STRUM UNGUENTI & STANS RETRO SECUS PEDES EIUS LACRIMIS COEPIT RIGARE PEDES EIUS & CAPILLIS CAPITIS SUI TERGEBAT. This is a quotation from the Vulgate (Latin Bible), Luke vii, 37–8, and the revised version reads 'she brought an alabaster cruse of ointment, and standing behind at his feet weeping, she began to wet his feet with her tears, and wiped them with the hair of her head.'

The next panel down shows Christ healing the blind man; under the figures is a large plain area of stone, possibly for an inscription which may have been carefully removed. The marginal inscription is damaged; it reads: (top of left side) ET PRAETERIENS . VIDI ... (T HOMINEM CAECUM); (top of right) A NATIBITATE ET SA ... (NAVIT EUM A) ... B INFIRMITATE. 'And passing he saw a man blind from his birth and he healed him from his infirmity.'

Underneath is a damaged panel, originally extremely fine, showing the Annunciation, with the angel (on the left) and Mary. The only part of the inscription remaining reads: ... INGRESSUS ANGEL ... which refers to the Vulgate, Luke i, 28: 'et ingressus angelus ad eam dixit: ave, gratia plena: Dominus tecum: benedicta tu in mulieribus'; 'and the angel came in unto her, and said, Hail, thou are highly favoured, the Lord is with thee: blessed art thou among women.' This would fit on the side margins.

The lowest panel on the reverse side has as its subject the crucifixion and it occupies the wider base, or plinth, of the cross which is 1·12 m high and 0·81 m wide. The sculpture has been very badly damaged and all inscriptions are effaced.

On the narrow sides of the cross is finely executed ornamentation of animals, birds and foliage. The latter includes bunches of grapes showing that the motif is intended to be the vine. This decoration on each face is contained within two long panels, the margins of which are covered with runic inscriptions. Those on the upper panels are badly defaced in part but on the lower panels the runes are clear. They are part of an Anglo-Saxon poem, the *Dream of the Rood*, the full version of which is known from elsewhere, and it seems fairly clear that the Latin and runic inscriptions were incised at the same time. The runic system of writing is of purely Germanic origin and close connections between the Ruthwell cross and Anglo-Saxon England are evident in this as in other ways. The character of the runes offers some evidence as to the date of the cross and points fairly clearly to an old Anglian, pre-Viking age for it, possibly late in the 7th century or early in the 8th. It has been suggested that the great cross may have been set up not long after the Synod of Whitby in 664 to commemorate this triumph of the Roman Church over the Celtic (p. 35 above).

It has also been suggested that Ruthwell was a preaching cross, a 'sermon in stone', whose finely carved scenes from the life of Christ could be used as illustrations in missionary sermons.

The 13th-century *Caerlaverock Castle* (NY/026656), 11 km south-south-east of Dumfries, is only 10 km from Ruthwell and can conveniently be visited on the same tour. The B725 runs west from Ruthwell, or south from Dumfries, and very close to it.

Nithsdale

Travelling NW from Dumfries on the A76 one passes close to the *Twelve Apostle stone circle* near Holywood (NX/947794). Take the B729 W at New Bridge 3 km from Dumfries and the circle is 300 m along in a field on the north side of the road. There are 11 stones of which only five remain upright. Thom has surveyed the site and finds it to be a large example of a Type B flattened circle. Half of the ring is a true circle with a diameter of 89 m or just over 106 megalithic yards; one side is composed of an arc of a much larger circle drawn from a point on the circumference of the first one.

Eight kilometres further north the impressively situated vitrified hillfort of *Mullach*, near Dalswinton, may be visited (NX/929870). Probably the best way is to take the NE farmroad from where the A76 joins the minor road to Dalswinton after crossing the Nith. Shortly before getting to High Auldgirth leave the road and walk SW for 1 km to the summit of the hill. The site commands an extensive view over the Nith valley to the Kirkcudbrightshire hills in the west. The fort is oval in shape, having two concentric walls about 30 m apart. The enclosed area measures about 91 m by 74 m and several masses of vitrified stone are visible in the rubble ruins of the walls. These were thus once stone walls with an internal framework of timber beams (p. 27) and the site is likely to date from some time between the 8th and 4th centuries B.C. It has not been excavated.

Proceeding N on the A76 one may see the well-preserved Norman *Motte of Dinning* (NX/892902). Take the W side road $\frac{1}{3}$ km north of Barburgh Mill (or at Closeburn if travelling S), and then turn left. Both motte and bailey are visible at this site, the former standing some 4·3 m high and the latter being defended by a ditch 3·7 m deep to the south-east.

Six kilometres further north is the *Nith bridge cross*, an Early Christian Anglian monument (NX/868954). Take the A702 W just north of Thornhill (or follow the minor road N from Dinning) and the cross is close to the south side of the road 1 km from this junction. It stands 2·75 m high but the transverse arms have disappeared and the decoration is difficult to see now because of lichen. The broad front and rear faces are ornamented with panels containing inter-twined foliage and animals and the sides have similar interlaced decoration. At the junction of the cross arms is a rosette pattern. The cross is dated approximately to the 8th century.

There is a fragment of another *Anglian cross shaft*, with interlace ornament, in the old church at *Closeburn* (NX/904923); a particu-larly fine decorated Anglian cross shaft used to stand somewhere in this village and is now in the Dumfries museum. Of white sand-stone, the slab is 1·07 m high with the broad face up to 0·37 m in width. The right side has ornamentation of intertwined foliage and birds very similar to that on the Ruthwell cross.

Annandale

Travelling N along the A47 from Carlisle one passes close to three well-known archaeological sites just south of Lockerbie. It is worth mentioning the important Early Christian site, with several fine stone crosses, that was at *Hoddom*, 4 km south-west of Ecclefechan, although there is little to be seen there now. Several fragments of the crosses are in the Dumfries Burgh museum and one is in the National Museum of Antiquities in Edinburgh. The pieces of the finest cross were however lost during the Second World War when Hoddom Castle was occupied by the military. This great 8th-century Anglian cross at Hoddom might originally have stood 6·1 m high.

At *Hoddom bridge* (NY/167727), 3 km south-west of Ecclefechan on the B725, the foundations of a church were exposed in 1915 in the north-east corner of the old graveyard which is east of the bridge and road; this church seemed to be of a 12th- or 13th-century type. In the early 1950s it was re-explored and traces of an even older building were discovered under the nave. A date of about A.D. 700 was suggested for this and part of the buildings of the Anglian monastery at Hoddom were probably thus revealed. Its importance is shown by the several fine stone crosses which came from the site. There is a great stone cross socket at the east end of the churchyard.

One of the largest and most important Roman forts in the south-west—*Blatobulgium* or *Birrens** (NY/218753)—is close by. The by-road to Middlebie can be taken from the A74 at Kirtlebridge Station or the B725 east from Ecclefechan. The site is west of this by-road at 1 km south of Middlebie. The fort stands on flat ground within the angle formed by the confluence of the Middlebie burn and the Mein water and the six concentric banks and ditches are now completely preserved only on the north side. The enclosed rectangle measures some 160 m north–south by 102 m east–west, but the south end has been partly eroded away.

The fort has been twice excavated, in 1895–6 and again from 1962 till 1967, and the stone buildings of the barracks and the central *Principia*, or headquarters building, were uncovered. Nothing of these is now visible, however. More than twenty inscribed stones have been found in the various excavations and most of them are in the National Museum of Antiquities in Edinburgh. One important dedicatory stone tablet was set up in A.D. 158 in honour of the Emperor Antoninus Pius by the Second Cohort of Tungrians and

Plate 2. Roman camp on the N side of Burnswark Hill, Dumfries-shire, seen from the hill: the far side of the camp runs along the edge of the wood.

it is likely that the fort was extensively rebuilt at about that time, when a general reconstruction of Scottish defences took place.

The excavations in the 1960s demonstrated that Birrens had been in existence, as a turf-ramparted camp, during the Flavian occupation of Scotland (about A.D. 80–100) as well as in the Antonine phase (about A.D. 140–80). Traces of the initial defence work, perhaps laid out by Agricola himself in his initial campaigns in A.D. 79–84, were also found under the permanent Flavian fort.

The fort stands on the main Roman route from Carlisle into western Scotland.

Four kilometres north-west of Birrens is *Burnswark* (Pl. 2), a large Iron Age hillfort, or oppidum, with two Roman 'siege works' beside it (NY/187788). The by-road due north from Ecclefechan leads straight to the hill, a conspicuous eminence rising some 285 m above the sea. The fortifications seem likely to have been enlarged at one stage, the primary defence-work being the oval enclosure on the summit at the south-west end. This measures some 275 by 200 m. The ramparts are most impressive on the north, the easiest line of approach. Here the rampart and ditch span from 13 m to 18 m but elsewhere the breadth is less, 9–10 m. The north-east enclosure evidently represents an extension at a later stage up to the precipitous face known as the Fairy Craig.

The fort was excavated in 1898 and again in 1966 and 1967. The recent work established that there was a wooden palisaded defence underneath the main rampart which was dated by radiocarbon to the 7th or 6th century b.c. It was also discovered that the paving of the central gateway in the southern rampart had been laid when the rampart was in ruins: the original surface of the gateway was much lower. It was concluded that the Roman lead and clay *ballista* artillery bolts which were found in both excavations were discharged at a dilapidated hillfort—in other words that the Roman camps were for practice attacks against an empty native stronghold, for field exercises for the troops stationed at the near-by fort of Birrens, probably in the 2nd century A.D. The sites of a number of timber roundhouses have been located inside the hillfort.

The southern Roman camp is the most impressive and four artillery platforms are visible as flat-topped mounds on the side facing the hill. In the corner of this camp is a small fortlet which belongs to an earlier period of Roman activity near the hillfort.

An exceptionally fine native Celtic bronze three-link bridle bit, decorated with coloured enamel, was found near the fort in the 18th

4

century and is now in the National Museum. Judging by its size the hillfort seems to have been an important one and may have been the capital of the Novantae tribe.

Travelling further up Nithsdale to Moffat on the A74, one can see the well-preserved *Auldton Motte* (NT/094058). A trench surrounds the motte at its foot on all sides and provided an inner defence if the bailey was overrun.

2. GALLOWAY

(Kirkcudbright and Wigtown)

Kirkcudbrightshire

Travelling W from Dumfries take the A710 to the 13th-century *Sweetheart Abbey*+ (NX/965663). The ruins of this Cistercian monastery are among the most attractive in Scotland and are situated next to the New Abbey burn along the minor road which leaves the main one nearly a kilometre north of New Abbey.

Close by the abbey is the Norman *Ingleston Motte* at NX/982651. It is reached by a side road 1·6 km south-east of New Abbey. Another Norman motte with the bailey attached is the *Mote of Urr* (NX/815647) on the A710 3 km north-west of Dalbeattie; it is one of the best preserved of its kind in the area and was owned by the de Berkeley family.

Continuing W along the A710 one reaches the Iron Age and Dark Age fortress of *Mark Mote* (or Mote of Mark) at NX/845540. The site is in a National Trust for Scotland area west of Rockliffe which is reached by the side road leaving the main road at White loch (NX/865544). The main rampart, now much denuded, is vitrified so that originally it must have been a massive stone wall with an internal framework of timber beams (p. 27 above). It could be as old as the Late Bronze Age and encloses an area some 82 m long and from 32 m to 16·7 m wide; it is sited on a conspicuous long, rocky hill near the shore of Rough Firth. New excavations began there in 1973.

The fort was excavated in 1913 and produced large quantities of animal bones, a piece of a rotary quern, clay floors or hearths and much evidence of metal working (crucibles) and iron smelting. Though the techniques of excavation practised at that time precluded precise stratigraphical observations, two fragments of Roman pottery which were found suggest that the timber-framed fort may have been in use until the 2nd century A.D., though the complete absence of other native Iron Age relics except the quern is striking. However, a great mass of clay moulds for objects of 8th- and 9th-century date shows that the ruins were re-used late in the Dark Ages and the many pieces of glass vessels of a similar or slightly earlier age also discovered confirm this.

Continuing W through Castle Douglas it is well worth visiting *Threave Castle**+ (NX/739623), 2 km west of that town, even though it is technically outside the scope of this guide. It was built in the middle of the 14th century by Archibald 'the grim', 3rd Earl of Douglas. To reach it from the A75 a walk of about a kilometre along a prepared path from Kelton Mains farm is needed and one is rowed across to the island by the custodian.

About 8 km east of Kirkcudbright, on the A711, is *Dundrennan Abbey**+ at the village of that name. It is situated in a most attractive, secluded and wooded valley. The fine architecture of the church stands out well but, as at its daughter abbey at Sweetheart (p. 50), a large part of the living area of the monastery is completely demolished and not even the foundations are exposed. Dundrennan was a Cistercian monastery, founded in 1142 by King David I and colonised by monks from Rievaulx Abbey in Yorkshire. Mary Queen of Scots spent her last night in her own country here in 1568. Dundrennan Abbey was saved from demolition in the mid-16th century after the Reformation by Lord Herries, who refused to carry out the orders of the Lords of the Congregation to destroy it. Sweetheart Abbey was preserved in the same way. Unlike Sweetheart, though, Dundrennan Abbey was not preserved after the church ceased to be used in 1742 and the buildings were used for quarry material thereafter.

The design and situation of the abbey reflect the strict rules of the Cistercian order. The soil was fertile for crops and orchards, the running water of the near-by stream was utilised in the drainage system and to work corn mills, and pasturage for the herds of horses and cattle was to be found on the slopes near by. The architecture is of an austere design and belongs to the period, called Transitional, when Norman or Romanesque designs were giving way to the Gothic 'first pointed' style of the 13th century. Round (Romanesque) and pointed (Gothic) arches are found together. Of the church the east end still stands well preserved but most of the rest is reduced to foundation level. It had a large aisled nave and an aisle-less choir. Various architectural features may be noted, such as the ornamented central doorway in the west end (though this has been restored), the round clerestorey windows of Norman character (above the aisle roof), the wheel stair in the north-west corner of the north transept (which gave access to the clerestorey and the tower) and the double piscina in the wall south of the main altar in the presbytery. Set in the west wall of the church is a stone effigy of an abbot, in a monastic robe and holding a crook. A small dagger just below the neck suggests that the abbot was murdered and a wounded figure at his feet may be the assassin.

The monastery buildings extended southwards from the church and followed the Cistercian plan with the lay brothers' range on the west of the cloister and the monks' range on the east. At some stage there were no more lay brothers in the monastery and their living quarters were changed into cellars, which are the buildings now visible. On the east side, running outwards from the south transept of the church, the library, the sacristy and the chapter house are visible. The rest of the buildings have vanished, many buried under the garden of the near-by manse. The chapter house was rebuilt in the 13th century and is in the distinctive 'first pointed' Gothic style. The mouldings of the windows and other pieces of stonework in the chapter house exhibit elaborate carvings. In the same building are decorated stone coffin lids of the abbots buried there and also a fragment of blue marble, from 14th-century Tournai, which was once part of a knight's tomb.

West of Kirkcudbright take the B727 to Borgue and then the minor coast road north-west of this village to see the Iron Age galleried dun *Castle Haven** (NX/594483). This ivy-clad ruin stands on the rocky foreshore and is visible from the road which one leaves about 300 m east of a tower-like building at Corseyard. The building is of dry-stone masonry, like the letter D in plan with the straight edge formed by the wall running along the edge of a low cliff on the west. There is a similarly shaped outer wall on the east which runs up against the central dun on the north and south sides; it is not certain that this was an original feature of the dun.

The fort was cleared out in 1905 and the exposed walls and doorways were to some extent restored and rebuilt so that the lintel stones visible are not necessarily in their original positions. A broad band of white paint was put on at the time to mark the junction between original and restored masonry, but little trace of this remains. In fact at the time of excavation the outer wall stood only from 60 cm to 1·2 m high and the north, east and south walls of the dun stood from 90 cm to 1·2 m. Only the foundations of the west wall remained.

The area enclosed by the central dun measures 10·7 m east–west by 18·2 m north–south. The main doorway, equipped with checks, is in the north wall, in line with that in the outer wall. The dun wall is built hollow, with three stretches of gallery running nearly all round it at ground level and communicating with the interior by six doorways. No trace of an intra-mural stair leading to upper levels of gallery (as in the brochs, p. 28) was found, but immediately east of the main entrance several steps of stone slabs project from the inside face of the wall and doubtless once led up to the wallhead. With this arrangement Castle Haven is distinguished from the many superficially similar galleried duns in Argyll and the Western Isles (Chapter 5). In fact the fort is the only one of its kind known in south-west Scotland. A narrow doorway leads through the southern wall to steps down a natural cleft in the rock to the beach; presumably the inhabitants' boats were beached here. The site is wrongly described as a broch on the 1 inch Ordnance Survey map.

Several characteristic Iron Age artefacts were found in the excavations, including two bronze spiral finger-rings, a bead of blue glass paste with a wavy white line around it, a piece of a polished stone disc and pieces of rotary querns. The bronze rings and the bead could indicate that the fort-builders, or some of them, had but recently arrived from southern England in the 1st century B.C. There were other objects which show that the dun was in use in much later, probably Medieval times. These included pieces of chain mail and a bronze penannular brooch of a late type with the pin missing.

Two kilometres north of Castle Haven is the village of Knockbrex where a minor road turns west to the shore of the Fleet estuary. Here is *Ardwall island* which excavations in 1964 and 1965 by Professor Charles Thomas showed to have been the site of an important Early Christian chapel and cemetery (NX/573495). Originally the site seems to have been an inhumation cemetery, dating perhaps to the 6th century A.D., and possibly grouped around an early shrine. This was followed by a small timber chapel or oratory which measured only 3·35 m by 2·15 m. There were more graves around this chapel and aligned on the same axis as it. Finally in Phase III, in the 8th century, a stone chapel measuring internally 7·02 m by 4·00 m was built partly over the foundations of the timber building and with a different orientation. The burials of this phase are aligned on the axis of the stone chapel and were thus distinct from the earlier ones. By about A.D. 1000 the stone church was in ruins and some late graves had been put inside it. The foundations of the church were later incorporated in the walls of a Medieval building. A low, stone-revetted bank—traces of which can be seen—surrounds the whole complex, which seems to have been an early church serving the local community. Men, women and children were buried within the enclosed cemetery. A series of carved memorial stones, both fragmentary and complete, were found at the Ardwall site, and can be seen in the Dumfries museum.

Travelling W on the A75 through Gatehouse of Fleet one passes the 16th-century *Cardoness Castle* on the north side of the road (a Guardianship site) and leaves the Norman *Boreland Motte*, held by the de Morevilles, on the south side (NX/585555). Two kilometres west of Gatehouse a minor road to Anwoth turns north and the small vitrified fort of *Trusty's Hill* can be visited from that village (NX/588561). A footpath leads due east of the cross-roads to near the fort.

The main timber-framed wall, now vitrified, is approximately rectangular in plan and measures some 27·5 m by 18 m. There are outer defences in the form of banks and ditches further down the slope of the knoll on which the fort stands. The site has not been excavated so no information about its history is available. However, the entrance on the east side is between two outcrops of rock and on the southernmost of these outcrops are carved three *Pictish symbols* (p. 33). These consist of a monster figure, a double disc with Z-rod and a unique circle with projecting curved horns and containing a stylised human face. Presumably these symbols were carved long after the timber-framed fort was built and destroyed.

Proceeding W from Gatehouse of Fleet along the coast road one passes the Auchenlarie caravan site. Two kilometres west of this a minor road turns north and leads to the farmroad and to the two *Cairnholy chambered cairns*[+] (NX/518541). Both sites were excavated in 1949 by Professor S. Piggott and Professor T. G. E. Powell. The southernmost, *Cairnholy I* (Pl. 3), is the most spectacular monument; the cairn runs east–west and measures some 51·8 m in length with a width of about 15·25 m. The east end is horned, having six tall stones set in a concave arc flanking the entrance to the burial chamber. This forecourt has some drystone walling between the orthostats. The back part of this chamber is composed of two huge side-slabs 2·7 m and 2·9 m long and up to 0·76 m high; the front part, or antechamber, is blocked off from the main chamber by a tall, thin slab 1·37 m high and a similar one forms the west end of the chamber itself.

Plate 3. Cairnholy I Neolithic cairn, Kirkcudbright: view of the façade.

Excavation in 1949 showed that five fires had been lit on the ground in front of the tomb entrance during the period of its use. The tomb-builders used leaf-shaped flint arrowheads and pottery which has affinities with that found in Ulster and the Isle of Man rather than with the Neolithic wares found in the chambered tombs of the Clyde area. However, pitchstone fragments from Arran were recovered from the site and more evidence of trade appeared in the form of a large jet bead and a fragment of a highly polished ceremonial jadeite axe. The dead were cremated before being put into the burial chamber and the latest of these interments were in the antechamber and were accompanied by Late Neolithic and Beaker (Early Bronze Age) pottery. The latter dates to the late 3rd millennium B.C. (p. 25). Finally the entrance to the tomb was blocked with a mass of stones. In the Middle Bronze Age another burial was inserted into the main chamber and this had a cup-and-ring marked stone set up beside it (p. 26).

The second chambered tomb, *Cairnholy II*, lies 150 m north of the first and the cairn is much more dilapidated. The tomb lacks a forecourt façade and the chamber and antechamber are formed of four large stone slabs. As with the first cairn the tomb had been blocked at the end of its use but the burial chamber had been completely cleared out before the 1949 excavations. Even so some

Neolithic sherds, a knife, a scraper and a leaf-shaped arrowhead of flint were found. There were also some Beaker sherds which showed that the tomb had been used at the beginning of the Bronze Age.

The Wigtown peninsula

Continuing W on the A75 one reaches Newton Stewart and the various roads into the Wigtown peninsula, one of the richest archaeological zones in the country. On the way south to Whithorn (A714 and A746) it is worth making a short detour 5 km west up the B733 from Wigtown to Kirkcowan to see the *stone circle and standing stones* at *Torhouse* (Pl. 4) (NX/383565). The circle, close to the south side of the road, consists of 19 boulders on the edge of a low mound and there are three other stones in a line near the centre. The ring is claimed as a Type A flattened circle by Thom, that is, most of the perimeter follows the circumference of a circle 19·8 m (24 megalithic yards) in diameter but part of it is constructed along the arc of a much larger circle 36·6 m (44 my) in diameter. The centre point of the larger circle is on the circumference of the smaller. There are other standing stones near by which may be part of another circle, and an outlying standing stone is 400 m to the south-south-east.

Plate 4. Torhouse stone circle, Wigtown.

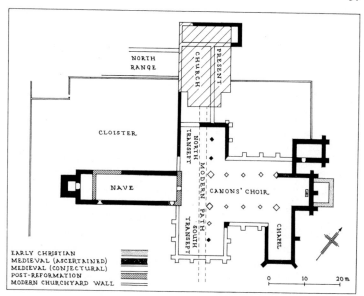

Fig. 6. Plan of the known and inferred remains of Whithorn Priory in relation to the modern church and churchyard wall. Scale 1:1000.

Continuing along the A746 one reaches the famous Early Christian and Medieval religious centre at *Whithorn Priory**+ (NX/445403) (Fig. 6). It is known that St. Ninian established the first church in Scotland at Whithorn in the 5th century A.D. (p. 35 above) and opinion has veered as to whether his white-plastered stone structure, the 'Candida Casa' of the historian Bede, was at Whithorn itself or at the Isle of Whithorn 5 km to the south-east (p. 61 below). What evidence there is seems to be entirely in favour of the former locality.

One approaches the site through a narrow lane, the Pend, which leads off the western side of the main street and under the arch of the old gatehouse of the Medieval priory. This arch dates to about 1500. The museum is along the same lane, just before the entrance to the churchyard. The visible ruins are but a small proportion of the original buildings and consist in fact solely of the much reconstructed and altered aisle-less nave of the priory church. There are also the crypt and vaults underneath the east end of the church which can be reached by a locked door (key in museum) in the southern chapel. This church formed part of a Premonstratensian monastery which was founded in the 13th century. Of the east end of the priory church, and of the traces of much earlier buildings of the Celtic Church which were found next to it, nothing appears above ground but the positions are marked on the plan (Fig. 6). The history of the site is most conveniently described in chronological order.

In 1949 Dr C. A. Ralegh Radford excavated on the site and re-exposed some early masonry—first explored by the Marquis of Bute at the end of the 19th century—at the east end of the priory church. As one approaches the modern church (built in 1822) the path cuts across the site of the Medieval church at the east (right) end of its nave so that the site of the transepts is along the line of the path and that of the choir and chapels to its right (Fig. 6): as we have said, these latter features are invisible now and the chapels at the east end of the church lie under the cemetery wall. It was here, at the east end, that the remains of the Early Christian building were found. These remains consisted of three walls 1 m thick projecting east from the priory church. The masonry was relatively crude and the stones were set in clay. Traces of a coarse cream mortar of poor quality were noted on the outer surface but none was on the inside. The building was 4·6 m wide inside and more than 4 m long, the west part having been destroyed when the priory church was built. No early finds were made in the building.

The mortar coating at once recalled to the excavator the description of St. Ninian's whitewashed stone church, and Dr Radford believed that he had in fact found 'Candida Casa'. Professor Charles Thomas, on the other hand, doubts this and believes the building probably to be 7th century or later in date, and to belong to a time after the site had become a monastery. In 1965 further excavations at the east end of the priory church revealed crushed skeletons in dug graves which may well belong to the period of St. Ninian. There seems little doubt that his church was built somewhere on this spot and that that is why the later religious buildings were erected there. The 'Latinus stone' in the museum (see below) could well belong to the period of Ninian himself.

After the Northumbrian conquest of Galloway during the 7th century, the local church had to be converted to the official Roman ways, notably over the date of Easter. The first of the new bishops was Pecthelm and doubtless the monastery at Whithorn was re-organised and rebuilt on Anglian lines. However, no traces of buildings of this period have been found, though two 9th-century crosses are in the museum (p. 59 below). The religious site seems to have continued as such after the Viking conquest of Galloway in the early 10th century but again no buildings are known. However, the large number of headstones and crosses of the 'Whithorn School' bear witness that the Viking rulers were being buried in the traditional way on traditional Christian sites.

The next major visible episode of building at Whithorn was the construction of a cathedral on the site in the 12th century, after Whithorn had been re-established as the seat of the local bishop (diocese of Galloway), with Gilla-Aldan as the first. This cathedral was a cruciform building of unknown extent of which the only visible features now are part of the south wall of the nave of the priory church and the reset Romanesque doorway near its west end. There are some stone fragments in the museum belonging to this building.

The Premonstratensian order colonised the Whithorn area in about 1177 from Soulseat, near Stranraer, converting the pre-existing monastery to their own use. In the following 13th century the monastery was rebuilt, and the nave of the church belongs mainly to this period, as does also the vaulted crypt under the east end. Fragmentary remains of the rest of the church and of some of the other monastic buildings have been excavated at various times so that part of the plan can be inferred (Fig. 6). There was only one main wing of domestic buildings and this ran parallel to the nave and further north. This range was linked to the north transept by the east range.

The nave itself is a simple rectangular structure which served as the local parish church until the 18th century. It now measures some 22 m by 6·7 m internally but was originally just over 26 m long; the west end was shortened and rebuilt in the 18th century. The original 13th-century walls are visible along most of the north side except the west end and at the west end of the south side. Two tomb recesses, dating to about 1300, have been reset into the east end of the north wall. As we have mentioned earlier, the fine, round-arched Romanesque or Norman doorway at the west end of the south wall dates to the 12th century and has been repositioned. Like the Romanesque cathedral before it, the great church of the Premonstratensian priory served also as the cathedral for the Galloway diocese. Presumably the nave was intended to have been enlarged to fit the east half of the church but for some reason never was.

In the *Whithorn museum**+ is a fine collection of Early Christian stone monuments and crosses, all of which have come either from Whithorn or from St. Ninian's cave 4 km away on the coast (p. 62

below). None has come from St. Ninian's chapel at the Isle of Whithorn and this is a strong argument against there having been an important Early Christian site there (p. 62). The Galloway Early Christian stones might usefully be divided into three groups according to their age and cultural context. The first or *British group* belongs to the period of the Celtic Church and is of 7th-century date or older. It includes, first, a stone belonging to near the time of St. Ninian himself in the 5th century and, second, stones belonging to the 6th or 7th century, to the time of the Celtic monastery which

Fig. 7. Five of the most important Early Christian stones from Galloway. From l to r: the Latinus stone (Whithorn), the memorial to Vaventius and Mavorius, that to Florentius, the 'initium et finis' stone—these three at Kirkmadrine—and the Peter stone (Whithorn).

is reported to have existed at Whithorn. The second or *Anglian group* of stones belongs to the period of the Northumbrian dominance of Galloway after about the middle of the 7th century, when the Anglian Church replaced the Celtic, while the third or *Viking group* —the products of the 'Whithorn School'—belongs to the period of the Norse dominance of Galloway from early in the 10th century onwards.

In the centre of the rear hall of the museum the best of these stones stand upright (Fig. 7). The most important of the British group are as follows:

(1) The '*Latinus stone*': this is a simple rectangular gravestone and dates to the middle of the 5th century, thus being the earliest Christian memorial known from Scotland. The inscription is in twelve lines and reads (omitted letters being in brackets): TE DOMINU(M)/ LAUDAMUS / LATINUS / ANNORU(M) / XXXV ET / FILIA SUA / ANN(ORUM) IV / (H)IC SI(G)NUM / FECERUT / NEPUS / BARROVA / DI. Translated this reads, 'We praise thee Lord Latinus of 35 years and his daughter of four years. The grandson Barrovadus set up this monument here.' The stone was found in 1891 at the priory and it is not impossible that it was put up in St. Ninian's lifetime.

(2) The '*Peter stone*': this is another rectangular slab, this time with an incised wheel cross the arms of which are made from arcs of circles. Underneath is an inscription which reads (L)OCI / PETRI / APU / STOLI, or 'The place of Peter the Apostle'. This stone used to stand by the side of the road south of Whithorn and the 'locus' referred to may well have marked a cemetery or oratory dedicated to St. Peter. The type of lettering is that used in Merovingian Gaul and is rare in Britain; a date in the 7th century, before the subjugation of Galloway by Northumbria, seems indicated.

Two fragments of cross shafts, numbers 3 and 5, belong to the early period of Northumbrian rule in the 9th century and show the characteristic Anglian interlace pattern. From the following period of Viking domination, starting in the 10th century, come the many stones of the 'Whithorn School' of which the only complete one is number 7 belonging to the 10th century. It stands in the centre of the central group and consists of a flat stone slab with a circular head forming the cross. The expanded arms of the cross are depicted in the usual manner by having cut-out circles between them, there is a central boss and the shaft is decorated with the usual interlace pattern in relief.

The *St. Ninian's cave stones*★ are also in the Whithorn museum and are simple crosses cut into loose boulders. Number C.1 is probably the earliest, a simple boulder with a cross on it which looks like a 7th-century type. The others, which include headstones and pillar stones, probably range from the 8th century (C.2) to the 10th and 11th centuries. The one with an inscription reading SANCT(O) NINIA(NO) probably dates in fact to later than 1500.

Going on 5 km further south-east to the tip of the peninsula one reaches the Isle of Whithorn, now converted to a peninsula by an artificial causeway. There is a sheltered inlet on the west, now the modern harbour, and this was probably always the landing point for

Plate 5. St. Ninian's cave, Wigtown.

pilgrims to Whithorn coming by sea. *St. Ninian's chapel**+ or *kirk* is
on the Isle, and was excavated by Dr C. A. R. Radford in 1949
(NX/479362). The building is a simple rectangular drystone chapel
7·7 m long by 5 m wide internally, with walls just under a metre
thick. The structure had been partly restored in 1898 by the Marquis
of Bute. Excavations revealed the foundations of an older chancel,
probably of 12th-century type, and the main building is assigned to
the 13th century. Nothing was found of the Early Christian period
and no stone monuments of this period have been recorded from the
Isle of Whithorn. The chapel was found to be surrounded by an
enclosure wall which was still standing 1 m high in places.

There is a *promontory fort**, presumably of the Iron Age, on the
peninsula at the south end of the Isle of Whithorn. It has not been
excavated.

To complete the trio of sites in the Whithorn area associated with
St. Ninian one may visit *St. Ninian's cave** (Pl. 5) near Glasserton
(NX/422360). A sign leads off the A747 and one can drive to Physgill
House; a walk of about 1 km down to the shore and then right along

the beach brings one to the cave, the floor of which is about 7·6 m above sea level. The cave has been associated with St. Ninian by tradition, and the discovery in 1871 on the rock face near the entrance of an incised cross of early type seemed to support this. In 1884 excavations took place and uncovered several stone pavements and floors; more crosses were found cut on loose boulders as well as on the walls of the cave. It appeared that even the earliest deposits were relatively recent and the height of the crosses on the walls suggests that the Early Christian levels had been destroyed: the floor at that time would have been at about the level of the present one. Several crosses are still visible on the cave walls, protected by iron grilles. They are done in the pecked technique characteristic of Early Christian memorial stones and were presumably executed by pilgrims visiting the cave.

There is another concentration of ancient sites of various kinds around Port William and Monreith, west of Whithorn. The area can be reached by the A747 from Whithorn (8 km) or by the A714 from Wigtown (12 km). If one travels parallel to the A714 along the B7005 and the minor road through Kirk of Mochrum one passes the well-preserved Norman *Druchtag Motte** just north of Mochrum village and by the side of the road (NX/349466). Approaching Port William

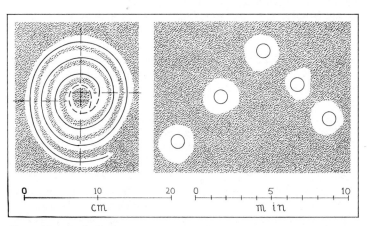

Fig. 8. Two Early Bronze Age rock carvings. On the left is the spiral at Knock, Wigtownshire, made up of half ellipses. On the right is the set of cup-marks on Gourock golf course, Renfrewshire, which form Pythagorean triangles of 3–4–5 and 6–8–10 megalithic inches. Scale 1:5.

from Wigtown one may pause to visit several *cup-and-ring marked rocks*. There are two groups on *Drumtroddan farm**+ (NX/363447) which are reached by going through the farm buildings and turning S. There are cups, cups with rings and others with connecting channels. The group of markings at *Big Balcraig*+ is just north of the B7021 and 1·5 km east of its junction with the A714 (NX/374440), and those at *Clachan*+ are about 500 m north-north-east of the last mentioned (NX/376445). In view of the claims that have been made about the accurate geometry underlying cup-and-ring marks, it might be of interest to look at the design on the sea-shore at *Knock* (NX/364402). One takes the by-road S to the shore from the A747 a kilometre east of Monreith, and goes straight on to the shore when this road turns left. One of the designs here fits a spiral built up from a series of five half ellipses (Fig. 8).

There is a fine Early Christian stone cross in the grounds of *Monreith House**+ (NX/355429). It is best to enter the south driveway which leads east from a minor road going south from the A714 1 km east of Port William. Carry on up the drive for 0·6 km and turn through the iron gates on the right. The cross has been set up on the lawn in front of the house but was originally on Court Hill at the Mower. Still standing 2·3 m high, the cross is a fine example of the interlace-decorated work of the 'Whithorn School' of sculptors in the latter part of the 10th century, while Galloway was under Viking domination. It has the disc-shaped head with central boss and the expanded arms of the cross are formed by four circles. The shaft is unusual in that the two narrow edges, as well as the flat faces, are covered with the interlace pattern so that the monument was conceived as a true shaft of the older type, and not just as a flat slab.

Not far away is the stone circle known as the '*Wren's Egg*'*+ (NX/361420). One takes the farmroad to Blairbuie further south-east along the same minor road that leads past Monreith House. Originally there was a double concentric ring of stones but only three remain. The 'Wren's Egg' is the large round boulder. Thom calls another group of *stones* 450 m to the south by this name (NX/362415) and suggests that an astronomical alignment was intended here. The stones point to the south-west to the island of Big Scare which, being on a bearing of $227\frac{1}{2}°$, gives a declination of $-23·6°$ suitable for midwinter sunset in prehistoric times. The writer does not know whether the near-by wood now blocks the view out to sea to the south-west.

The A747 to Port William runs along the coast after Monreith and it is convenient to pause at Barsalloch point. The post-glacial raised beach is very clear here and to the north of the road the old sea-cliff rises sharply. Mesolithic sites have been discovered at various places along the top of this cliff and one at Barsalloch yielded a hearth with charcoal which gave a radiocarbon date of 4050 ± 110 b.c. Evidently small bands of hunter-gatherers occasionally camped on top of the cliffs while the sea washed at their base.

At the point is *Barsalloch Fort**+, sited on top of the cliff (NX/347412): the notice-board can just be seen from the road. One can either clamber up the steep slope straight to it or go up the valley at the houses to the south. This latter route is doubtless one of those used by the Mesolithic people to get down to the beach. The defences of the fort are impressive and consist of two ramparts with a wide, deep ditch between. These curve round to form a D-shaped enclosure against the edge of the cliff, which forms the straight side of the D.

The same coast road leads on towards Glenluce and the remains of *Chapel Finnian**+ may be visited beside it some 8 km beyond Port William. The site consists of a mortared rectangular stone chapel, measuring some 6·7 m by 4·1 m internally and buttressed. It is surrounded by a drystone wall enclosing an oval area which contains a well (just inside the gate in the road wall). The chapel is named after the Celtic St. Findbar and is dated to the 10th or 11th century. Its situation near the shore suggests that it was for the use of pilgrims after they had come ashore at some near-by landing place.

The Rhinns of Galloway

Travelling W along the A75 from Newton Stewart, or the A747 from Port William and Whithorn, one reaches Glenluce and the vicinity of the extensive sandhills around Luce Bay which have yielded a vast haul of archaeological finds of all periods.

Half a kilometre farther along the A75 the minor road to New Luce leads to *Glenluce Abbey**+ (NX/185587), a Cistercian monastery founded in 1192 by Roland, Earl of Galloway and colonised by Cistercian monks from Dundrennan or Melrose. Excavations took place here in the late 1940s and a small site museum shows photographs of the work and some of the finds.

The general design of the monastery is a cruciform church with the cloister garth situated against the south side of the nave. The rest of the buildings surrounded the other three sides of the square.

5

Of the church, most of the nave and the north transept have been completely razed to the ground but the south wall remains, with the door to the cloister walk at the east end. Holes for the beams of the timber roof of the cloister walk are visible in the upper part of this wall. The nave measured 35·7 m long internally by 17 m wide. The south transept has an aisle on its east side separated from the rest by two arches; enough of the pier remains to show that these are in the 'first pointed' style and date to the second half of the 13th century. The raised door in the south-west corner of the transept, its sill 2·1 m above the floor, once had the stone night stair running up to it and it led to the monks' dormitories above the east claustral buildings. Little remains of the north transept.

The east wing of the claustral buildings abuts on to the south transept and the vaulted chapter house is the second building along it. This is the most complete surviving fragment of the monastery, and is later than the rest: it was probably built in the 16th century to replace an earlier chapter house.

Carry on further up this road to see the two *Mid-Gleniron Neolithic chambered cairns* (NX/187610). A little less than 2 km beyond the abbey a farmroad turns off east and the cairns are a further kilometre up that. They were excavated between 1963 and 1966 by Dr John Corcoran and are of particular interest because they were the first to yield clear information about the successive stages of enlargement that cairns of this kind often underwent while they were in use.

The first site lies to the north (left) of the track leading to Mid-Gleniron farm and before excavation it appeared to be a horned long cairn with three chambers in different parts of the mound. Excavations showed that the oldest structure was an oval cairn with a chamber which now forms the rear part of the mound. A second similar one was built close in front of it while the third stage involved incorporating these two mounds in a single long cairn, adding a curved façade to the north side of the north one and inserting a third chamber between the two round mounds. Nine cremations in inverted cinerary urns, belonging to the Bronze Age, had been inserted into the body of the cairn in its final state. The burials in the various chambers had all been removed at some earlier time but the sequence of alterations to the cairns doubtless took place at intervals during 4th and 3rd millennia B.C. The entrance to the north cairn was finally blocked up and the nine Bronze Age burials were presumably put in later, during the 2nd millennium B.C.

The second cairn, *Mid-Gleniron II*, is about 100 m to the south-east at NX/188609, on the other side of the farm road. This too appeared to be a multi-period cairn in which a simple, east-facing oval, chambered cairn was enclosed within a larger, rectangular cairn with a façade and chamber facing south.

These two excavations were the first in Scotland which showed how much useful information about the development of Neolithic burial sites could be obtained by carefully analysing the structure of the cairns.

Travelling W again along the A75 continue on it to Dunragit and turn S along the A748. A well-preserved *Norman motte*, that of *Droughdod*, can be seen at the edge of a wood on the east (left) along the A748 before it joins the A715 (NX/148569). Continue along the A715 and then take the A716 through Sandhead, turning on to the minor road to the west, 1 km south of the village, to *Kirkmadrine church**+ (NX/081484). Take the first right turn and the church is at the top of a track running north through a wood, 2 km from the main road.

Set in a glass-fronted porch or recess in the outside wall of the west end of the church are a number of important *Early Christian stones** three of the finest of which are Celtic and belong to the earliest of the three periods suggested above (p. 60), to the time of St. Ninian himself or soon after (Fig. 7). These stones, and a number of other pre-Norman cross fragments, have been found in the church and churchyard at various times and indicate that the place was probably a Celtic monastery up to as late as the 10th or 11th century. The name suggests that the site was dedicated to St. Mathurinus, a 4th-century saint; the earliest stone belongs to the 5th century.

The first stone, K.1, is a squarish gravestone with a slightly expanded-arm cross inside a circle carved at the top. The upper arm of the cross has a loop at the right side, converting the whole into the Chi-Rho monogram, and the inscription below, in six lines, reads: HIC IACENT / S(AN)C(T)I ET PRAE / CIPUI SACER / DOTES IDES / VIVENTIUS / ET MAVORIUS. This reads: 'Here lie the holy and chief priests, Ides, Vaventius and Mavorius.' It has been suggested that 'chief priests' means 'bishops' so that Kirkmadrine was an important ecclesiastical centre. The stone is dated to the 5th century from the style of the lettering which is straightforward, well-cut roman.

Stone K.2 is a similar pillar with the same encircled cross incorporating a Chi-Rho monogram. Below is the damaged inscription . . . S ET / FLOREN / TIUS / meaning '(Here lie) . . .s and Florentius.' This memorial is dated to the late 5th century.

The third stone, K.3, is again similar in shape but the encircled ·cross is thicker with more markedly wedge-shaped arms. Below is the inscription INITIUM ET FINIS, 'The beginning and the end'; this refers to Revelation, xxii, 13: 'I am Alpha and Omega: the beginning and the end, the first and the last.' This stone is dated to somewhere near the year A.D. 600.

There are a number of other fragments of stone monuments which have been found at Kirkmadrine over the years and these belong to later times, to the Northumbrian (Anglian) and Viking periods.

If one continues along the by-road running south-west from south of Sandhead one can visit the *Ardwell broch*★ (NX/066466). Follow the straight road right down to the nearest point to the shore: the broch is about 300 m further south and round the point. This broch is one of the more convincing of the four or five examples claimed in Wigtownshire; it is reasonably well preserved, unexcavated and is characteristically situated on a rocky knoll close to the sea. The inside wallface can be seen above the rubble and various intramural features are apparent. There is an entrance passage facing the sea and what is probably a secondary entrance on the opposite side. The site is defended by a wall and ditch cutting off the neck of the promontory, with a built causeway spanning the ditch.

There are two well-preserved Norman mottes in the same area. *Ardwell Motte* (NX/107455) is 200 m west of the A716 at Ardwell while *High Dunmore Motte* (NX/139359) is just north of the B7041 1 km south-west of Drummore.

3 · South-east Scotland

(Roxburgh, Selkirk, Peebles, Berwick, the Lothians and Edinburgh)

The terrain in the border counties of Roxburgh, Selkirk and Peebles varies between uplands of wild, rolling hills and grass-covered moors and the great lowland basin of the river Tweed in which there are many attractive, winding river valleys and luxuriant woods. This country, like Galloway, is far from crowded even in the summer holiday season and the minor roads have very little traffic. The border towns of Melrose, Jedburgh, Kelso, Hawick and the rest are ideal centres from which to explore the numerous archaeological remains, particularly the spectacular ruined abbeys for which the region is famous.

1. ROXBURGH

The Hawick area

A stone circle, of some interest geometrically, is *Burgh Hill* (or *Allan water*) 8 km south-south-west of Hawick (NT/470062). Take the by-road SW out of Hawick itself: it forms a triangle with the A7 and the circle is about 2 km from the southern tip along the east side, 300 m west of the road at a height of 950 ft near the summit of Burgh Hill. There are 25 stones, 13 of which still stand; in plan the setting is sub-oval, 16·5 m from south-east to south-west and 13·4 m transversely. Thom classes it as a Type 1 egg-shape, the figure being based on two opposed Pythagorean triangles of $5\frac{1}{2}$, $6\frac{1}{2}$ and $8\frac{1}{2}$ megalithic yards (Fig. 9). The wide part of the 'egg' is a half-circle 16 my in diameter, the long sides are arcs of circles 27 my in diameter and the tip fits a segment of a circle 10 my diameter centred on the apex of the triangles.

In Hawick itself is a well-preserved *Norman motte** (NT/499141). It is situated in Mote Park, reached from the street called Loan

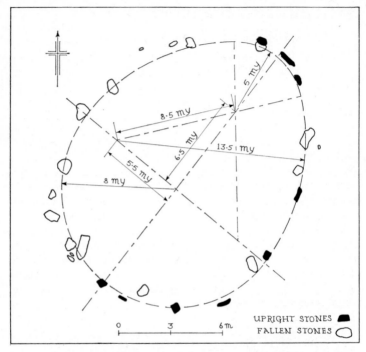

Fig. 9. Plan of the Burgh Hill (Allan water) stone circle, Roxburghshire. The suggested egg-shaped geometrical construction is shown in dotted lines, standing stones in black and fallen stones white. Scale 1:200.

which runs south-west from Drumlanrig Square. The mound is a truncated cone 7·6 m high with a flat top 12·5 m in diameter; it is apparently entirely artificial. The ditch round the base is scarcely visible now but excavation in 1912 showed that it was 8·5-4·3 m wide, flat-bottomed and 1·2-2·1 m deep. Pottery and a coin of Henry II (1154-89) recovered from it suggested a 12th-century date: at this time a member of the Lovel family held Hawick.

Six kilometres west of Hawick, on the B711 to Roberton, can be seen one of the rare Pictish symbol stones in the lowlands at *Borthwick Mains** (NT/437140). A stone pillar 1·5 m high and roughly square in section with each face measuring about 36 cm across, it is situated on the lawn in front of the house at Borthwick Mains farm. The figure of a fish, 94 cm long and with the tail downwards, is cut into the stone with pecked lines, a standard Pictish technique. Eyes, gills and dorsal and ventral fins are all clearly marked. A hole near the top of the pillar suggests that it was once used as a gate-post. The absence of careful dressing and of Christian symbols indicates that this is a Class I stone datable approximately to the 6th or 7th century A.D.

A few kilometres south-east of Hawick along the A6088 is Bonchester bridge and overlooking it is the well-known fort on *Bonchester Hill*★ (NT/595117). One convenient way up is from a field gate in the main road about 0·7 km south of the bridge. The hilltop, 1,020 ft above the sea, commands an extensive view to the north-east and north-west. The fortifications consist of an outer encircling ring of earthworks below the base of the knoll which actually forms the summit of the hill, and enclosing the steep scarp slope on the south side. The area defended by these ramparts, which excavations in 1950 showed to be the final of three phases of fortification, measures some 290 m north–south and 240 m east–west. There are some circular hut foundations within this rampart on the west side, beyond the modern wall.

The second stage of the defences is represented by traces of an inner grass-grown bank; this is inside the modern wall on the west and it starts at the top of the steep slope there and runs round the northern side to end at the top of the same steep slope on the east. Here the bank is close to the Phase III rampart just described. The primary fort was a stone-walled enclosure within this, built round the top of the summit knoll to enclose an area of 105 m north–south and 85 m east–west. The main wall was originally from 3·0 to 3·7 m thick at base and does not seem to have been timber-framed. Finds probably associated with this fort included an early La Tène (Ic) brooch and an iron crook-headed pin. A date in the 5th century B.C. for it would not be impossible and the two other phases of fortification would presumably fall between that time and A.D. 80, the time of the first Roman conquest.

Jedburgh

In the museum of the famous Augustinian abbey in this town, described below, are some *Early Christian carved stones*★ of Anglian type which show that there was a shrine on the site in the 8th or 9th century. The finest piece is a large squarish fragment of creamy white sandstone some 66 cm wide and 82 cm high which has been identified as part of the gabled end of a *stone sarcophagus*. The piece

includes the right border, decorated with pure Anglian interlace ornament between plain margins, and most of the central panel with
intertwined vines with birds and animals. The fragment is dated to
about A.D. 700. The slight notch at the upper end of the right margin
has been interpreted as the point from which the steep gabled top
part of the end of the sarcophagus, like an inverted V, sprang up. On
the back of the slab is a groove against which one of the long sides of
the sarcophagus rested. It has been argued that this tomb might have
been made for St. Boisil, one of the early abbots of Old Melrose (p. 82
below), whose bones were removed from there to Durham.

Also in the museum is part of the head of a large *Anglian cross*
with interlace decorations of late 8th- or early 9th-century type, and
several other early fragments. There is also a large piece of a decorated *stone coffin cover* dating stylistically to about the middle of the
12th century. The length is now 1·37 m but it was probably originally
about 1·7 m long. On it is sculpted a tall cross with a stepped base,
the head is missing. This is flanked by two borders of simple plaited
strands. It has been suggested that this slab might have covered the
tomb of Bishop John of Glasgow (p. 107 below) who died in 1148
and was buried in the church of the new abbey of Jedburgh.

Jedburgh Abbey*+ (Pl. 6) was founded for the Augustinian order
in about 1138 by David I, although it is clear from the stones in the
museum (described above) that there had been a church on the site
since at least the 9th century. No part of this has survived but it is
thought to have occupied the position of the six east bays of the
present nave. This is deduced from the placing of the first, small
cloister garth against it (below).

The abbey church is well preserved in part, the pier arcades of
the nave, on pillars, being entire up to the level of the roof, as also is
the tower over the crossing. The claustral buildings are badly ruined;
they extended south from the nave down a slope towards the river
Jed which formed the southern boundary of the site. The west end
of the nave opens on to the street and is almost intact: it is of late
12th-century date and built in the Transitional style (between
Romanesque and early Gothic or Pointed). The round arch of the
doorway has six decorated orders and is unusually high. On the inside
of this doorway are entrances to two staircases within the flanking
buttresses. Immediately inside the entrance to the north stair is a
lintel which is a re-used Roman stone. The inscription reads: I(OVI).
O(PTIMO). M(AXIMO). VEX/IL(L)ATIO. RAETO/RUM.GAESAT(ORUM)
/Q(UORUM). C(URAM). A(GIT). IUL(IUS)/SEVER(INUS *or* US). TRIB

Plate 6. Jedburgh Abbey, Roxburgh: the nave and crossing from the SW.

(UNUS) /. It translates as 'To Jupiter, best and greatest, a detachment of Raetian spearmen under the command of the tribune Julius Severinus (or Severus) (dedicated this altar).'

The nave has eight pairs of pillars forming nine bays and the surviving masonry is also of late 12th-century date. The aisles are fragmentary and the outer walls badly broken down; the south wall is higher but has been extensively restored. Two round-arched processional doorways are in this wall, the one on the east being late 12th century and the one on the west a modern restoration. The nave actually replaces a smaller late 12th-century structure and abuts against the Romanesque transepts which remained unaltered when the church was thus enlarged. At the crossing only the north-east pier is Romanesque and on each side of the north transept there are Romanesque archways opening into the nave aisle and the east chapel. The outer part of this transept has been re-roofed to serve as the burial place for the Earls of Lothian.

The choir is unique in Scotland in that the triforium is incorporated within the pier arcade, creating a soaring effect in the columns and arches. The west part of the choir is mid-12th century Romanesque and the east part is later Transitional work: the junction between the two styles can be clearly seen.

The conventual buildings are now badly ruined but the remains have been excavated and left open for inspection. The original cloister was 12·5 m square and is too small for the present nave. It presumably fitted against the pre-Norman church, mentioned earlier, which the Augustinian canons used for a while after they came. The cloister was later extended westwards when the larger nave was built and the two successive bordering alleyways can be traced on the west and south sides of the cloister garth. The east range contained the sleeping quarters over the chapter house, a room which may have been the treasury, and other rooms further down the slope. It extended beyond the south range so that the reredorter (latrine) could be over the stream running away from the abbey mill. This range was more or less left unaltered and is mostly of 12th- and 13th-century date. The west range, however, was moved two bays outwards in the 14th century after the nave had been enlarged, so that it was aligned with the west façade of the church. The west range contained the frater (refectory) and the 12th-century undercroft of this is visible next to the cloister. The 14th-century enlargement of the cloister resulted in the new south alley running along where the frater had been and in the latter being transferred to an upper floor.

On the other side of the road along the south side is the mill stream, beyond a wall which is monastic up to a height of 3·7 m. The outlet of the west drain from the monastery can be seen in this wall.

Kelso

Kelso Abbey*+ was founded by David I about 1128 for a convent of reformed Benedictine monks, the Tironensians, who had originally settled at Selkirk in about 1119 but had found that site unsuitable. They came to Selkirk from the mother house at Tiron in France. The new site was on flat land on the left bank of the Tweed. Only the west end of the church remains partly standing: the rest of the church and all except one of the claustral buildings—which were on the south side—have vanished in the various destructions which have overtaken the abbey. The church is unique in having had double transepts, a pair at each end, and also two towers, one over each crossing. It was founded in 1128 and dedicated in 1243. The west end was built at about 1190 and in the same style as the original

Romanesque design although with its architectural details in the then current Transitional style. The remains thus comprise one of the largest fragments of Romanesque architecture in the border area.

The gable of the north transept is still complete and presents an impressive façade to the street. Half of the west gable has collapsed but a fragment of the fine, round-arched doorway remains. The south arcade of the nave can be seen from the outside, as the south aisle wall has been demolished, and its wall is preserved to roof height. The angle of the roof of the nave can be seen on the east and west sides of the tower. Spiral stairs lead up from the west outer corners of the transepts and there is a piscina recess in the south transept.

The only remaining fragment of the claustral buildings is the outer parlour, which is next to the south transept. It is a barrel-vaulted room in which are the remains of an elaborate arcade on the south wall.

The Cheviots and the Border

An instructive excursion to see a variety of archaeological sites in wild border country can easily be arranged from Jedburgh or Kelso. From Jedburgh take the east by-road 6 km to Oxnam. The left fork 1 km after that village leads, after another 5 km, to another left fork and 1·5 km beyond that are the *Pennymuir Roman camps** (NT/755138), the *Roman road* known as *Dere Street** and the *Iron Age hillfort* on *Woden Law** (NT/768125). Dere Street is the Saxon name for the main Roman road which runs from the Tees to the Forth, the east of the two major routes into Scotland. The road comes down the gully to the east (left) of Woden Law and there is a good stretch south of this point, towards Hunthall Hill. The road there is a conspicuous causeway mound 8·2 m wide and about 1·2 m high. On the descent from Woden Law to Tow ford the mound is quite well preserved and it leads straight to the modern road which follows its course, across the ford, and up past the Pennymuir camps. After that it leaves the modern road and runs away north-west beside the field wall up to the summit of the moors. At 200 m north of Pennymuir farm there is a 100 m length of mound 6·4 m wide. For those with an imaginative cast of mind it is extremely easy, in this wild and quiet border country, to visualise the legions marching down Dere Street past Woden Law and across the ford to bivouac in Pennymuir camps.

Two of the three *Pennymuir temporary camps** are in the angle between the road north from Tow ford and the west arm of the T-junction to which it leads. The third camp is bisected by the eastern bar of the T-junction about 350 m along the road from it. They are the best preserved of their kind in Scotland and are delineated by long, straight ramparts with an external ditch. The larger and earlier of the first two camps, close beside Dere Street, is approximately rectangular in shape and is 520 m long (north–south) and 329–52 m wide. It encloses 0·17 km² (42 acres), enough to accommodate two legions of 5,000 men in tents. Where it has not been destroyed by cultivation (along most of the south side and on the south half of the east side) the rampart is well preserved, standing up to 1·2 m high and being about 4·6 m thick at base. The ditch in front is about 4·6 m wide and up to 1·2 m deep. Five gates are now visible, one each in the north, east and south sides and two in the west. Each is between 17·4 m and 20·7 m wide and is protected by a traverse in front.

The smaller, later camp occupies the south-east corner of the larger one, utilising the defences of the latter on the south and east sides, and its rampart and ditch can be seen to override those of the larger camp at the two junctions. It measures 293 m north–south by 125 m east–west and the east and west sides are in good order. Four gates now remain, two on the west, one on the north and one on the east; the last has lost its traverse. Three gates are about 8·5 m wide but the more northerly of the two west ones has subsequently been reduced to 2 m for some reason.

The third camp is not so well preserved as the other two.

The near-by multivallate hillfort on *Woden Law*★ (NT/768125), although only partly excavated, is of considerable interest both because of the excellent state of preservation of its rampart and ditches and also because of the Roman siege-works—also well preserved—which surround them (Fig. 10). The hill stands 1,388 ft high and the north-west slope descends steeply towards the Tow ford. The easiest ascent is to follow Dere Street up the gully to its flank and then to go straight up the hill. The hill is strategically situated; the pass through which Dere Street runs is the most convenient way through the northern flank of the Cheviots for many miles on either side.

A limited amount of excavation was carried out on the ramparts of both the hillfort and the siege-works in 1950 and it showed that the former had been constructed in three phases. In Phase I the fort consisted of a single stone wall, without a ditch, enclosing an oval area some 137 m long with a maximum width of 53 m. Its entrances were

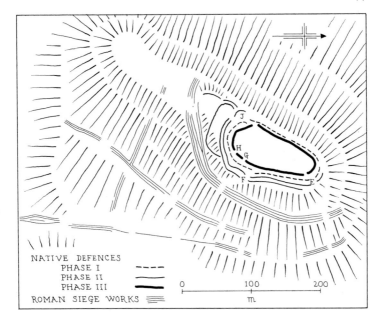

Fig. 10. Plan of the Woden Law hillfort, Roxburghshire, showing the three phases of the native defences and Roman siege-works. Dere Street passes the hill at lower right. Scale 1:5260.

NATIVE DEFENCES
PHASE I
PHASE II
PHASE III
ROMAN SIEGE WORKS

0   100   200

m.

probably at J and F, the rampart being sharply turned in at the former point. The stone for this wall seems to have been obtained from the quarry at the northern end of the summit. In Phase II two outer ramparts, with a ditch between them, were added to create defence in depth. It seems that the inner rampart was faced with stone taken from the original fort wall, and that the outer one was faced with timber. Three undug causeways crossed this line of defences at E, F and J. Both these ramparts were systematically destroyed not long after construction and this event is likely to be linked with the building of the Roman road by Agricola. The first stone-walled fort could have been built some centuries earlier.

The third phase of fortification seems to have taken place in post-Roman times when a boulder-faced rubble wall some 2·75 m thick was built within the previous defences (III on the plan). The resulting enclosure is roughly oval and measures 121 m long with a maximum width of 49 m. The entrance to this fort is at G, where the earlier ditch has been filled in. There are traces of four round huts within the fort.

Several clear lines of outer banks and ditches are visible, which are Roman constructions. They all appear to have been dug in separate sectors in the Roman manner, and all are unfinished. The innermost line consists of three ditches with two banks between them which run at a distance of 30–12 m from the hillfort, mainly beyond the effective range of hand-thrown spears (though the sector 12 m distant on the south-east side is too close for safety). Several stretches of the outer banks have been flattened and excavations showed that these had been reinforced by ballasting with stone: they are likely to have been artillery platforms.

There are three other lines of siege-works further out, one at right angles to the other two, and none seems to have been completed. The second circuit cuts across the line at right angles to it and was built later. The whole arrangement is interpreted as the results of training exercises for Roman troops and there can be little doubt that the Pennymuir camps were built to accommodate the units who practised on Woden Law on at least two occasions.

With some fairly extensive walking up Dere Street to the north of the Pennymuir camps one can see some much earlier sites. By following the Roman road for 1·2 km one finds the *Black Knowe cairn**★* at the summit of the rise and a few metres west of the stone wall which forms the parish boundary (NT/751155). This is a small round cairn some 8·2 m in diameter with five boulders around its perimeter. There are four more outlying boulders which may have been moved from the cairn. The possibility of the cairn being a marker for a distant astronomical foresight is dramatically brought home on a clear day if one approaches the site from the south. As one gets to the summit of the ridge on which it stands the view to the north-west suddenly opens out and the three Eildon Hills are strikingly silhouetted against the sky 26 km away.

A short journey 5 km north from Tow ford to Hownam brings one close to two interesting sites, some rows of standing stones and a hillfort close together. There is a track just north of the bridge leading east from the village and this takes one 1·3 km to the summit of the hill. *Hownam Rings* hillfort (NT/791194) is about 400 m north along the top of the hill from the track and the *standing stones* are in the same line about 100 m nearer (NT/792193). The latter are marked on the 1-inch Ordnance Survey map as a row of dots but are not labelled. They are not mentioned in the Royal Commission's *Inven-*

tory of Roxburgh although they are labelled on the map in the back pocket.

Hownam Rings was excavated in 1948 and was the first site of its kind in southern Scotland which was shown, by skilful interpretation, to have gone through several periods of occupation. The fort stands on the raised north end of the elongated plateau formed by the hilltop and the slopes leading up to it are steep on all sides except the south-south-east. The first phase of the defences was a wooden palisade, the post-holes of which underlie the Phase III ramparts. At the time of excavation such a wooden defensive enclosure was thought likely to have been built in the 2nd century B.C. at the earliest, but radio-carbon dates from similar sites have since shown that they are more likely to be of 6th or even 7th century date, belonging to the last phase of the Scottish Late Bronze Age.

As at Woden Law (p. 76 above), the second phase involved the construction of a stone wall 3–3·7 m wide at base. This ran round the hilltop and enclosed an area some 75 m north–south by 90 m east–west. The gateway was in the south-east and was 1·2 m wide. The wall was destroyed, only the foundations remaining, when the Phase III defences were built. These are the visible banks and ditches round the site and consist of a multivallate system of earth-works evidently designed, as at many other hillforts, to combat long-range weapons (probably the sling) by creating a defence in depth. There are up to four ramparts, the outer two being very fragmentary and adequately visible only on the west side. The innermost and second ramparts now stand about 1·2 m high; the former was built of stone from the Phase II wall and the second with material scraped up from a shallow ditch in front of it.

The excavations showed that the system of multiple ramparts had hardly been completed before it was falling into ruin. In Phase IV the site was an open settlement with numerous hut circles which lay both in the fort interior and over parts of the defences. One such hut, on the northern arc of the defences, was excavated and yielded 3rd-century Roman pottery as well as native wares. There are traces of a rectangular homestead, measuring about 33·5 m by 26 m, overlying the ramparts at the east end of the fort. There was an earlier hut circle inside it, 7·3 m in diameter, which yielded a few finds suggesting a late Roman or early post-Roman date.

It seems reasonable to suppose that the multivallate defence works were hastily built to combat the threat of the rapid Roman advance through England after A.D. 43 which culminated in Agricola's invasion of Scotland in about A.D. 80. The fort would then have been destroyed or have surrendered and the open settlement would reflect the establishment of the *pax Romana* in the area.

The rows of standing stones near by, the *Eleven Shearers*, have been planned by Professor A. Thom, who for many years has been engaged on accurate surveys of standing stones throughout Britain with the object of deciphering their possible astronomical uses. They now consist of about 16 low stones running more or less due east-west (on azimuth 94·5°) with suggestions of two more lines diagonal to this on an azimuth of 109·2°. The lines point to distant hill horizons and give astronomical declinations which could refer, in the case of the main row, to the equinoctial sunrise and, in the case of the diagonal, to an intermediate solar calendar date.

The Melrose area

Melrose is situated at a strategic cross-roads in south-east Scotland and has been an important centre since prehistoric times. The river Tweed and the flat country round it provide an open route to the sea on the east; the routes south to Newcastle skirt the east end of the Cheviot Hills along the coastal plain. To the west, past Galashiels, is the pass known as the Biggar gap which leads to the upper valley of the Clyde and so to Glasgow and the west coast. To the south-west is Liddesdale, the pass to Galloway and Carlisle, while the A7 runs to Edinburgh through the pass to the north. There are fords across the Tweed both above and below the sharp bend in which lies Old Melrose (p. 82 below). In and near Melrose are four major sites— dating from the Iron Age, Roman, Early Christian and Early Medieval periods—which bear witness to this strategic situation. Unfortunately only the earliest and latest are at all visible above ground.

The great Iron Age oppidum of *Eildon Hill**+ sits on top of the north of the three hills of that name which form an isolated group overlooking the town (NT/555328). The series of ramparts encircling the slopes around the shallow dome-shaped summit are conspicuous from several kilometres away. Although the fort has not been excavated the remains of ramparts and hut circles on the hilltop are very clear. The fort can be approached from the north or south. In the former case one follows the first part of the 'Eildon walk' which is signposted, starting from the B6359 to Lilliesleaf a short way up from the centre of the town. This involves a stiff climb up the upper slopes. There is a cart track suitable for Land-Rovers leading to the top from the south side and to reach this one approaches along the

B6398 from Newtown St. Boswells, or takes the minor road from Eildon on the A6091 3 km out of Melrose.

The oppidum is the largest hillfort in Scotland, enclosing 0·16 km² (39 acres), and is placed in a situation of great natural strength. The summit inside it is 1,327 ft above the sea and nearly 1,100 ft above the river. The enclosed area consists of, first, a flattish summit area with traces of numerous hut circles all over it; secondly, a broad plateau below this on the south side, a good part of which is encircled by a stone-faced bank (probably for a fairly recent plantation); thirdly, a series of gradually descending terraces running south-west from the top towards the col joining Eildon Hill North with the middle hill, also with numbers of hut circles on them; and fourthly a sloping plateau below the summit on the north-west side, also covered in circular hut platforms.

The Royal Commission's careful survey suggests that the fortifications surrounding all this went through several stages of development. The largest and best-preserved ramparts form the outermost, and latest, system which is nearly circular in plan and almost 1·6 km in circumference. This system runs along a natural shoulder which borders the various plateaux described and separates them from the steep slopes below. There seem to have been three concentric ramparts originally but large parts of these have slid down the hill. In many places only flat terraces are left on which the ramparts were originally sited. Five entrances can be traced through these defence works, on the east, east-south-east, south-south-west, west-south-west and slightly east of north.

The oppidum in this its final phase was evidently a small native town, since a total of 296 circular hut sites have so far been identified inside the ramparts and there must have been many more on the south terrace—obliterated by the plantation—and on flat ground where they would leave little trace. Most are level, circular platforms created on a slope by hollowing out the uphill half-circle and using the debris to form an artificial semi-circular platform on the downhill side. Thus a sheltered, round, level floor was made.

Traces of the ramparts of two earlier, smaller hillforts can be seen. Fragments of a terrace about 2·4 m wide for a rampart can be seen on the north, west and south sides; it seems to have enclosed the whole of the summit area and the uppermost of the series of natural terraces on the south-west. Finally there is a fragmentary rampart which enclosed an elliptical area on the south side of the summit, along the edge of which there is no trace of it. This might be the

6

earliest fort on the site and is difficult to see on the ground: it is clearly visible on air photographs.

At the west end of the summit is a circular ditched enclosure 10·7 m in diameter inside which, revealed by excavation, had stood a wooden *Roman signal tower* which was presumably an outpost of *Newstead Camp*. Of this great fort, one of the largest and most important of Roman Scotland, no traces survive on the surface although it was extensively excavated from 1905 to 1909 and explored again in 1949 (NT/571344). The site is near the modern village of Newstead and can be reached along the B6361 taken from the centre of Melrose or from the A68 2·5 km north of Newtown St. Boswells. The north ramparts of the main, almost square camp run along parallel to and partly under the north side of the B6361 from a point starting about 400 m east of the Y-junction immediately east of the village and they continue for some 290 m. The main fort underlies the field to the south of the road and in certain seasons areas of soil coloured black by charcoal can still be seen. Many important inscribed stone altars and other pieces were found during the excavations and are now in the National Museum in Edinburgh together with a mass of pottery and other finds. The site was occupied both in the Flavian and Antonine periods.

The second unexcavated and almost invisible yet archaeologically important site is *Old Melrose**—*Mailros* of the historian Bede—an Early Christian Celtic monastery which was founded between A.D. 635 and 650 by St. Aidan who was a monk of Iona and bishop of Lindisfarne. This monastery was burned by Kenneth MacAlpin, King of Scots, in A.D. 849.

The site is the long, broad promontory formed by a wide bend in the Tweed 2 km north of Newtown St. Boswells. On the opposite, outer side of the curve are steep cliffs below Bemersyde Hill on which is Scott's view (p. 89 below). The ground on the promontory is private and reached by an old road which runs to the house called Old Melrose east from the A68. It leaves it just north of the bridge over the railway and 1·5 km north of Newtown St. Boswells. About 320 m before this house is reached the road forks and passes through a ditch and bank earthwork which has been traced all the way across the promontory, which is at its narrowest here. This is believed to be the remains of the outer defence of Mailros.

There was a stone chapel close to the house dedicated to St. Cuthbert. Its foundations are reported by the present owner to be underneath the greenhouse. St. Cuthbert came to Mailros in 651 when Boisil was prior; parts of the latter's finely carved stone sarco-phagus or shrine have been identified at Jedburgh (p. 72 above). The chapel itself probably dated to the late 11th century, after the Celtic monastery itself had been burned and abandoned. There is a fragment of a 12th-century corbel of red sandstone from this chapel in the Melrose Abbey museum.

Melrose Abbey*+ is in the town of that name (NT/549342) and is the fourth of the notable archaeological sites of this area. It is the earliest Cistercian monastery in Scotland, having been founded in 1136 by David I and colonised by monks from Rievaulx Abbey in Yorkshire. These evidently decided that the ancient monastic site of Old Melrose was unsuitable and chose a better-drained, more open spot 4 km further west. The abbey stands on level ground about 300 m from the river Tweed. The surviving remains of the church are impressive (Pl. 7) but most of these belong to the recon-structions of the 15th century. The general plan shows the abbey church aligned as usual east–west with the claustral buildings in an unusual position on its north side, nearer the river. The stream which used to serve as the main drain for the abbey, along the west side, has been diverted and the channel is exposed and dry.

The earliest 12th-century church was largely destroyed and replaced, but traces of it can still be seen. It was a simple, austere structure, completed ten years after the foundation in 1246 and dedicated to the Virgin Mary. In the late 14th century it was largely taken down and the present spectacular church, in the late Decorated and early Perpendicular style, was built. In general the later church followed the same plan as the early one, but a series of aisles were added to the south side of the nave, extending it outwards. The foundations of the early church were exposed in 1923 but the only visible masonry of that period is the base of the west gable of the nave where the 12th-century stonework includes the lowest part of the sides of the central doorway. As with the later church, the nave of the early one was presumably divided in two parts, with the lay brothers using the west half—which had a night stair leading to their residential wing—and the monks the east half.

Part of the original lay brothers' range, in 12th-century masonry, are visible on the west side of the cloister. Their building was two-storeyed, frater below and dorter above, and the lay brothers, or 'conversii', had their own separate cloister on the west side of this. The water trough in the central room of this range is a later feature, introduced when the lay brothers' range was enlarged and extended northwards, to a total length of 108·3 m, in the early 13th century and the frater had been transferred there. The northern extension, built with a vaulted undercroft of 14 bays and a central row of pillars, was evidently not too well constructed as strengthening buttresses had to be added to the inside of the walls at a later date. The northern part was used as cellars. The main drain ran under the northern end, and under the reredorter which apparently extended west of this point. There are two tiled tanning pits in this wing. The number of lay brothers living in the abbey had risen to about two hundred in the 13th century, which explains the need for the extension to their living quarters.

The east range extends north from the north transept for 54·9 m. In it, from south to north, were the sacristy, the chapter house, the inner parlours (the only part of the monastery where conversation between the monks was permitted), and an undercroft with two aisles with seven bays which may have been the monks' day-room. The masonry is 12th century with 13th-century alterations. The reredorter extended east from the range over a drain with running water. The monks' dorter was on the first floor and was reached by a day stair to the cloister next to the chapter house. The night stair to the church led up from the north transept to the dorter, the outline of the roof of which can be seen on the gable of the north transept.

The chapter house is particularly noteworthy in being one of only two in Scotland with tiled floors. The other is at Glenluce Abbey (p. 65 above). The second abbot, St. Waltheof (or Waldere), was buried in the chapter house and three fragments of a monumental stone tomb which might have belonged to him are now in the abbey museum. There is a lead casket still under the floor containing a mummified human heart: this recalls the story that the heart of Robert the Bruce is buried somewhere in Melrose Abbey.

The northern range runs beside the road and contains a warming house on the east, a second frater projecting north from the centre (extending to the north of the road) and the kitchen at the west end. The original 12th-century frater ran parallel to the church along the northern range but in the 13th century the second one was built out at right angles to it.

The architecture of the present abbey belongs mainly to the 14th- and 15th-century reconstructions and is notable for its elaborately decorated stonework, ornamented with flowers, gargoyles, traceries, figures of Christ and saints and many others. The Cistercian monks had gradually abandoned the austerity which the founder of their

Plate 7. Melrose Abbey, Roxburgh; view from the SW.

order had enjoined on them and turned more to outward show, presumably reflecting in stone the increasing wealth and worldliness which ultimately attracted to the monasteries the wrath of the Reformed Church. However, the sackings of the abbey by Sir Ralph Evers and the Earl of Hertford in 1545 were grievous blows from which Melrose never returned to its former glory.

For a description of the near-by Scott's view see p. 89 below; *Dryburgh Abbey* can be conveniently visited from the A68 nearby (p. 90).

2. SELKIRK

One of the few brochs in south-east Scotland is within easy reach, 10 km west of Melrose on the A72. About 3 km west of the junction with the A7 in Galashiels a farmroad winds north up the hill to Torwoodlee Mains. One goes through the farm, straight up the track to the top of the ridge and then turns east (right) along it. *Torwoodlee broch* and *hillfort** are to be found at the west end of a wood about 300 m east of the top of the track referred to (NT/466384).

The broch was cleared out in 1891, at which time a large quantity of Roman pottery and glass was found inside it. It was properly excavated in 1950 and its relationship with the hillfort, and the associated Roman material, was then successfully established. The site is now somewhat overgrown but the inner and outer wallfaces, and the various intramural features, can be easily traced. The circular, drystone structure is reduced to less than a metre in height all round and measures 23·2 m in overall diameter. The wall is 5·2 m thick so that the diameter of the central court, almost exactly circular, is from 11·9 m to 12·2 m. The entrance to the broch is on the east side and there is a check for the door in each wall of the passage. A doorway from the central court in the south-west side leads to the few remaining steps of the stair in the wall, rising to the right, and to a cell at the foot of the stair on the left. The broch is unusual in being surrounded by a ditch, with a causeway in front of the entrance. Excavation showed this to be V-shaped in section, some 2·7 m wide and 1·6 m deep, and also that it had been deliberately filled with rubble from the broch wall not long after it had been dug and before any silt had accumulated in it. The broch had evidently been systematically destroyed.

Cuttings through the wall of the broch showed that it had been built on top of Roman pottery and glass similar to that found in the interior in 1891. Most of this was Flavian material, belonging to the first Roman occupation of southern Scotland (about A.D. 80–100). The implication seems to be that a solid-based broch of a type common in Caithness and Sutherland was built, with several others, in south-east Scotland after the Romans withdrew in about A.D. 100 and that the Torwoodlee broch was thrown down not long afterwards, probably by a Roman expedition preparing for the reoccupation of A.D. 140. The many fragments of Roman material in the broch might be explained as loot from the great camp at Newstead a few kilometres away (p. 82) which was abandoned in about A.D. 100.

The excavation also showed that the broch was built partly over the filled-in ditches of the hillfort, whose defences are crossed just to the west as one approaches the broch. Possibly this hillfort was overthrown, and the ditches filled up, during the initial Agricolan campaign in about A.D. 80.

3. PEEBLES-SHIRE

Continuing W along the A72 after Torwoodlee one is traversing the pass leading to the Biggar gap, a valley 11 km long which provides an easy route through the mountainous country which separates the upper reaches of the Tweed from the Clyde valley to the west. There are several archaeological sites strategically situated in this pass. At Innerleithen is a fragment of an *Early Christian cross*,★ set up outside the east end of the parish church (NT/332369). Turn N up the B709 in the centre of the town and the church is on the left 200 m from the junction. The cross shaft is a rectangular block of stone, decorated on all four faces with pecked designs of cup-shaped hollows surrounded by double circles linked in dumb-bell patterns. A date in the 9th century has been given to this fragment, which was found in the foundations of the old parish church when this was demolished in 1871.

In Peebles itself is the *Cross Kirk*★+, the ruins of the church of a Trinitarian friary founded in the late 13th century (NT/250408).

The fort on *Whiteside Hill* is a few kilometres north-west of Peebles (NT/168461) and can conveniently be seen if following the A72. Follow the B7059 for 3·7 km north of its junction with the main road: there is a minor road to the east just before the 16th-century parish church of Newlands. This takes one to within about 400 m of the fort on the summit of the hill (1,200 ft). It is one of the most conspicuous and best preserved in the Lowlands, standing on a spur projecting from the east side of the valley of the Lyne water. Fine views are to be had from it.

Careful survey has shown that the hilltop was fortified in several stages. The first fort was a single rampart and ditch enclosing an area some 73 m in diameter. Two more concentric ramparts and ditches were added outside this in the second phase, but in the third phase a reduction in size occurred and a stone wall was built inside the first rampart enclosing an area some 61 m across. Finally a fourth phase saw this area drastically reduced again: the ruined wall of this fort occupied only the east corner of the earlier ones. There are outer defences on the north and south and traces of hut platforms inside belonging to some phase prior to the last.

If one follows the Tweed into the pass along the B712 one reaches Stobo. Here is the 12th-century *Stobo church*, the most important parish church in the region in Medieval times (NT/182376). The whole of the rectangular nave and chancel, together with the tower at the south-west end, seems to be of Romanesque origin but so many changes and additions to the structure have been made that it is difficult to see the original masonry. An extensive restoration took place in 1863. The side chapels are later additions but there are two original windows in the north wall of the chancel.

Next one can visit the spectacularly situated fort and settlement on *Dreva Craig*, where there is a rare example of an outer defence formed by *chevaux de frise* (NT/126353: the fort). When 3 km south west of Stobo take the minor road to the left (or from Broughton on the A701 from Edinburgh to Moffat), and the right fork uphill on that. Where the road crosses the summit of the ridge it is only 200 m from the fort which can be clearly seen to the south across level ground. From the fort one has extensive views up and down the valley.

The *chevaux de frise* is a device to break up a charge of horsemen or chariots, an alternative to rows of pits (p. 118 below). They consist of rows of stones or stakes set upright in the ground, usually arranged outside the main defences of a stronghold and protecting a vulnerable point. In the last war concrete pillars were designed to stop tanks in the same way. Prehistoric Iron Age forts with this type of outer defence have a wide distribution but are comparatively rare; stone examples occur in Shetland, southern Scotland, Wales and Ireland and in Spain in large numbers.

The fort consists of two stone walls, the inner one encircling the summit of the knoll and 3·7–4·3 m in thickness at the base. This encloses an oval area about 42 m by 53 m into which there is an entrance 3·7 m wide arranged through a natural gully on the east-south-east. There are traces of a secondary occupation within this wall in the form of four stone rings, presumably hut foundations, about 6 m in diameter and built partly in the debris fallen from the wall.

The outer wall is similar in construction—with a dry rubble core faced with boulders—and lies near the base of the knoll. It is best seen on the arc from north-west round to south-east where it is at its maximum distance of 30·5 m from the inner wall. There are traces of one side of an entrance on the north.

The *chevaux de frise* is on the south-west side of the fort (opposite to that facing the road) and beyond the outer wall. It consists of about 100 still upright earthfast boulders with as many more fallen or broken, and occupies an area about 30 m by 21 m. The tallest stands about 0·8 m high. It is possible that a *chevaux de frise* also protected the opposite approach along the ridge, on the north-east: here there are a number of unusually large upright boulders in the settlement which has been built at this point.

There are several clusters of hut foundations near Dreva which, one might assume, comprised an open village occupied either under the *pax Romana* or in later times. One cluster is close to the north-east end of the fort and another larger one will be found at the foot of the slope on the north-west side, starting some 45 m beyond the outer wall. No part of the site has been excavated.

4. BERWICKSHIRE

The Dryburgh area

The town of Melrose, and the four major sites described earlier, can be well seen from above from the fine vantage point of *Scott's view*★ (NT/594344), on the west side of Bemersyde Hill. This is also the road to Dryburgh Abbey (below). The viewpoint is reached along the B6356 from Earlston to St. Boswells. At the latter place one turns off the A68 on the B road; but, if coming from the north, take the east side road just north of the bridge over the Tweed at Leaderfoot, near Newstead (p. 82 above), and keep turning to the right. Immediately below the viewpoint is Old Melrose, and this is the best place to see the site of that Celtic monastery. The oppidum on Eildon Hill North is straight in front and the east end of Melrose Abbey can be seen among the trees to its right. The site of Newstead Roman Fort, too, can be easily picked out, especially in August if the field under which it is has been sown with corn. The old red stone railway viaduct at Leaderfoot is to its right and just visible above the trees.

The small village of Dryburgh is 2·5 km south of Scott's view and *Dryburgh Mains farm** is in it, just north of the abbey (NT/591321). This farm has produced one of the largest concentrations of Mesolithic flints in south-east Scotland from its fields along the banks of the Tweed. A large collection is in the Hunterian Museum of the University of Glasgow and another is in the National Museum in Edinburgh. The flints include many microliths, tiny geometrically shaped pieces which may have been attached to the shafts of weapons as barbs. The Tweed valley sites probably date to between about 4500 and 2500 B.C.

The beautifully situated *Dryburgh Abbey**+ is close by (NT/591317). It was founded in 1140 as the first monastery in Scotland of the Canons Regular of the Premonstratensian order. The 6 km detour from St. Boswells, and the longer one from Leaderfoot, can be avoided by taking the by-road marked 'Dryburgh footbridge' from the A68 1 km north-west of St. Boswells. A suspension footbridge crosses the cliff-bordered, tree-filled Tweed valley and a pleasant walk of a ½ km downstream leads to the abbey. Dryburgh lies within one of the Tweed's many great horseshoe bends, on a sheltered stretch of fertile, low ground and beside a river that is full of fish. There was a ford to Melrose a short distance upstream, presumably where the bridge is now.

The abbey is built on a slope and for that reason is constructed on three stepped levels. The church, on the north, is highest; the cloister is on the next level and the east range and other buildings are lowest. The abbey church has been badly wrecked; only the north transept remains to any height. However, a large part of its masonry and that of the claustral buildings is the original late 12th- and 13th-century work so, unlike Melrose, the abbey is a good example of a relatively unaltered early Medieval building.

The Premonstratensian canons had come from Alnwick in Northumberland and Dryburgh is laid out on a similar plan to the parent house. There is an aisled cruciform church on the north side 57·3 m long, a cloister 27·5 m square abutting on to the south side of the nave, a short southern range next to this containing the monk's frater (with undercroft and kitchen below), and a long east range with vestry, parlour, chapter house, day stair, warming house and novices' room; the canons' and novices' dorters were on the first floor of this. There was a high wall on the west side of the cloister instead of the more usual west range.

The plan of the abbey church is traceable by the exposed foundations which show six bays in the nave. The west entrance is a round-arched 15th-century doorway decorated with mouldings and rosettes of leaves. The foundations of the screen separating the canons' choir from the nave can be seen two pillars west of the crossing. The transepts are the only parts of the building which stand to any great height. The north one, and the eastern half of the church in general, are built in the 13th-century Transitional style with the first use of the pointed arch. The north transept is now used as a burial vault for Sir Walter Scott, and Earl Haig's vault is close by. There are bullet marks on the outside face of this transept, no doubt originating in some skirmish with the English.

The lower part of the south transept and the whole of the east range are the earliest parts of the abbey and are built in the late Romanesque style of the latter part of the 12th century. The remains of the night stair to the canons' dorter are visible in the south-west corner of this transept, going through a raised, round-arched doorway.

The east range of the claustral buildings has a row of Romanesque round-arched doorways opening on to the cloister. Beside the processional door from the church is a wall press for books for reading in the cloister. The north doorway from the cloister leads to a barrel-vaulted chamber, the library and vestry. The next room is the parlour (not open to the public), the only place where conversation was allowed. The chapter house, with a fine round-arched door, is next to this: this barrel-vaulted room contains traces of wall paintings on the east wall and on the vaulting of the north window. There is a fine, carved stone basin in this room.

The remains of the day stair up to the canons' dorter on the first floor are next to the chapter house, with the canons' warming house south of this. Here a fire was allowed. The original fireplace was in the east wall but was converted to a window in the 14th century. The novices' day-room, with their fire, was to the south. The dorter was on the first floor, above these rooms, and a night stair led down from this into the south transept of the church. The outline of its roof can be seen on the transept wall.

The south range of buildings contained the dining-room, or frater, with the undercroft of two vaulted cellars underneath. The old water channel is to the south of this with the late 15th-century gatehouse beyond. No trace of the abbey's precinct wall remains.

Lauderdale

The A68 from Newcastle to Edinburgh runs through Jedburgh and Newtown St. Boswells and then north through Lauderdale. Travelling N one can turn E on to the A697 1 km before Lauder to see *Haerfaulds hillfort* (NT/574500). Follow the A697 to Cambridge and there take the by-road to the NE. At 1 km up this a farmroad turns off north-west to Blythe and about ½ km beyond the farm turn off due west across the moor. The fort lies 1 km from the road. Its remains are impressive, consisting of the stone rubble spread of a ruined wall which encloses an oval area about 116 m by 73 m. There is no visible evidence of the kind of wall this was but the quantity of rubble remaining, despite robbing, suggests that it was at least 3 m thick. The fort is sited in open moorland on the edge of a steep drop down to a stream.

There are a number of circular stone hut foundations inside the fort, some built in the fallen rubble and being therefore later than the ruin of the wall.

The stone circle of *Borrowstone Rig* is in the same area (NT/560521): it is best reached by following the A697 for 4 km north of the junction with the A6089 near Lauder. At Newbigging Walls there is a farm road going north-east. At 2·5 km along this, past Burncastle farm, strike off to the SE for 1 km. The setting is an interesting example of Thom's Type II egg-shape, though the 10 surviving upright stones are inconspicuous, some barely showing above the heather. Many more fallen ones are visible and some buried examples were located by probing. Most of the stones lie on a true circle 41·5 m (or 50 my) in diameter. The west segment is formed of an arc of a circle 25·6 m (31 my) in diameter, the circumference of which passes through the centre of the main circle. The perimeter is completed by straight lines which join the arcs of the two circles.

The Duns area

The B roads joining Duns and Haddington pass through hilly country and near several interesting archaeological sites. The remains of *Edrom Old Kirk*+ are worth visiting for the fine Romanesque doorway (NT/828558). Take the A6105 E of Duns and the minor road to Edrom turns north 2·5 km west of Chirnside bridge. The church is 0·4 km west-north-west of the village and the only remaining part is the doorway which now leads into a burial vault. It is a large door, measuring 1·42 m between the jambs and 3·35 m from the ground to the soffit of the round arch. The arch is decorated with three carved orders in the late Romanesque style. It may have been rebuilt in its present position.

The well-known hillfort, broch and settlement of *Edinshall*+ is 3·6 km north-west of Preston, itself 3 km north of Duns. The most convenient approach is along the farmroad past Cockburn farm, which runs north from the junction of the B6355 and the B6365 2·5 km west of Preston. The site is signposted. It stands on the north-east slope of Cockburn Law, just above a fairly steep slope down to the river Whiteadder. The *hillfort* consists of a double rampart, each line with an external ditch, enclosing an oval area some 134 m east–west and some 73 m in maximum breadth north–south. On the north side the defences continue as stony banks at the top of the slope. The entrance has been in the west-south-west.

The next structure to be built on the site was a massive, round drystone fort usually described as a broch. The structure has been excavated and the walls still stand up to 1·5 m high in places. The entrance is on the south-south-east and has door-checks as well as two guard cells opening off it further in. Three large mural cells open on to the central court which is 16·8 m in diameter. The cell on the south has the remains of a stone stairway at its north end which presumably rose to the wallhead. The wall is 5·2 m thick so that the overall diameter of the building is some 27 m, very large for a broch. A rectangular chamber attached to the outside of the wall at the entrance is a secondary addition, but there are traces of ruined walls which were outer defence works.

The final phase of occupation on the site is represented by an open settlement, consisting of a number of circular hut foundations in the west half of the hillfort. Many of these override the hillfort ramparts and are therefore later than they are, and probably later than the broch as well.

It may be supposed that the hillfort belongs to the pre-Roman Iron Age, that the broch was probably built—like Torwoodlee—in the forty-year interval (from A.D. 100) between the two Roman occupations of southern Scotland, and that the open settlement was perhaps an undefended village under the *pax Romana* of about A.D. 140–180. At that time this was the territory of the Votadini and Edinshall is the only broch in it.

One of the rare long cairns in south-east Scotland is the *Mutiny stones* (NT/623590). At Longformacus, 10 km north-west by west of

Duns, take the minor road NW, which can also be reached on the B6355 8 km east of Gifford. At 4 km from the latter junction a farm-track crosses the road: follow it S for 2·5 km and the cairn is about 100 m to the west. It is aligned north-east–south-west and is an impressive pile of stones about 85 m long and up to 23 m wide at the broader north-east end. Here the cairn still stands about 3 m high. It appears to have no chamber and may be a northern counterpart of the unchambered long barrows of south and east England.

5. THE LOTHIANS AND EDINBURGH

East Lothian

Continuing NNW along the B6355 one may visit two standing stone sites. *Kell Burn* is 100 m to the south of the road, 200 m before the minor road leading north-west to Garvald (NT/643642). It consists of a good alignment of stones and declinations of the resulting azimuths (129·8° or about south-east and 309·8° or nearly north-west) have been measured. The results were −19·7° in the former case, which could indicate a lunar 'solstice', and +23·5° in the latter, which is near the summer solstice sunset.

The *Kingside Hill stone circle* is 2 km further on (NT/627650): take the cart track due N for 350 m and the circle is close to the east. It consists of 30 small boulders forming a circle about 11·9 m in diameter; the highest is only 0·4 m above the ground. There is a large boulder in the centre of the circle, which appears to be lying in the middle of a low cairn some 3 m in diameter. Whether the circle and cairn were built together, or whether the latter was inserted into the circle as at Cairnpapple Hill (p. 102), is not clear.

The other eight sites to be described are all in the lowland area south of north Berwick on the Firth of Forth and can conveniently be visited from Edinburgh. *St. Martin's church*+ is on the east side of Haddington on the A1; it is most easily reached by turning S down the A6137 and then E across the river near the mill. The church dates from the beginning of the 12th century and was a simple, rectangular, Romanesque structure consisting of nave and chancel of which only the nave remains; it measures internally 5·03 m by 16·9 m. Excavations in 1912 failed to reveal the foundations of the chancel. Part of the slightly pointed, barrel-vault roof remains on the west end and this was probably put on in the 13th century; the buttresses added to the outside of the wall date to this time and were doubtless needed to support the new heavy roof. There are three narrow, round-headed windows with possibly a ruined one in the west wall. The chancel arch is also semicircular and there is a piscina to the south of it.

In the south wall of the parish church at Morham (NT/556726) is built a fragment of an *Early Christian Anglian cross shaft* with inter-lace decoration. Take the B6369 south of Haddington for 2 km and then turn E along the minor road for 2·7 km at which point a by-road leads NW to the church.

By continuing either along the minor road, or by going E along the other one direct from Haddington, one passes close to the great oppidum on top of the isolated hill *Traprain Law* (Fig. 11). It can also be reached from East Linton. The hillfort, which went through a series of reconstructions, was extensively excavated at intervals between 1915 and 1921 but the sequence of layers, which yielded

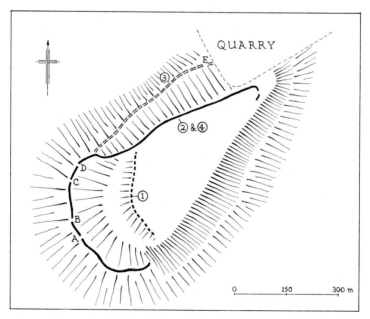

Fig. 11. Plan of Traprain Law hillfort, East Lothian, showing the ramparts of the four successive phases of fortification. No. 1 is the earliest 20 acre enclosure, 2 the first of 30 acres, 3 the largest 40 acre fort and 4 the final enclosure reduced again to 30 acres. Scale 1:10700

large quantities of finds, could not at that time be adequately defined nor related to the ramparts. Subsequently careful surveys and some limited excavation on the ramparts have established a structural history for the hillfort, but how the finds relate to this is still not clear. The situation of the site is commanding, overlooking as it does a wide stretch of fertile farmland and having formidable natural defences. In Roman times the surrounding territory was that of the Votadini whose capital was doubtless Traprain Law.

The finds recovered from the excavation indicate a millennium of possibly continuous occupation, from the Late Bronze Age in the 7th or even 8th century B.C. down to post-Roman times. The site produced rare examples of Late Bronze Age metalwork—socketed axes, knives, chisels, spears and so on—apparently in association with pottery (a plain, gritty ware) and stone hut sites. Judging by other dated examples there may well have been a wooden palisaded enclosure on top of the hill at this time. The great mass of objects recovered from the upper levels belong to the pre-Roman Iron Age and to Roman times and they include a spectacular hoard of Roman silver. This, with many of the other finds, is on display in the National Museum in Edinburgh. In general the ramparts run round the hill from south through west to the north-east end: the long straight precipitous edge on the south-east side seems to have been a sufficient protection on its own and lacks ramparts.

The defences of the earlier phases of the hillfort are naturally inconspicuous, having been robbed of material for the later ones. The most striking to the visitor is the latest which is a wall 3·7 m thick with a turf core faced with stone. This extends for some 1,070 m round the hill, encloses about 0·12 km² (30 acres) and overlies all the other ramparts. It seems to represent a reduction in size of the oppidum from the previous phase and, belonging to the latest phase of occupation, may have been used until about the middle of the 5th century.

The previous rampart evidently enclosed an even larger area to about 0·16 km² (40 acres). It followed the course of the final rampart except along the north face of the hill; it diverges from the former at the west end and runs diagonally down the north slope towards the quarry. Near the quarry is an entrance through this rampart near which relics of the 1st century A.D. were found in 1915. The 40-acre oppidum may have been built early in that century but a construction several centuries earlier is equally possible. The site must have been a barbarian town at that time, with numerous thatched wooden or stone-walled huts and many specialist craftsmen plying their trade. Bronze craftsmen were concentrated there, judging by the numerous ornaments of that metal, many enamelled, which were found. Many iron weapons and agricultural implements give a valuable picture of the equipment of a wide section of the community.

The previous (second) phase of the hillfort seems to have occupied the same area as the fourth but its remains are naturally difficult to disentangle from those of the latter. The earliest fortifications appear to be represented by the now incomplete remains which run along the west end of the highest part of the hill, on the crest of the slope. This would elsewhere have followed the course of the second and fourth lines of defences and perhaps enclosed 0·08 km² (20 acres). Since the trenches which discovered the Late Bronze Age settlement were further west at the foot of this slope it would seem that the first hillfort is later than that phase.

There is no doubt that if Traprain Law was stratigraphically excavated, the sequence of defences worked out and linked with the sequence of finds, it would be a key site for the archaeology of northern Britain.

The *Kirklandhill standing stone* is not far away, close to the east side of the A198 (NT/616776) near its junction with the A1 2 km east of East Linton. The stone is a large one, 3·36 m high and approximately square in section. Its sides are about 0·5 m long at ground level. It is interesting that the isolated hill of North Berwick Law is prominently visible almost exactly in the north-west, although only 9 km away. It is possible that the Kirklandhill stone may be a marker for a summer solstice site.

Close to Traprain Law is the 13th-century *Hailes Castle*+ which is reached by the SW by-road out of East Linton along the river Tyne (NT/575758).

If travelling N towards the Firth of Forth from Haddington visit the *Chesters hillfort* (NT/507782). Take the B1377 east of the A6137 4 km from Haddington and a by-road leads S to near the site. The fort is on rolling ground about 400 ft (122 m) above the sea and is one of the best-preserved examples of a multivallate system of prehistoric earthworks in Scotland. It is however in what appears to be a highly unsound situation strategically in that it is immediately under a steep scarp 15 m high from which any lethal missile can be hurled or shot into the interior of the fort (see the Ardifuar dun, p. 149). The enclosed area measures about 116 m by 46 m and is surrounded by slight traces of a ruined rampart. Another one surrounds this

7

with traces of six others further out. No doubt this fort, like others, underwent several phases of reconstruction with the multivallate system perhaps belonging to the latest phase. It has not been excavated.

Continue on the A6137 to Aberlady and take the A198 to see the 13th-century *Dirleton Castle*,+ which is in the village of that name (NT/516839).

Midlothian and Edinburgh

There are several monuments older than A.D. 1200 within Edinburgh itself. The *Abbey of Holyrood* is at the foot of Canongate (NT/269739), next to the Palace and 1 km east of Waverley Station and Princes Street. The present palace was built by Sir William Bruce for Charles II and was started in 1671 on the site of an earlier one. The abbey was founded by David I in 1128 for Canons Regular of the Augustinian order who had come there from St. Andrews Priory in Fife (p. 123). All that remains of the splendid Abbey of Holyrood is the ruined nave of the monastery church, next to the palace. Of the transepts and the presbytery to the east nothing remains but some foundations are marked on the ground. Similarly the monastic buildings around the cloister on the south side of the nave have also vanished almost entirely. The existing Gothic nave is the enlarged church of the late 12th and early 13th centuries. Of the original Romanesque 12th-century church nothing appears above ground, but its aisle-less nave is thought to have occupied the southern half of the later Gothic nave. The only fragment of the Romanesque church of David I is the blocked east doorway from the cloister to the church.

The *standing stone* known as the *Caiystane* can be seen near Oxgangs Road (NT/242683) on the east side of the city. Take the A702 through Morningside and turn W along the B701 5·5 km south of Princes Street. The stone is some 500 m from the junction.

In Holyrood Park, a short distance south of the abbey, are traces of three Iron Age fortifications two of which are worth visiting. On *Salisbury Crags* (NT/270732) there is a stone wall defending the south-east end of the crags; its total length is about 595 m and it encloses an area of about 0·08 km² (20 acres). The south end of this wall comes close to Radical Road on the south-west edge of the park, about 350 m north-west of the junction with the Queen's Drive. Traces of a pair of once-massive ramparts can be seen on the east slopes of *Arthur's Seat* and Nether Hill (NT/278729); these run for about 340 m and also enclose about 0·08 km² (20 acres). When intact these hillforts would have been comparable in size and importance with Traprain Law (p. 95) and Eildon Hill (p. 80).

Travelling W on the A90 to South Queensferry one can visit the *Roman fort** at Cramond (NT/190768): turn N at the roundabout along Whitehouse Road and, at the village, follow the sign to Cramond kirk. The exposed part of the fort is next to the church, only a few metres from the shore of the Forth. This fort is about 18 km east of the east end of the Antonine wall at Bridgeness and was excavated in 1961. There is a model of the fort in the Huntly House museum. Cramond was built in the mid-2nd century as part of the Antonine wall defences and served as an important port in the Severan campaign in the 3rd century (p. 31).

West Lothian

About a ½ km along the shore west of the Cramond fort just described is the *Eagle rock*+*. The rock, also known as Hunter's Craig, contains a niche cut in the seaward face about 3 m above the beach. The niche is just under 1 m high, 0·76 m wide and about 22 cm deep. Within this niche there was once a sculptured carving, said to have been an eagle, but all the details of this have been eroded away. The outlines of the relief figure can be seen still and it looks something like an eagle standing upright. A figure of Mercury is an alternative suggestion. The sculpture is likely to be Roman in view of the nearness of the Cramond fort.

Continuing along the A90 to Queensferry one reaches *Dalmeny church** in the village of that name, the best-preserved Romanesque church in Scotland (NT/145775). The plan is tripartite with a simple, rectangular nave some 12·7 m long and 5·4 m wide, a slightly narrower chancel and a semicircular apse at the east end. There has been a square tower at the west end where two massive buttresses incorporate the remains of its side walls. A modern aisle has been added on the north side, the west gable has been renewed and the belfry is modern. The roof was renewed in the 18th century. In spite of these alterations the south side of the exterior, with its round-headed openings, appears much as it did when it was built in the latter half of the 12th century. The masonry is ashlar, faced with closely joined, finely dressed blocks.

The entrance on the south has a round arch with two decorated orders of which the inner may incorporate zodiacal signs. The round chancel arch inside is heavily decorated with chevron ornament as is that leading to the apse. There are no ancient monuments in the churchyard except for an early, massive stone coffin opposite the south door.

Continuing on the A904 W of South Queensferry one can visit *Abercorn church* with its *Early Christian stone cross shaft* (NT/081791). The church itself was originally Romanesque and a built-up round-arched doorway of this period can be seen in the south wall. The plan then included a nave and chancel; the aisles were added later. At the head of the stairs leading to the gallery on the north side is a fine Anglian cross shaft set in a modern base. It had been in use as a window lintel and was rescued during alterations. The fragment is 1·37 m high and sculptured in relief on all four faces. The motifs include Anglian interlace ornament and intertwined foliage: the cross is dated to the 9th century. There are also two hog-back gravestones (p. 108) and several early cross fragments in the vestry.

The ecclesiastical site at Abercorn is a very old one; it was mentioned by the historian Bede ('Aebburcurnig') and Bishop Trumwine made it his seat soon after A.D. 680. There are still traces near the church of the bank which surrounded the early monastic site and excavations in 1967 on part of it within the churchyard showed that it had probably been a stone-faced rampart.

If one is continuing W along the A904 to Grangemouth it is worth pausing on the site of the Mesolithic shell mound at *Inveravon*★ (NS/952798). Take the B904, either from Polmont on the A9 or from the A904 3 km east of Grangemouth: 600 m west of the latter junction a farmroad turns north up a hill, passing a wood on the east (left). The shell heap is on both sides of this by-road at the crest of the slope, and under about 0·6 m of plough soil. It was breached by a mechanical excavator close to the west side of the road in the spring of 1970 and large oyster shells are still visible in the field here and on the east side of the road. The shell heap extends for many metres and is about 2 m thick. Recent radiocarbon dates have shown that it was accumulating by 4000 b.c. and ceased to be used at about 2100 b.c.

This vast midden is the food debris of Mesolithic hunters who lived on the shores of the Forth estuary when it was greatly enlarged during the period of the high post-glacial sea-level (p. 24). The shore of the estuary was then at the base of the slope, 1 km away from the present shore, and the hunters had only to carry their harvest of shell-fish a few metres up the slope to their camp site.

There was another shell heap 300 m to the south at Polmonthill but no trace of this is now visible.

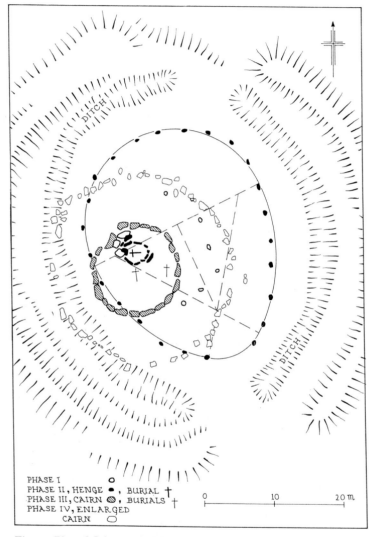

PHASE I   o
PHASE II, HENGE ● , BURIAL †
PHASE III, CAIRN ◎ , BURIALS †
PHASE IV, ENLARGED
     CAIRN   ◯

0   10   20 m

Fig. 12. Plan of Cairnpapple Hill, West Lothian, showing the main features of the first four phases. The suggested geometry for the sockets for the stone circle of Phase II has been added. The modern concrete dome covers the area of the first round cairn of Phase III. Scale 1:525.

One of the most important Neolithic and Bronze Age sites in Scotland is *Cairnpapple Hill*[*][+] near Torphichen, 3 km north of Bathgate (NS/987718). It can be reached most conveniently from the A706 which runs from Linlithgow to the A8 west of Bathgate. Two B roads lead to Torphichen and a minor road leads east from there to the hill. Alternatively the minor road due north from Bathgate runs straight to it. Cairnpapple Hill was excavated in 1947 and 1948 by Professor S. Piggott and revealed a complex sequence of ritual and funerary structures spanning the period approximately from 3000 to 1400 B.C. (Fig. 12). The structures have been laid out by the Department of the Environment and there is a small museum.

The site is on a hilltop over 1,000 ft above the sea with immense views in several directions. To the north one looks across the Forth to the Ochil Hills, and the summit of Schiehallion, 87 km away in the north-north-west, is visible on clear days. To the west, Goat Fell on Arran 150 km away can be sighted if conditions are perfect. These long views, and the many distant mountains that can be seen, suggest that the site may have been chosen partly as an observatory, though no work on this possibility has yet been done.

In its first period Cairnpapple was a cremation cemetery. An irregular arc of seven holes was dug and handfuls of cremated bones were found in six of them. A bone pin of Late Neolithic type was found in one of the pits and on the old ground surface was one chip from the cutting edge of a stone axe from the Neolithic factory at Great Langdale in the Lake District and another fragment from that at Penmaenmawr in North Wales. The former factory has been given a radiocarbon date of about 2700 b.c. There seems to have been a setting of three large stones in front of these pits.

In the second period an oval ring of 24 standing stones was erected: some of the sockets for these are excavated and displayed. They run in a broad arc around the west side of the site, just grazing the inner kerb of the first Bronze Age cairn (below). Outside this was a rock-cut ditch with an external bank, and with entrances in the north and south. The stone setting measured 35 m by 28 m and it fits neatly round one of Thom's Type I egg-shapes drawn round two opposed Pythagorean triangles of 12, 16 and 20 my (Fig. 12). The site was in fact a double entrance henge monument with a stone circle in it and this would have been the observatory if there ever was one on Cairnpapple Hill.

Within the stone circle were two Beaker graves of the Early Bronze Age. One of these, the north grave, is reconstructed under a concrete barrow (representing the Phase III cairn, below) into which one can descend. The grave was a rock-cut pit with a standing stone at the west end, containing a crouched burial (disintegrated) and two Beakers; there was an oval stone kerb round the grave. It appears to be a ceremonial burial made within the stone circle presumably some time after this had been erected. Another Beaker grave was found near stone-hole 8 on the east side.

In the following third period the site underwent a complete change of function. A large Bronze Age round cairn, about 13·7 m in diameter, was built in the west part of the henge, overlapping several of the sockets of the stones of the circle. These stones must therefore have been removed earlier and were in fact used to build a massive stone kerb for this burial mound. The north Beaker grave, with its standing stone, was buried intact in the body of this cairn. At the centre of the cairn was a short cist grave, lined with stone slabs and dry walling and sunk into the ground. This contained a food vessel, which had been placed on a small shelf, together with a crouched inhumation burial. There was also a stone with three cup-marks. A second cist was found under the cairn, nearer the kerb, but this contained only cremated human bones.

In the fourth period the cairn was enlarged to a diameter of about 30 m and a new kerb of rounded boulders was built around this. Material for this cairn seems to have been robbed from the bank of the henge, most of which lacks its upper part (it is intact only on the south-east side). Two cremated burials under inverted cinerary urns were found in pits in the old ground surface within the area of the enlarged cairn. An antler pin was found with one.

The final period at the site is represented by four full-length inhumation graves on the east side, between the kerb of the second cairn and the bank of the henge (not shown on the plan). These may well belong to the Iron Age.

Part of the fascination of Cairnpapple Hill lies in its being a classic example of how skilled excavation techniques can disentangle a complex history from a superficially unpromising site. Part of it also lies in the tantalising glimpses one has of significant changes in social activities taking place on the hilltop in the 3rd and 2nd millennia B.C. The stone circle was doubtless a ceremonial site of some importance, and we now know that it may have had astronomical functions as well (p. 154). The grave of a Beaker chieftain (as one supposes he was) was put into this and the unique provision of a standing stone marker next to it may suggest some close connection between the dead man and the circle. The use of the site as a burial ground for chiefs continued without a break into the Bronze Age. Most cinerary urns were in unmarked graves but the two at Cairnpapple were under a huge cairn, suggesting persons of high status. Yet while the Beaker grave of the second period was carefully incorporated into the first Bronze Age cairn, the stone circle was completely wrecked to provide kerb-stones for that cairn. It seems that this must have been an event of major significance. One might speculate that the site shows the continuity of a chiefly dynasty contrasting with the destruction of the power of a priestly class. Unfortunately we shall never know for certain.

4 · Central Scotland

(City of Glasgow, Renfrew, Dumbarton, Lanark, Stirling and Fife)

The Central zone of Scotland, being largely a heavily populated, industrial belt, seems at first glance unpromising ground for archaeological remains. Nevertheless there are a number, though they tend to be of the more indestructible kind. The most famous and noteworthy sites are undoubtedly the Roman turf wall—the northernmost frontier of the Empire built under the Emperor Antoninus Pius—and some of the Early Christian and Medieval sites. Glasgow has one of the finest and most complete Medieval cathedrals in Britain and, at Govan, an exceptionally fine collection of Early Christian stones.

1. GLASGOW AND ITS ENVIRONS

It is convenient to visit most of the monuments in the west part of the Central zone from a base in Glasgow.

City of Glasgow

Glasgow Cathedral*+ lies in the heart of the old city and is most easily reached by the High Street N from Tollcross (on the A74) or E along Cathedral Street, an extension of Bath Street (NS/602656; Fig. 13). The present cathedral is mainly of 13th-century design although it was not completed until about the middle of the 14th. It has remained substantially unaltered since that time and is a rare example of an intact major religious Medieval building.

The history of the site as a Christian one goes back to St. Kentigern (St. Mungo), the patron saint of Glasgow, who died probably in A.D. 612. At that time south-west Scotland was part of the British kingdom of Strathclyde, with its capital at Dumbarton rock (NS/401744). There is a suggestion that Christianity had already taken hold in Strathclyde in the 5th century but St. Kentigern is the

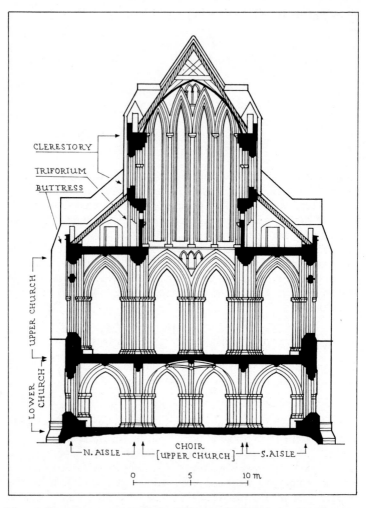

Fig. 13. Elevation across the choir of Glasgow Cathedral showing the five vertical levels—lower and upper churches, triforium, clerestory and roof—and the three horizontal zones—two aisles and choir. The E windows are also shown in the upper half of the choir though these are not of course on the cross section. Scale 1:320.

most famous of the early missionaries of the Celtic Church. It was he, according to the 12th-century sources, who set up a church and a monastery of Celtic type at Glasgow of which he was the first bishop. No trace of this monastery has been found, nor have any inscriptions or carved stones. The contrast with Govan church (p. 108 below) is striking and the only explanation that has been offered is that the Early Christian memorials still lie hidden in the fabric of the cathedral. The tomb of St. Kentigern is traditionally held to be below the lower church in which a shrine now marks the spot.

The 12th century saw the introduction to Scotland of the feudal system and the reformed Roman Church by the Canmore kings (p. 36). The small Celtic cathedral was rebuilt by Bishop John (who was buried at Jedburgh Abbey, p. 72) and consecrated in 1136. No trace of this church is visible but it may have been, like that at Whithorn (p. 57), cruciform in plan with a short, aisle-less nave; it probably lies under the present nave. Bishop Jocelyn enlarged and extended the east end and this work was begun at about 1160 by the Augustinian canons. This was the first stage in the construction of the great Gothic cathedral which was not finally completed for about two hundred years.

The cathedral is of unusual design in two ways, first in that its east part is two storeyed and second in its rectangular plan: there are no projecting transepts. It is built on ground which slopes down to the east towards the Molendinar burn (now subterranean). Along its length of about 100 m the ground falls about 4·6 m so that the east end is far higher than the west. The lower church is here almost entirely above ground because of the slope, and the floor of the choir is raised 0·9 m above that of the nave to give more room below (Fig. 13).

The basic structure can be seen in the elevation of the east end of the choir (Fig. 13). The usual high-roofed nave and choir are present with lower aisles: the transepts do not project at all but are roofed at the upper level, thus interrupting the aisle roofs. The aisle continues right round the east end of the church—another unusual feature—to form an east ambulatory. The church is stone-vaulted except for the central alleys of the nave and choir which have a steep roof of wood and slate. There are thus no flying buttresses to take the outward thrust of a high stone vault as at Melrose (p. 83). The cross-section shows the three stages of the vertical construction—first the massive pillars of the choir, second the triforium above these and third the clerestory, with its windows above the level of the aisle roof, leading up to the wooden roof.

The lower church is reached by two flights of stairs between the massive pillars supporting the crossing tower and spire. The vaulting of the lower church is 5·9 m above the floor and that of the choir is 22·7 m above the upper floor. St. Kentigern's tomb is held to be under the shrine in the centre of the lower church. The Blacader aisle, which leads south from below the south transept, is an addition of the early 16th century. The foundations of the Bishop's Palace lie under Cathedral Square, in front of the Royal Infirmary.

Govan church is on the south side of the Clyde, 4·9 km from the cathedral as the crow flies (NS/553659). It lies between the river Clyde and Govan Road (the A9 to Greenock) and is reached either E from the Whiteinch tunnel or W from the city centre. Within the church and the graveyard is one of the finest collections of *Early Christian stones*★ in Britain, if not in Europe, dating from the 10th and 11th centuries. The church is open on weekdays from about 9 a.m. to 12.30 p.m. and from 2 to 5 p.m. (mornings only on Saturdays). There are 24 stones within the church and there were 17 more along the east wall of the graveyard. Some of these were unhappily damaged in 1973 when the neighbouring factory was demolished and have been removed to the City museum. Inside the church there are now one sarcophagus, five hog-back gravestones, two cross shafts and many recumbent grave slabs. The stones are numbered after the list of Romilly Allen (p. 287).

Number 1 is the *sarcophagus*, carved from a single block of sandstone and decorated on four faces with sunk panels of ornament in relief. A hunting scene is on the back with animals reminiscent of the Pictish style and other animals are on the front. Panels of Anglian interlace ornament separate the groups and a date in the 10th or even the early 11th century has been suggested. The grooved edges suggest that the sarcophagus had a tiled gabled roof cover, like the earlier one at Jedburgh (p. 72). Three such sarcophagi were present at Govan church in the 18th century and one doubtless contained the relics of the particular St. Constantine to whom the church is dedicated.

The five *hog-back tombstones* are of an Anglian type which was evolved in northern England, apparently as a solid imitation of the gabled sarcophagus or tomb-shrine, an example of which was described above. After the Danish settlement in northern England hog-back stones were evidently adopted as tombstones for prominent men and the Govan examples were probably for such. The design like roof-tiles in fact represents a sarcophagus roof and the roof-ridge is represented on number 3. The gabled ends can also be seen in the end panels, especially on number 11. The crude interlace ornament on the Govan stones suggests a 10th-century date, or even in the 11th century for number 2.

Two fragments of *cross shafts* are present, one unnumbered and one number 29. Both have lost their heads but number 29 is quite similar to the Thornhill cross in Dumfries-shire (p. 47). The shaft of the first has a horseman in the Pictish style (Meigle, p. 185) and both have interlace ornament. Number 29 is damaged but shows two seated figures, apparently St. Paul and St. Anthony in the desert, so much better seen on the Ruthwell cross. A date of about A.D. 900 has been suggested for the Govan crosses and they should be the earliest monuments in the group.

Numbers 4 and 5 are upright *cross slabs*, the former having a spear-carrying horseman on the front and, on the back (facing towards the centre of the church now), a boss with four serpents emerging from it (the so-called 'sun stone'). The swastika-like arrangement suggests Norse influence and a date in the 10th century. The rest of the stones (numbers 6–9, 13–28, 30–8) comprise 29 flat *grave covers*, usually with a cross carved on them and flanked by interlace orna-ment. None shows Romanesque ornament so they all ought to date to between about A.D. 900 and the early 12th century. Many of the stones have been re-used in recent times and bear added names.

Renfrewshire

Travelling W on the south side of the Clyde one can see several sites in this county. There was another early church at *Inchinnan*★, now within Abbotsinch airport, and the three stones found there are at the new church a mile from the old (NS/477691). It can be reached by following the M8 and turning off at Renfrew to join the A8. One kilometre after the steel bridge over the Black Cart water take the minor road NW through Inchinnan: the new church is on the left. The largest stone (number 3) is a rectangular slab 1·6 m long, appar-ently the stone cover for a sarcophagus like that at Govan: this is shown by the decorated edges, which do not occur on grave slabs. It has been dated stylistically to about A.D. 900 or soon after. Above the plain cross on the upper surface are two pairs of beasts and, below it, a standing figure with four beasts—presumably Daniel in the lions' den. (See Meigle number 2, p. 185.) The other two stones are part of a cross (number 2) and a grave slab, the former being of 10th-or 11th-century date and the latter of a similar age.

Paisley Abbey★ is in the centre of that town, which is most easily reached along the M8 to Greenock (NS/485640). It was founded for the Benedictines (Cluniac order) in 1136 and the monks came in 1169. However, the original church was burnt by the English and the present fabric is almost entirely mid-15th century and later reconstructions. The choir was revaulted in the 1920s. The cloister garth of the monastery adjoined the south side of the nave and the adjacent houses, the Place of Paisley, were built on the foundations of some of the old monastic buildings.

The *Early Christian Barochan cross*★+ is 12 km west of Paisley (NS/405690) and can be reached by following the A761 to Bridge of Weir and then the B789 N through Houston. Alternatively take the M8 and turn SW at Bishopton. The cross stands on a hill and is visible from the road. It has evidently been broken since being described by Allen in 1893 and struts of concrete now obscure some of the decoration, which occurs on all four faces. On the front of the shaft is a scene with five men, one with a spear on horseback, one with a drinking horn and one with an axe. On the reverse are, or were, four men blowing horns. A 10th-century date is suggested.

Continuing along the A701 one can visit the vitrified hillfort in *Craigmarloch Wood*★ (NS/344718). At 1 km north-west of the village of Kilmacolm take the minor road to the left (west) beside the railway. The fort is just inside the wood about 900 m from the junction and about 300 m from the road. The main fort consists of a stone wall enclosing an oval about 26 m by 49 m. There appears to be an outer enclosure against the north side and possible outworks on the south. Excavations in the 1950s showed that a wooden palisaded enclosure antedated the stone wall and much pottery and other finds were associated with this. A radiocarbon date on charcoal from this earlier phase, when converted (p. 22), suggests a date in the 8th–6th centuries b.c. The date of the building of the timber-framed stone wall—subsequently burnt and vitrified—is not clear.

In Gourock, on the golf course south-west of the town, there is an interesting group of *cup markings* carved on rock (NS/229762). A sign points uphill to the course at the west end of the town on the main road. From the club-house, where permission to visit the site should be sought, cut left and then uphill along the stream at the east edge of the course to its south-east corner on the hilltop; the 8th tee is close by. The rock outcrop is 21 m south-west of the 8th

(Championship) tee and 12 m west of the wall. There are two groups of five and nine clear, deep cup marks (Fig. 8). Five of the cups fall exactly on the corners of superimposed 3–4–5 and 6–8–10 Pythagorean triangles. This is a rare and plain demonstration of the interest in geometry current in the Early Bronze Age.

One *chambered cairn*, not very well preserved, may be visited at Cuff Hill in Ayrshire, 6·9 km east-north-east of Beith (NS/386551). Take the A736 through Barrhead, the B776 W from Caldwell Station for 3 km and then the minor road W for just over 1 km: the site is 300 m north-west of the road on pasture land. The cairn has been badly disturbed and robbed but several features can be made out. The long axis, running south-east–north-west, measures about 45 m. Three chambers can be seen, the one on the north having lintels still in position. Traces of wallfaces are apparent between it and the cists to the south so the structure may well be composed of one or more small cairns combined into a long one. The chambers were looted at various times in the 19th century and human bones were reported found.

If travelling S on the A77 past Maybole it is possible to visit the well-preserved 13th-century *Crossraguel Abbey*★+ (NS/275083).

Dunbartonshire (west)

Two well-preserved lengths of the stone base of the *Roman wall*★ are visible in the cemetery at New Kilpatrick (NS/556723). Take the Bearsden road (A809) N from Anniesland, the A81 at the Canniesburn roundabout and turn E along the B8049 1 km after that (signposted). The cemetery is 800 m along this, the Boclair Road. There is a gutter in each of the sections and one has a step built into it to increase the stability of the turf wall which once rested on it. As it crosses the summit of the hill in the cemetery the wall bends sharply towards the south so that the second exposed stretch—on the east slope of the hill—is not in line with the first. Another stretch of *wall base*★, with the *ditch*, can be seen W of Bearsden, on the northern flank of a hill in 'Roman Park' (NS/534725). Take the A810 through Bearsden to a little W of the junction with the Stockiemuir road (A809) and then cut S through the housing estate.

Between these two sites excavations at the *Roman fort* of *New Kilpatrick*★ in 1973 have uncovered the foundations of the garrison's bath-house and this may eventually be laid out on display (NS/546721). The site is immediately north of Roman Road in Bearsden, 0·3 km east of the junction with the A809.

Continue W either along the A810 or the Great Western Road (A814), to the minor road north at Milton 14 km west of Anniesland Cross. This road leads to a *vitrified fort*★ and a fine *cup-and-ring rock carving*★. Take the minor road N for 600 m and then fork right along the farmroad to Greenland farm. The *rock carvings*, in two groups, are in the middle of the low, flat ground about 400 m south of the farm (NS/435746). The largest group has 22 sets of concentric rings, 106 cup marks and one spiral. The second rock is 60 m east and has five cup-and-rings and some cups.

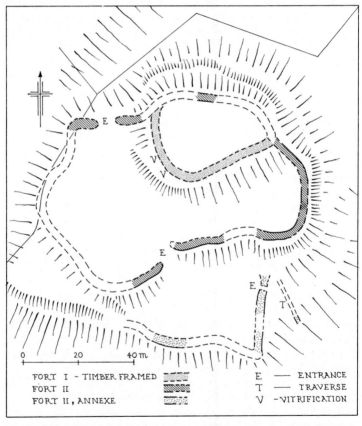

Fig 14. Plan of the two hillforts on Sheep Hill, Dunbartonshire, showing the three enclosures. Scale 1:1330.

Plate 8. Dumbarton rock from the S bank of the river Clyde.

The *Sheep Hill vitrified fort*** is on the isolated rock knoll (a basalt volcanic plug) about 200 m south of the rock carvings (NS/435746) (Fig. 14). Excavations from 1966 to 1970 showed that it was a two-period fort, the earlier and smaller being the vitrified fort on the very summit of the knoll (Fig. 14). One stretch of vitrified core is visible on the south-west but most of the rubble from the wall, reddened by heat, was removed to build the rampart of a larger enclosure which can be traced around the edges of the lower rock terraces. This later fort also has a triangular, lower enclosure on the south with a gateway visible in its east wall. A short traverse protects this gate from an assault along the slope of the hill. Some midden material was found under the second rampart and gave gritty pottery and some clay mould fragments, probably the debris deposited by the occupants of the timber-framed fortlet. The later fort yielded many jet bracelets and a tiny blue glass bead and could thus date to the 1st centuries B.C. and A.D. The site commands a splendid view up and down the Clyde.

Continuing W take the A814 to Dumbarton where *Dumbarton rock*[+] may be visited in a splendid situation on the shore of the Clyde (NS/400745) (Pl. 8): it lies 0·5 km south-south-west from the centre of the town. This isolated volcanic plug is traditionally held to be what the name suggests, the 'dun of the Britons', the

8

capital of the ancient British kingdom of Strathclyde (p. 32 above). The top of the rock is now cluttered with recent fortifications and buildings but must once have been a fairly large and very strong Dark Age fortress like Dunadd (p. 147).

If taking the A82 past Loch Lomond visit the church at *Luss* where there are several *Early Christian stones*★ (NS/361929); the church is near the shore and east of the centre of the village. Of particular interest are two *hog-back tombstones* (p. 108) in the churchyard which appear to be in their original situations (although raised up and secured in the 1920s). One is finely carved with a representation of a tiled roof and, on each side, with a round-arched arcade in the Romanesque style; this presumably dates the stone to the 12th century, late for its class. There are also three *early crosses*, one— against the north wall of the church—a free-standing monument sculpted on both faces and the others simple incised crosses on slabs. On Inchtavannach, south of Luss, lived the 6th-century St. Kessog who was one of the earliest martyrs for the new faith in Scotland.

Lanarkshire

The famous 13th-century *Bothwell Castle*+ should not be missed: it is conveniently reached by taking the A74 south-east of the city to Uddingston where a minor road leads SW for 1 km to the castle.

If one is travelling between Glasgow and south-east Scotland (Chapter 3) two Norman mottes can be seen. *Coulter Motte Hill*+ is on the A72 about 1·5 km south-west of Biggar and next to Coulter Station (NT/019363). *Carnwath Motte* is just south of the A70, about 1 km west of Carnwath (NS/975466).

2. STIRLINGSHIRE

The Forth valley

A variety of interesting sites can be seen in a day's tour N from Glasgow, E through the Forth valley and back to the city along the A80. Take the Aberfoyle road (A81) through Strathblane and a private minor road to the left 4 km beyond that village to visit the *Duntreath standing stones*★ (NS/533807). This road is just north of the conspicuous, tree-covered conical hill (a volcanic plug) in the middle of the valley bottom to the left (west), and a track leads south along the east flank of this hill to the field in which the stones are.

There is only one stone still standing, four more are lying nearly flat and one boulder looks as if it has been added recently. The standing stone has a flat face exactly aligned on a hill notch to the east. This notch has a declination of $+1°\ 21'$ which indicates the sunrise point two days after the spring equinox or two days before the autumn one. Excavations around the stones in 1972 produced a few small flint and jasper implements of Mesolithic type and a spread of ash and charcoal. The latter gave a radiocarbon date of 2860 ± 270 b.c. (about 3300 B.C.).

Continue along the A81 for 9 km and then take the Stirling road (A811). At Arnprior one can travel N alongthe B8034 and W along the A81 past the Lake of Menteith (in Perthshire) to see the beautifully-situated 13th-century *Inchmahome Priory*★+ on an island in that lake. The custodian runs a boat to the island from April to mid November and a guide pamphlet is available. Parts of the ruins are well preserved and there are traces of the monastic gardens. Mary Queen of Scots spent a short time at the priory when a child. Return to the A811, and there is a long straight stretch soon after Kippen; 2·6 km along this a narrow private road turns south along a stream for 1·2 km. From the bridge at the T-junction follow the path S through the woods to the *Leckie* Iron Age *broch and promontory fort*★ (NS/693940). The site is now (1974) in the early stages of excavation and has already proved to be of considerable interest and importance. It stands on the end of a rock promontory between the confluence of two streams, a crater-like depression among rubble. The northern half of the site seems to be the remains of a solid-based broch in which part of the stair is visible; it was evidently burned and destroyed in the latter part of the 2nd century and many finds were on the floor. Occupation continued in the ruins and later—perhaps during the Severan campaigns of the early 3rd century (p. 31)—another emergency evidently arose and a promontory fort was built across the south part of the site. There are clear signs that this was still unfinished when the native fortifications at Leckie were thrown down for a second time and the site was thereafter abandoned.

On the east edge of Stirling stand the scanty remains of the 12th-century *Cambuskenneth Abbey*+, in a fine situation close to the river Forth (NS/809939). The site is probably most easily reached along the minor road which runs south to it from the A91 to Alloa, 0·6 km east of Causewayhead. The abbey was founded by David I for the Augustinian canons in 1140 but the fragmentary remains now visible suggest that most of the building took place in the 13th century. The free-standing bell tower is the only complete (restored) building and belongs to the late 13th or early 14th century. Fragments of the monastery church are preserved, including the complete west door of the nave, and also part of the refectory on the south side of the cloister. A guide pamphlet can be obtained at Stirling Castle.

Close to the north of Stirling is *Dumyat* (pronounced Doom-eye-at), a hillfort about 300 m high which can be reached with a stiff walk (NS/832973). Take the A997 and A91 to Alva from Causewayhead (on the A9): at 600 m east of Blairlogie a farmroad turns north and winds round the east side of Dumyat Hill. The fort stands some 500 m south-west of the summit, at the edge of a precipitous crag which bounds it on its north, east and south sides. The name almost certainly means Dun Myat, the 'dun of the Maeatae', a tribe recorded by the Romans as living in this area in the 2nd century A.D. The innermost enclosure appears to be a ruined, oval stone dun measuring about 17 m by 27 m internally. This dun, judging from comparable examples (Dun Lagaidh, p. 214, and Dun Skeig, p. 131), was probably inserted into a ruined hillfort the remains of the double rampart of which can be seen curving round on the west side, cutting off what is in effect the neck of a promontory. The entrance through the hillfort defences is about 33 m west-north-west of the dun.

The excavated Iron Age dun at *Castlehill Wood** lies 6 km south-west of Stirling and can be visited with a walk of about 800 m (NS/751908). Take the minor roads south-west of the town through Torbrex and then the western loop that runs to join the hill road to Carron Bridge and Kilsyth. Just over 2 km along the loop is an army range and, if this is inactive, one can strike up this just N of W to the dun (the farmroad to Shielbrae leaves the main road at the same point). The dun was excavated by Mr R. W. Feachem in 1955 and is oval in plan, the interior having axes of about 15·25 m and 22·9 m. The wall is built of angular blocks with a rubble core and the entrance, equipped with door-checks, faces east. A stone projecting from the inner wall about 2·4 m north of the entrance may be the base of a flight of steps to the wallhead. The gallery-like passages opposite the entrance were interpreted as a corn-drying kiln: they may have been flues leading to small oven chambers in the wall. The few finds suggest that the dun was used in the 1st or early 2nd century A.D.

Take the A9 from Stirling to Falkirk to see the *Torwood broch**, the best preserved of the few brochs in southern Scotland

(NS/833849). At 1·5 km after Plean take the minor road back NW for 500 m to the top of the hill. The broch lies 500 m to the south-west at the summit of the ridge. A plantation now prevents direct access but by following the track which runs S from the minor road below (south of) the hilltop one can cut NW from it and reach the broch along the south edge of the plantation (though the going is rough). The broch stands on the edge of the steep northern face of the ridge and has an extensive view to the north: it was cleared out in 1864 and the outer face is largely concealed by debris. The lin-telled entrance passage, 6·25 m long and with door-checks and bar-hole, faces east; about 0·8 m of debris now lies in the passage and the bar-hole thus appears to be close to the floor.

The interior is somewhat egg-shaped in plan with a maximum and minimum diameter of 10·6 m and 9·7 m, and the lintelled door to the mural stair is at about 8 o'clock. A ledge scarcement is in the wall, which still stands some 2·7 m above the debris, and there are a num-ber of cupboards, or aumbries, in the wallface. The remains of two concentric outer walls are clear on the north-east, south and south-west.

This massively built, solid-based broch is closely similar in its design and architectural features to Carn Liath in Sutherland (p. 216) and it may well be that its designer came from the far north.

The Antonine wall

A short distance south of Torwood are several well-preserved sec-tions of the Roman Imperial frontier of about A.D. 142–80. Continue S down the A9 to the centre of Larbert and then take the road W to Bonnybridge. Alternatively Bonnybridge can be reached directly from the dual carriageway from Stirling to Glasgow (A80). In Bonnybridge itself the roads and track to the *Rough Castle Fort and wall**+ are signposted (NS/843799) (Fig. 15). More than 2 km of the ditch and wall are well preserved here, the irregular turf mounds of the latter being clearly visible. The stone base is not exposed. Rough Castle is the best preserved of the forts which housed the garrison of the Antonine wall and was excavated in 1903 and 1932–3; it is currently being explored and consolidated by the Department of the Environment. The fort lies just to the east of where the Rowan Tree burn crosses the course of the wall. The main fort consists of a turf wall on a stone foundation enclosing a square area 65·6 m across, the north rampart being formed by the wall itself (Fig. 15). There is a sally-port through this with a causeway across the ditch in front of

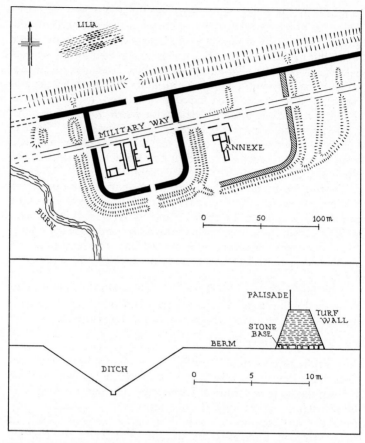

Fig. 15. (*top*) Plan of Rough Castle Roman Fort, Stirlingshire, with annexe on E side and Antonine wall on the N. Scale 1:3150.
(*bottom*) Diagrammatic section of Antonine wall and ditch. Scale: 1:3150.

it. About 30 m beyond the ditch is a series of defensive pits, or *lilia*, in 10 parallel rows; each pit was originally about 2·1 m long, 0·92 m wide and 0·76 m deep. Obviously the *lilia* were designed to break up any attacks by horsemen or chariots on the sally-port and causeway and to give the soldiers emerging from it time to deploy and form up.

Two ditches are outside the main rampart of the fort, and the whole is bisected by the military way running parallel to the wall.

Three stone buildings were uncovered inside the fort in 1903 but only mounds and rubble can be seen now. Fragments of a stone tablet were found in the ruins of the headquarters building, showing that it was built by the 6th Cohort of the Nervii. To the west is the granary with the commanding officer's house beyond. To the east of the fort is the annexe containing a bath-house and defended by a turf wall and three external ditches on the west. The section (Fig. 15) illustrates the defensive capacities of the Roman frontier.

Another well-preserved length of the ditch is a little to the east at *Watling Lodge+*, near Falkirk (NS/862798); the B816 leads right past it. The wall has been destroyed but the V-shaped section of the ditch is clear. A third stretch is at *Seabegs Wood+* (NS/814793), a short distance west of Rough Castle; the B816 again runs right past it. About 200 m east of the wood traces of the Seabegs Fort were recently located by excavation though nothing is visible on the surface.

3. DUNBARTONSHIRE EAST

The Antonine wall

Travelling towards Glasgow from Stirling or Falkirk one can visit three well-preserved sections of the Antonine wall and ditch. At *Castlecary*, just to the east of where the motorway runs under the railway and beside the B816, is the *Roman fort+* of that name (NS/790783). Some parts of the ditch are visible to the east of the fort and immediately north of the B road.

West of Castlecary the ditch is almost continuously visible for 6·5 km where it runs across open country. The *Westerwood Fort+* is well preserved (NS/761774) and can be reached by following the B816 for a short distance west of Castlecary and turning N to the track which runs along the course of the wall towards Dullatur. Further west at *Dullatur Colliery+* is another well-preserved section of the wall (NS/753773). A walk of 1 km along the wall west of Dullatur brings one up on to *Croy Hill* on the summit of which is the only original gap in the ditch (NS/733766). The underlying rock is so hard that even the Roman army had to give up at this point. There are two *beacon platforms* on the west brow of the hill from which, as might be expected from such features, there are some fine views to be had.

4. FIFE

The county of Fife can be entered across the Forth road bridge from Edinburgh or by way of Kincardine bridge from Glasgow and the west.

The south coast

Taking the A985 along the Firth of Forth one can see the 13th-century *Culross Abbey*[+] (NS/989863) and *Dunfermline Abbey*[*+] 10 km further east (NT/ 090873), south of the road and at the west end of the town. The latter has a fine 12th-century Romanesque nave which is well worth a visit (Pl. 9); the rest of the church is modern and the monastic buildings are 14th century. This Benedictine abbey was founded at about 1070 and the foundations of the small, aisle-less church of that time were revealed beneath the present nave in 1916. The outline of this is marked on the floor of the nave—in lighter-coloured flagstones between metal strips—and fragments of the early masonry can be seen through the gratings (ask for the sub-floor lighting to be put on). This early church consisted of a rectangular nave with a square tower and a choir with a semicircular apse; it is very similar to the well-preserved 11th-century church at the Brough of Birsay, Orkney (p. 246). The impact of Norman architecture on Scotland in David I's time can be well visualised by comparing this small 11th-century church with the vast Romanesque one which succeeded it and which was dedicated in 1150. The first abbot, Geoffrey, came from Canterbury.

The aisled nave has eight massive, cylindrical pillars the decoration on which is closely similar to that in Durham Cathedral; masons from Durham doubtless worked on the new church at Dunfermline. The round, decorated arches resting on the pillars support the rows of similar round arches of the triforium and clerestory above. The central roof is of wood and tile—not stone-vaulted as at Durham—and the vaulting of the aisles is later. The north and west doors into the nave are the original 12th-century ones, the west door being most impressive. The nave of Dunfermline Abbey church is one of the two most complete fragments of early Romanesque architecture in Scotland, the other being the nave of St. Magnus's Cathedral in Orkney (p. 240). The whole of the contemporary monastery, on the south side of the nave, was burnt and levelled by Edward I in 1303: the existing buildings post-date that event.

If one is travelling along the A92 to Aberdour a motor-boat can be hired to visit *Inchcolm Abbey*[+] on the island of that name

Plate 9. Dunfermline Abbey, Fife: interior of the nave looking E.

(NT/190826). The abbey church was founded early in the 12th century but was added to extensively in later times. A guide-book is available. On the crest of the knoll immediately west of the abbey is a decorated *Early Christian hog-back gravestone*, comparable to those at Govan (p. 108 above).

Further east the Early Christian cross known as the *Dogton stone*+ can be visited by turning N up the A910 from Kirkcaldy for 8 km (NT/236969). Take the B922 at Cluny and, after 1·5 km, the minor road W to Dogton. The cross is 1·5 m high and sculptured on all four faces, though the designs are now badly weathered. Interlace pattern can be seen, together with animals and a horseman with a spear (on the east side).

There is a *Norman motte*, the 'Maiden Castle', inland from Methil near Windygates (NO/349015); the A916 to Cupar passes close to it.

Continuing E along the coast road (A921) one passes Lundin Links with two *standing stones* 4·3 m high just north of the road (NO/405027); there is a smaller stone about 100 m to the north. From the stones the Bass rock can be seen 24·8 km away to the southeast (azimuth 127°) and the moon rising near its most southerly position would just graze the rock. The stones could thus have been a lunar observatory in the Early Bronze Age.

In the gateway of the parish church in Upper Largo, just north of the A92, is a badly weathered Class II *Pictish symbol stone* (NO/423035). On the front is a large cross with two intertwined animals with fish-tails next to it and, on the back, a scene with horsemen, hounds, deer, and the 'elephant' and double disc and Z-rod symbols.

St. Andrews

There was a Celtic monastery at St. Andrews and a fine collection of Early Christian stones in the site museum, dated to the 8th–10th centuries, shows how important it was. The monastery held what were believed to be the relics of the Apostle St. Andrew, which are reputed to have been brought to the place by the founder, St. Regulus, during the reign of Angus I, King of the Picts (about A.D. 731–61). No trace of buildings of the Celtic foundation are preserved although married monks of the Celtic Church, the Culdees, lived near the new Augustinian monastery for some two centuries after the establishment of the latter in the 12th century. The 12th century foundations of the *church of St. Mary of the Rock*+, east of the cathedral and close to the cliff, are probably those of the latest Culdee church.

The first church of the Augustinian canons was *St. Regulus'* or *St. Rule's*[+] (NO/514167), only 40 m south-east of the cathedral which replaced it. It is a fine example of early Medieval architecture with its splendid square tower of Norman type. Some of its architectural details are unique in Scotland but closely matched in the tower at Wharram-le-Street in Yorkshire, and it is known that Robert, Bishop of St. Andrews from 1126 or 1127, came originally from Nostell Priory, Yorkshire, to which the Wharram-le-Street church belonged. It seems probable that Robert brought north to Scotland with him a master mason who combined Saxon and Norman features in his work.

The church consists of a choir 7·9 m long with the square tower attached to the west end and a sanctuary on its east: no trace of the latter remains except marks on the east wall of the choir. The tower stands 39·92 m high but the present wallhead is of 16th-century date. The choir has massively built, high walls and arches—all Saxon characteristics. The date of the church has caused argument but somewhere between 1127 and 1144 seems likely. It is an example of the pre-Conquest architecture of Yorkshire with some Norman features added.

The adjacent cathedral and monastic buildings were constructed in the late 12th and 13th centuries to replace St. Regulus' church and are described in detail in the official guide-book.

In the site museum is a collection of more than fifty *Early Christian stones*[+] which have been found near by—some in the churchyard, some as fragments in the walls of the cathedral and many in the foundations of St. Mary of the Rock. Most of the stones are upright grave slabs (decorated on both faces) but there is a broken *cross shaft* and a *sarcophagus*. The latter is one of the most complete of its kind in Scotland and consisted originally of four massive, grooved corner stones and four side and end slabs fitted between these: three of the stones are missing but one complete side and one end are preserved. The central panel of the front side is carved with a scene showing David rending the lion on the right and various other figures in hunting scenes including a horseman with a hawk being attacked by a lion and a man below with a spear and wearing a plaid and kilt. The end panels show complicated interlaced serpents. The foliage and the classical draperies of David could indicate an 8th-century date for the sarcophagus, which shows an interesting blend of Pictish and Northumbrian artistic traditions.

The fine Romanesque *Leuchars parish church* lies 8 km north-east of St. Andrews on the A91, on a knoll east of the village (NO/455214). Most of the church is modern but the chancel and apse, each entered by their original, round-arched doorways, are of late 12th century date and one of the finest examples of Romanesque buildings in Scotland. The ashlar masonry, with large, rectangular dressed blocks, is typical of the period and the outer wallface is ornamented with round-arched arcading on two levels. The apse is stone-vaulted and supports the bell tower above.

The Newburgh area

At the east end of Newburgh, just south of the railway, is the *Clatchard Craig hillfort* (NO/244178); unfortunately it is partly quarried away but a quarry road leads to it. There are at least two, possibly three, forts but the uppermost has been almost completely destroyed; it may have been of Dark Age date. Up to five other ramparts enclose the summit and it is possible that the innermost of these is a timber-laced wall since burnt beams from it have been reported. The other ramparts may represent the later conversion of the defences to a multivallate system (see Hownam Rings, p. 78).

Further east is the Lindores Class I *Pictish symbol stone*, which is worth a visit (NO/262169); it stands beside the A913 to Cupar on the west side of Lindores, and is built into the garden wall of a cottage. At the top is a triple disc and cross-bar with a crescent and V-rod below. The latter has an attractive, rare infill of curved lines but has unfortunately been defaced by a government surveyor's bench mark.

The great hillfort on *Norman's Law* can be visited next (NO/305203): follow the A913 E from Lindores for 4 km at which point a farm road turns north to Denmuir and Denmuirhill. The fort is about 800 m north-north-east of the latter farm and commands some splendid views. The summit of the hill is defended by a ruined stone wall about 3·7 m thick enclosing an area 30 m by 52 m; this appears to be the latest defence on the site. Another stone wall encloses the whole of the hilltop—an area of about 210 m by 75 m—and there is a large annexe on the south-west side of this the wall of which extends up to 140 m from the main wall. Probably the earliest structure was the hilltop fort, which then had the annexe added to it; no doubt these are of Iron Age date. The final, smallest, fort could have been built when the rest was in ruins, possibly in the Dark Age.

5 · Western Scotland and the Western Islands

(Bute, Argyll, western Inverness and the Western Isles)

1. BUTE

Isle of Arran

This attractive island, reached by car-ferry from Ardrossan, is geologically and geographically a miniature version of Scotland as a whole. The highland northern half is rugged and mountainous while the lowland southern half, containing most of the archaeological sites, has much lower and more rolling terrain.

If one takes the B880 W from Brodick one can visit the remarkable complex of stone circles and standing stones on *Machrie Moor*★+ (NR/911325). When descending towards the west coast take the minor road forking left and then go S again along the coast road. Just after this crosses the Machrie water a farmroad runs east and runs 1·5 km to the circles (Fig. 16). *Moss Farm road circle*★+ is reached first and has a cairn inside it: it is immediately to the left of the track 0·6 km from the main road (NR/900326) (no. 10).

A *Bronze Age short cist grave* lies 600 m further on and 200 m east of the double *circle 5* ('Fingal's Cauldron Seat'), in many ways the most interesting structure on the site. The inner ring, of eight granite boulders, is laid out precisely around a true circle 11·56 m (14 my) in diameter. The outer circle, also of granite, is a geometrically constructed egg-shape. The fact that the inner ring is a perfect circle disposes of the argument—sometimes heard—that the non-circular stone rings are the results of accidents of nature (soil movement) or of the builders' carelessness. From the centre of this double circle one can see almost all the other circles and standing stones in the area. Stone 1 in the outer circle has a hole in which the giant Fingal is supposed to have tied his dog Bran while he cooked his cauldron on the inner circle. A ruined cist was found in the centre but contained no relics.

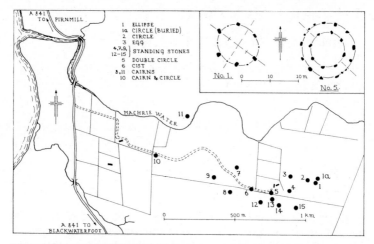

Fig. 16. Plan of Machrie Moor, Isle of Arran, showing the positions of cairns, stone circles and standing stones. Scale 1:25600. The inset shows plans of circles 1 and 5. Scale 1:1300.

The other four visible circles are marked on the plan (Fig. 16): *circle 1a* is buried under the blanket of peat which now covers the whole site and has submerged the lower parts of the stones. *Circle 3* has one tall stone remaining and the stumps of three other sandstone slabs still show (NR/910325); the snapped-off upper parts of these are still there, under the peat. There are nine stones in all, forming the same geometrical egg-shape as the outer ring of circle 5. The axis of symmetry (north-east–south-west) is 15·56 m long, or just under 19 my. There was a cist in the centre containing an 'urn' with some flint flakes and a second cist had a crouched burial also with some flint flakes.

Circle 1 (NR/912324) lies to the east of circle 3, just beyond circle 2. It is set out around a precisely drawn ellipse of eccentricity one half the axes of which are 12·69 m and 14·58 m long (a little under 15 my by 18 my); stones mark the ends of three of these axes (not one end of the short one). Granite blocks and sandstone slabs are set alternately round the ellipse, though a slab seems to be missing on the north-east. No cist was found in this circle. *Circle 2* (NR/911324) has three tall stones remaining and two slabs lying inside it—one perforated—which have apparently been cut from a fallen monolith.

A cist was found at the centre containing a food vessel and four flint flakes but a second cist near by was empty.

The completely buried *circle 1a* is just north of the ellipse and was found by probing. There are also several outlying standing stones which are marked on the plan. The various graves found seem to point to an Early Bronze Age date for the circles and the alignments between them and the single stones appear to point to several notches in the mountainous horizon which are astronomically significant. Although the site has yet to be systematically excavated and fully understood there can be little doubt that it is one of the most important of its kind in Britain.

Travelling S along the coast road to Corriecravie farm, 6 km south of Blackwaterfoot, one may visit the *Iron Age dun Torr a' Chaisteal*[+] (NR/922233); it is on an eminence 400 m south of the road but is now largely buried. At 4 km further east along the coast road is Lagg and 0·5 km after crossing the Kilmory water the farm road to Torrylin turns south. The *Torrylinn or Torlin chambered cairn*[*][+] is about 300 m north-west of the farm, on and close to the edge of the raised beach (NR/955211). The cairn has been disrupted so that its original shape is not clear but the segmented stone burial chamber is visible on the north: it has at least four compartments separated by slabs. Two of the compartments were ransacked of human bones in the later 19th century and the third or innermost one was more carefully explored in 1900. It was undisturbed and revealed skulls and bones in separate groups, indicating that the bodies had disintegrated and been rearranged before the tomb was finally blocked. One interesting feature about this site is that the axis of the burial chamber points almost due south directly at Ailsa Craig 20 km away. This orientation of a structure towards a distant landmark, presumably deliberate, recalls the stone circles of a later time. The similar *chambered cairn of Clachaig* is 400 m to the west (NR/949211).

Three kilometres further east is *East Bennan* farm and the *chambered cairn*[*] of that name (NR/993207); it lies close to the stream and about 400 m south of the farm buildings. This is a trapeze-shaped cairn with a semicircular forecourt and façade at the west end. The burial chamber has five compartments and is 6·7 m long: it was ransacked long ago.

Just before Lamlash a minor road turns west up the Monamore Glen and a Forestry Commission track turns south from this, across the river, a few hundred metres from the junction. This track winds its way for about 1 km to the south and comes in sight of the

*Monamore chambered cairn** on the slope on the opposite side of a side glen (a stream must be crossed: NS/017289). The compartmented burial chamber and the tall portal slabs of this tomb are still visible but the crescentic façade, exposed by the author in 1961 and built of upright stones with dry walling between, is now buried again. The excavations in 1901 and 1961 revealed few finds but the cairn has the distinction of being the first of its kind in Scotland to receive radio-carbon dates. One from a fire lit in the forecourt at an early stage in its use was 3160 ± 110 b.c. (about 3800 B.C.) and another fire, lit just before the tomb was blocked, was dated to 2240 ± 110 b.c. The cairn falls in the middle of a typological sequence which has been devised for the Neolithic tombs of south-west Scotland, in which cairns without façades are supposed to be earlier than those with. It should, according to this, date to about 2500 b.c., and doubt has therefore been thrown on the reliability of the earlier date. However, no reasons for doubting the charcoal sample concerned were noted at the time of the excavation.

From Lamlash or Whiting Bay boats can be taken to Holy island during the holiday season and the *Early Christian cave cell* of St. Molaise inspected (NS/059297). A path runs from the pier at the west end of the island along the west shore and a walk of about 1·5 km is needed. The cave was excavated in 1908 and a mass of occupation debris removed. There are runic inscriptions cut into the walls, one of 11th-century date and six others of 12th- or 13th-century date. One of the latter refers to the expedition of King Haakon of Norway in 1263 (which culminated in his defeat at the battle of Largs).

Between Lamlash and Brodick is a *stone circle* close by the road (NS/018336) and the *Sannox vitrified hillfort* is 9 km north of Brodick (NS/017462.)

Isle of Bute

This island is easily reached by car-ferry across the Firth of Clyde from Wemyss Bay. *Rothesay Castle*+, lying in the centre of the town south of the pier, was built early in the 13th century and is one of the best preserved Medieval castles in Scotland (Pl. 10) (NS/088546). This is a castle of *enciente* consisting of a massive circular curtain wall fortified with four drum towers projecting from it, all built of the finely coursed ashlar masonry typical of the castles of the time of Alexander II and III. The circular plan of the castle, enclosing an area about 41 m across, is unique in Scotland. It is surrounded by a deep moat and the entrance tower which projects into this is a

Plate 10. Rothesay Castle, Isle of Bute: the gatehouse, NW tower and moat.

later addition of the time of James IV (1488–1513). The adjacent
sectors of the curtain wall were heightened at the same time, pre-
serving the original battlements.

In 1230 Rothesay Castle was besieged by the Norsemen who,
having failed to storm it, chopped through the curtain wall with axes.
There are signs of disturbances and rebuilding in the wall on the
east side and this may well be the spot where the Norsemen broke in.

There are various buildings inside the castle including a chapel
on the east and, opposite it, what has been identified as a forge.

Travelling S from Rothesay along the coast road one reaches
Kingarth and 400 m further west of it a minor road turns south
beside a church. There is a *stone circle* close beside this road on the
east in a wood 600 m from the main road (NS/092556) and *standing
stones* 700 m to the south-west by west (NS/085554). Two kilometres
further south on the main road is Dunagoil with an *Early Christian
monastic site* and a *vitrified hillfort* close by. *St. Blane's church* is
about 500 m due east of Dunagoil House, at the southern tip of a
wood, and the numerous carved stones which have been found there
at various times show that it was an early monastery of some importance (NS/095534). The surviving church is a fine 12th-century

9

Romanesque building, consisting of a nave and chancel, and the chancel arch has the Norman geometrical, zig-zag ornamentation. The east end of the chancel appears to be of inferior masonry and may be a later rebuild. Eight Class III *Early Christian sculptured stones* and *cross slabs* have been found there and several are visible at the site. The design and extent of the pre-Norman monastery at St. Blane's have not yet been established.

At a distance of 800 m south-west of *Dunagoil* is the *vitrified fort* of that name, on a narrow and steep-sided ridge close to the sea (NS/085530). A heavily vitrified wall encloses an area about 91 m by 23 m. The hillfort was extensively explored in the late 19th and early 20th centuries and yielded large quantities of tools and ornaments of iron, bronze, bone, stone and jet which have never been systematically published. The finds suggest that the fort was occupied in the last few centuries B.C. but it could have been built as early as 700 B.C. (p. 27).

Also on the shore 400 m north of the last mentioned site is the smaller *Iron Age fort Little Dunagoil* which was partially explored in the early 1960s (NS/086534). The foundations of two *Norse longhouses* can be seen near the ramparts.

There is another Early Christian site on *St. Ninian's isle* on the west coast opposite Rothesay (NS/035612). The small rectangular chapel, only 4·9 m by 6·7 m internally, was excavated in the early 1950s and yielded a stone altar at the east end with what may have been a relic cavity inside it.

There are several Neolithic chambered tombs on Bute which have been excavated and yielded important finds but none is spectacular to look at now. The one at *Glenvoidean*, on the north-west coast (NR/997705), was excavated during the 1960s and produced some intact pots which are now in the museum in Rothesay. The cairn is trapezoidal with a flat façade and a segmented chamber behind. Two lateral chambers have been discovered. It is reached by following the A844 through Port Bannatyne to its end and then by taking the farmroad north up the west coast. The *Glecknabae cairn* is the first to be reached along this coast road and is now a grass-grown stony mound with few visible constructional features (NS/007683). On its excavation in 1903 it was found to be resting on an earlier Mesolithic shell midden and pottery was found in the two burial chambers. A short cist at the north-west end of the cairn, still complete, shows it to have still been in use in the Early Bronze Age.

The *Carn Ban long chambered cairn* is 1 km further north at the south-east corner of Lenihuline Wood (NS/005693): the despoiled cairn is about 55 m long and has a chamber at each end with a lateral chamber on the south side.

2. ARGYLLSHIRE

Kintyre

By taking the road W from Glasgow by way of Loch Lomond and Loch Fyne Lochgilphead is reached and turning either N or S there leads one to a rich archaeological zone. The Kintyre peninsula is important as being one of the first landfalls for ships coming up through the North channel and also in that the Mull of Kintyre is only 20 km by sea from Ulster.

Travelling along the A83 one passes East and West Loch Tarbert and at Clachan can turn NW up the side road before the village to see the *Dun Skeig hillforts and dun* (NR/757572). The forts stand on an isolated hill 143 m high at the entrance to West Loch Tarbert. The earliest fort consisted of an enclosure about 113 m by 36 m surrounded by a stone wall which has been severely robbed, presumably to obtain material for the later duns. Traces of its outer face are best seen at the north end. At the south end is a large oval dun enclosing an area some 26 m by 18·5 m, the wall of which is

Plate 11. Raised beach at Bellochantuy, Kintyre, Argyll: looking N.

vitrified, showing that it was originally built with a timber-framed wall. Evidently the builders of these Late Bronze Age and Early Iron Age forts had developed tiny, dun-sized forts by the time they reached Kintyre and such diminution in size, from the huge vitrified hillforts of the eastern mainland (p. 189) to the tiny ones of the west, may well show in general how the Iron Age dun itself was evolved. A well-preserved such drystone dun stands on the north end of the hillfort. It encloses an area 14·6 m by 12·8 m and the entrance, with door-checks and traces of a bar-hole, is on the east side. This may be assumed to be the latest structure on the site.

About 1 km after the road comes down to the coast, where it runs along the old raised beach (Pl. 11), is the impressive *Corriechrevie cairn*★ on an eminence just east of the road (NR/738540). It is the largest in Kintyre, 27·5 m in diameter, and appears to be intact in spite of some quarrying. About 1·5 km further south is an iron farm-gate and a track leading up the old sea-cliff to a large white barn. In the field behind this are the *Ballochroy standing stones and cist*★ (NR/730524). There are three stones, two with one flat face, set in a north-east line which, if extended, passes through a massive mega-lithic cist 36·5 m to the south-west. The cist was once covered by a large cairn. It has been suggested that the south-west alignment of the stones was meant to indicate an astronomical foresight formed by the west end of Cara island: this has a declination of $-23° 53'$, suitable for a midwinter sunset at about 1800 B.C. However the cairn over the cist would certainly have blocked this view when it was intact. More impressive is the clear orientation of the central stone to Corra Beinn on Jura, 30 km to the north-west. The right slope of this peak, when seen from the stones would give a declina-tion for the sun when its edge is just showing of $+23° 54'$ (Pl. 12). This would have happened only on midsummer evening in about 1800 B.C. At the present time the yearly swing of the sunset position does not reach Corra Beinn and the midsummer sun sets between it and the mountain to the left. These stones are a convincing pre-historic observatory for the summer solstice although a puzzle is provided by the orientation of the shorter, right (north-east) stone which points at the right slope of Beinn a'Chaolais, the furthest left of the four Paps of Jura. The declination of this slope is well inside (to the south of) the modern midsummer sunset position and is hard to understand.

Nine kilometres further south, just beyond Killean, the farmroad to Beacharr turns east and just west of the farm is the *Beacharr Neo-*

Plate 12. Ballochroy standing stones, Kintyre, Argyll: view to the NW with the Paps of Jura in the background.

lithic chambered cairn* and standing stone* (NR/692433). The cairn is now a grass-grown mound and the stone slabs of the segmented burial chamber, 6·25 m in length, are visible. When excavated in 1892 the chamber yielded two pots in each of its three compartments; these have since been used as the basis for an analysis of the development of the West Scottish Neolithic wares. In 1959 and 1961 the cairn was re-excavated by Mr J. G. Scott and a forecourt façade was found; the entrance, in the middle of this, was found to have been deliberately blocked in the usual manner.

The standing stone near by is 5·03 m high, the tallest in Kintyre. It is reported to have been used as a site for fertility-inducing rituals not long ago and vestiges of this may be seen in the fact that eggs are still rolled down the near-by hill at Easter. It has also been suggested that the stone marks the position of a prehistoric lunar observatory. The foresight would be the sharp dip between Beinn an Oir and Beinn Shiantaidh, 37 km away on Jura, which could have marked the moon when it set at its greatest northern declination.

There are several sites to be seen on the east coast road, the B8001 and B842, which leaves the main road a few kilometres south of Tarbert: it can be taken north from Campbeltown. The early 13th-century *Skipness Castle* is on the east coast, at the end of the B8001 4 km north from the junction with the B842 (NR/907577).

Travelling S again turn E to Carradale and S along the minor road from there: a walk of 1 km S of the end of this across moorland brings one to the *vitrified fort* on the summit of Carradale point; it is cut off at high tide. The fort is an elongated oval about 56·5 m by 23 m internally and impressive masses of vitrification, up to 1·5 m high, are preserved along the east wall. The entrance may be on the south-east and there are various short outworks blocking the approaches to the main fort.

Six kilometres south of the Carradale road are the fragmentary remains of the 12th-century *Saddell Abbey*, near the mouth of Glen Saddell (NR/784320). The buildings are situated about 500 m just south of west of the road bridge and immediately above the junction of the Saddell water and one of its tributaries, the latter doubtless being used for drainage. The abbey was founded for the Cistercian order probably in about 1160, and was colonised from Mellifont Abbey in Armagh. The site consisted of a church with an

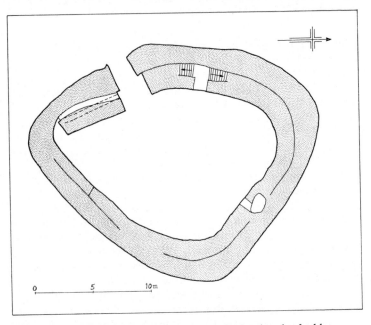

Fig. 17. Plan of Kildonan dun, Kintyre, Argyll, showing the double stairway in the wall, the length of mural gallery and median wallfaces. Scale 1:312.

Plate 13. Kildonan dun, Kintyre, Argyll: the entrance and stairs from the NE.

aisle-less nave and the conventual buildings round a cloister to the south of this. The only standing portions now are the 12th-century presbytery, the adjacent north transept (reconstructed in the 13th century), a fragment of the south range of the conventual buildings about 25 m to the south-west and the 12th-century undercroft (cellar) of the refectory. The rest of the abbey is a series of grass-grown mounds of rubble. A number of late carved stones from the abbey are in the Campbeltown museum and there are more in the presbytery.

Four kilometres south of the abbey the well-preserved *Kildonan dun** is seen 50 m east of the road (Fig. 17) (NR/780277). It was excavated between 1936 and 1938 and some rebuilding was then carried out, especially of the outer wallface on the west. The dun is triangular with the wide main entrance on the west complete with door-checks and a bar-hole and socket (Pl. 13). The area enclosed measures 19·2 m by 13·1 m and the wall is as much as 4·3 m thick. The dun is skilfully built on the summit of a rocky knoll and its outer face is founded everywhere at a lower level than the inner. Presumably to increase the stability of the dry rubble core on this slope the wall was constructed in two halves with a built, inward-facing revetment in its centre running nearly the whole way round.

This median face can be seen forming the outer side of the double intramural stair north of the entrance and it emerges as the north door-check in the entrance passage. On the south side of the passage is a short stretch of true mural gallery, again probably another device to ensure stability. There is a small cell in the wall opposite the entrance. The finds made during the excavations suggested that the dun had been built in the Iron Age, probably at some time between 100 B.C. and A.D. 200, and that it was occupied at intervals up until the 9th century A.D. Thereafter it was abandoned until a period of re-use in Medieval times, in the 13th century.

Kildonan dun has aroused some interest because of the supposed link with the brochs seen in its short stretch of galleried wall. However the double stair shows clearly that the wall was never very high and that the defenders went up these stairs to an open, parapeted wallhead to defend their dun. The entrance, too, is wider than that in the brochs and the triangular plan and revetted wall core increase the contrast with the tower-forts. Some 'galleried duns' on Skye provide more plausible broch prototypes (p. 162 below).

On and near the extreme south coast—the Mull of Kintyre— there are some interesting sites; they are reached by the A83 and B842 to Southend or by the minor coast road leading south-east from Campbeltown. At 1·5 km before Southend on the B842, and 600 m after the T-junction, one can walk 300 m SW up the hill to see *Cnoc Araich*, the largest hillfort in Kintyre (NR/693097). The remains of the ramparts are now very denuded but consist of three lines of defences enclosing an area about 204 m by 177 m. It is possible that this was the tribal stronghold of the Epidii who are mentioned on Ptolemy's map of the 2nd century A.D.

Taking the minor road E 1 km before Southend brings one, after 2·5 km, below the hill on which stands the *Blasthill chambered cairn* 400 m north of the road (NR/720092). This horned cairn is quite well preserved, 24·5 m long and standing up to 1 m high. The con-cave forecourt at the east end is marked by several upright stones and appears to have been blocked with rubble, a feature found in many Neolithic tombs of this type. The burial chamber is visible behind the façade and there is a second, transverse chamber further back.

One of the best-preserved duns in Kintyre is at *Borgadel water* (NR/625061), reached from the road west of Southend leading to the Mull lighthouse (itself a spectacularly situated structure dating from 1788). A walk of up to 2 km is required and it is probably best to follow the west side of the glen containing the Borgadel water: the dun stands on a rocky bluff overlooking the sea. In plan it is round, an area 13 m to 13·5 m in diameter being enclosed by a drystone wall 3·4 m to 4 m thick: this wall stands up to 1·8 m high. The entrance is on the west and one door-check remains.

At a distance of 1·3 km further west along the precipitous coast is the spectacular multivallate stone-walled small fort *Sròn Uamha* (NR/612060). On a rocky knoll at the edge of the sheer cliff a small area 32 m long is defended by three stone walls; the inner one is 3·7 m thick and follows the shoulder of the knoll, the two outer ones, lower down, are 2·1 m and 1·5 m thick respectively.

Isle of Islay

This attractive island is reached by car-ferries from west Loch Tarbert. Archaeologically it is one of the least well-documented regions of Scotland though certain classes of monuments like the Early Christian and Medieval carved stones have been well described (Dr W. D. Lamont's book should be consulted for a detailed account of these: p. 291). Islay is clearly an important island for Early Christian archaeology as the numerous old chapels and place names beginning with 'Kil' attest. Standing stones are also numerous but few have yet been surveyed for potential astronomical significance.

The MacBrayne's steamer docks at Port Ellen and the road east may be taken to see several sites. At Lagavulin, 3·5 km east of Port Ellen, a farmroad turns north-west and from it one can walk 400 m to *standing stones* (NR/389461) and, 200 m to the north of these, to the *Ballynaughton long chambered cairn* (NR/390464). The chamber, with four compartments, is visible though the cairn has been almost entirely removed. That the burial chamber had already been disturbed when it was excavated in 1901 was shown by the discovery then of a hoard of coins dating to 1450–1550 at the bottom of the west chamber.

Further east is the famous *Kildalton chapel and cross*★ 6 km beyond Ardbeg (signposted: NR/458508). This is the only complete freestanding wheel-cross in Scotland though there are two very similar ones on Iona. The cross consists of a single block of local stone 2·6 m high and, though weathered, the elaborate Celtic carving in high relief is still clear. This decoration, usually dated to the early 9th century, makes it one of the finest Early Christian monuments in the country.

The front face of the cross (facing east, away from the trees:

Plate 14. Kildalton cross, Islay: the E face.

Pl. 14) shows several biblical scenes. The top arm has a scene with a pair of angels and, below them, David or Samson rending the lion. At the end of the left arm is Abraham preparing to sacrifice Isaac and, on the right arm, Isaac's sacrifice. At the base of the lower arm are the Virgin and Child. On the lower part of the shaft is a characteristic Celtic composition consisting of curves and spirals. Anglian interlace work surrounds the boss at the centre of the cross and is seen again on the rear west face. This is also elaborately decorated with beasts and serpents and Celtic curvilinear ornament.

The cross is linked to the great high crosses of the Irish Celtic Church both in its form and its Celtic ornament and it shows an interesting mixture of Celtic and Northumbrian (Anglian) traditions in its design as well as its decoration. The shape of the arms, with slightly concave outer parts, is similar to the Ruthwell cross (p. 42) and the interlace ornament, the biblical human figures and the motifs of birds and grapes also originate in Northumbria. The cross would thus belong to a time when the influence of the Northumbrian sculptors was impinging on Islay.

At 2 km further north-east along the road one can walk 600 m E to the point at the south end of Claggain bay on which is the *Trudernish vitrified fort*★ (NR/467526). However the author could find no vitrified stone there in 1969.

Following the B8016 N from Port Ellen one can visit the well-preserved small hillfort *Dun Nosebridge*★ (Pl. 15) (NR/371601). Take the minor road NE from 2 km south of Laggan bridge or, alternatively, the same by-road direct SE from Bridgend. A farm track can be taken immediately north of the bridge over the river Laggan and runs right past the site. The fort stands on an isolated eminence overlooking the Laggan valley and consists of a well-preserved rampart enclosing an area 17 m by 29 m from crest to crest. There is an entrance in the middle of the north end and outworks defend the central citadel everywhere except on the east where the rock face is sheer. These outworks are particularly impressive and consist of two outer banks and ditches except in the south-west where there are four. The rectangular shape may mean that this is a small timber-framed hillfort which has not been burnt and vitrified.

Take the A847 W of Bridgend for 3·5 km, then the B8017 for 5 km to Gruinart and finally the minor road N up the west side of Loch Gruinart to see the *Kilnave cross*★ which stands in an old burial ground by the shore of the loch (NR/286715). This fine though weathered high cross still stands on its original site and exhibits

Plate 15. Dun Nosebridge hillfort, Islay, seen from the NNW.

sculpture on one face which is in the pure Celtic tradition. It was evidently set up before the arrival of Northumbrian influences and is usually dated to about A.D. 750. The single piece of slate is 2·6 m high and is ornamented with curvilinear Celtic decoration in a tradition which goes back one thousand years earlier to the La Tène decorated metalwork of the prehistoric Iron Age. The large circular medallion is very similar to designs in the *Book of Durrow* and the *Book of Kells*. The panels on the top arm and on the shaft closely resemble the design on the base panel on the Keills cross in Knapdale (p. 144 below).

Although it is sad to see this magnificent 1,200-year-old Celtic cross slowly weathering away there is something compelling about its quiet and lonely situation in an old chapel cemetery which contains quite recent tombstones. These include one set there in 1969 for his ancestor by a New Yorker of Islay origins. The sense of continuity with the past is very strong here.

Returning from Kilnave, turn right (west) along the B8017, then right and left round Loch Gorm towards Saligo bay (where there is a fine beach). *Ballinaby* farm is 1·5 km east of Saligo and above it is a huge *standing stone*★ about 5·4 m high (NR/220672) with a smaller one 200 m to the north-north-east and a third, very large one—now broken off short—above the crags in the same direction. The tall stone is very thin and clearly aligned towards two conspicuous crags 2 km away in the north-west (329°). Professor Thom believes the site to be an important lunar observatory. In the 17th century B.C. the upper edge of the moon setting at its extreme northerly declination should have just reappeared at the base of the right slope of the right-hand crag. Some of the other notches could also have been used for detecting the tiny nine-minute 'wobble' of the moon which is superimposed on its other motions and a knowledge of the periodicity of which could give a clue to the prediction of eclipses.

In the Port Charlotte area, in the Rhinns of Islay, a dilapidated *Neolithic chambered cairn*★ can be seen just to the east of the road less than 1 km south of the village (NR/247575). It has the remains of a chamber 6·7 m long which originally had four compartments. The best preserved of these tombs on Islay is high up on the hills west of *Nereabolls*★ (NR/210564) and can be reached with 2 km of rough walking N from the top of the Octofad road. The whole segmented chamber is exposed—7·7 m long—with two huge, displaced capstones lying in it; a portal stone and fragments of the horned façade are also visible. There are no records of anything having been found in either of these tombs, both of which appear to have been emptied.

About 6½ km north of Portnahaven on the west (minor) road is the *Cultoon stone circle**, 100 m west of the road. In 1974 excavations began at this site, where only two stones remain standing, and revealed at least twelve more lying partly or wholly buried. The stones lie quite well round an ellipse measuring 50 × 40 my, and based on a 3–4–5 Pythagorean triangle of 15, 20 and 25 my, but not enough of the stone sockets have yet been uncovered to determine whether this was the shape intended by the builders. The excavations showed clearly that peat began to grow over the site in Bronze Age times *after* the circle was in ruins: empty stone sockets were covered by this peat and monoliths were lying on the old ground surface below it. The cause of this apparently deliberate prehistoric destruction is unknown at present but the 1975 season of excavation may shed more light on it.

In the vicinity of Port Askaig (from which there is a car-ferry to Jura) is Islay's solitary *broch, Dun Bhoreraic** (NR/416658). Take the farmroad SE from Ballygrant for 2 km to Lossit farm and the broch stands on top of a low hill 500 m north-east of the farm; the site has a splendid view in several directions. The entrance is visible on the south-east, with what appears to be a guard cell on its left. The broch is well preserved though largely hidden under its own rubble.

Kilmartin and Knapdale

A few kilometres north of Lochgilphead lies one of the richest archaeological zones in Scotland, the Kilmartin valley and its adjacent regions. The sites may be conveniently visited by using the map (Fig. 18) on which there are numbers and symbols referred to in the text.

The A816 leads north from Lochgilphead and one can turn right along the farmroad 1 km from the town to Achnabreck. From there a forestry track continues north-east and the *Achnabreck cup-and-ring marked rocks*+ (1) are in the wood some 400 m beyond the farm (NR/856907). Two large areas of rock carvings are on the hillside showing elaborate pecked designs including double spirals. About 1·5 km beyond the farm on the same track is the *Auchoish chambered cairn** (2) (NR/870911). The site is a horned cairn some 40 m in length with the remains of a concave façade of orthostats at the north-east end. The chamber here has been completely wrecked, only the

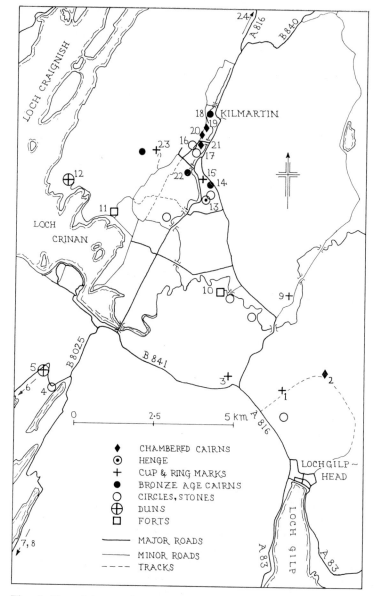

Fig. 18. Map of the zone between Lochgilphead and Kilmartin, Argyllshire, showing the location of sites described in Chapter 5. Scale 1:113640.

back slab remaining, but there is a lateral chamber further west which is quite well preserved. The site was excavated in 1931 but no finds were made.

Near the junction with the B841 to Crinan are the *Cairnbaan cup-and-ring rocks*[+] (3), 300 m north-north-west of the hotel (NR/838910). The carvings are in two groups and show cups, cup-and-rings and some grooves. Continue along the Crinan road and take the B8025 to Tayvallich. About 2 km along this the minor road forks left to Castle Sween (below) and at the junction is a fine copy of the Kildalton cross. At the sharp turn in the road 700 m further on is the *Barnluasgan stone circle*[*] (4) immediately to the left of the road in a clearing in the wood (NR/783907). There are erect stones on the north-east and south-west sides but none visible on the east. Before afforestation the site had a wide view to the east. About 1 km further on the road bends sharply to the left again and the *Druim an Duin dun* (5) is on a high ridge to the left after this (NR/781913). There should be a track up to the fort on the left of the road starting about 400 m after the stone circle mentioned. The dun stands on the edge of a precipitous crag and is roughly oval in plan measuring internally 14·6 m long with a maximum width of 10 m. There are two opposing entrance passages, both with door-checks; the south-west one has a bar-hole and socket and a guard cell on the right. Excavations in 1904 produced some standard Iron Age relics and the dun is likely to have been built at some time between 200 B.C. and A.D. 200.

The road continues for 13 km through Tayvallich to the end of the peninsula where the *Keills Medieval chapel* and Class III *Early Christian cross*[*+] (6) are situated (NR/690806: signposted). The cross, about 100 m north-east of the chapel, is of blue slate, stands 2·2 m high and is sculpted on the front face only. In the centre of the head is a large boss covered with Celtic curvilinear ornament and similar decoration is on the base of the shaft. This ornamentation closely resembles that on the Kilnave cross in Islay (p. 139). On the top arm is an angel treading on a serpent and, on the bottom one, a priest or saint giving a benediction. Interlace work and key-pattern decoration occur and the cross thus shows a mixture of Celtic and Northumbrian motifs. The central boss, usually described as the 'bird's nest with three eggs', marks it as one of the 'Iona group' of crosses of which Kildalton, Islay, is another (p. 137). A late 8th or a 9th century date might be indicated.

The chapel is a simple, early Medieval rectangular structure with

Plate 16. Castle Sween, Argyll, seen from the SSE.

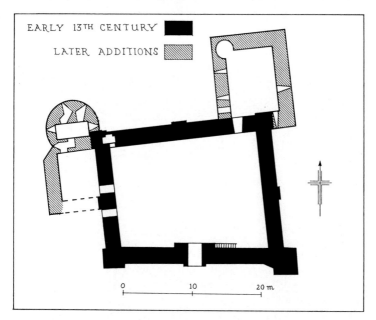

Fig. 19. Plan of Castle Sween, Argyllshire, showing the primary masonry and later additions. Scale 1:525.

10

one round-arched window in the east wall. It and the graveyard are full of fine Medieval grave slabs.

Taking the minor road left 1 km before the Barnluasgan stone circle described above brings one down along the east shore of Loch Sween and, 15 km from the junction, close to *Castle Sween*⋆⁺ (7) 400 m to the right down on the shore (Pl. 16; Fig. 19) (NR/713789). This, together with the Castle of Old Wick in Caithness (p. 228) and Cobbie Row's Castle in Orkney (p. 254), is one of the earliest stone castles in Scotland, having been built in the 12th century. The original structure is the oblong Norman tower or keep with large buttresses at the corners: it measures internally about 21·5 m long and up to 16·8 m wide. The kitchen wing was added to the north-east side at a later date, as was the structure at the north-west corner. Castle Sween is reported to have been built by Dougall, third chief of Craignish and was destroyed by Colkitto Macdonald in 1645.

Four kilometres further south along the road, at the mouth of Loch Sween, is *Kilmory Knap* (8), a Medieval chapel and cross with some *Early Christian stones*⋆⁺ among the Medieval ones in the burial ground (NR/702750). There are four early cross slabs, all having a ring connecting the arms. If a boat can be obtained to visit *Eilean*

Plate 17. Bronze Age rock carvings at Kilmichael Glassary, Argyll.

Mor a *Medieval chapel*[+] can be seen there with an *Early Christian cross slab*[+] 30 m east of it (NR/666754). The arms of the cross are broken away but the front face of the shaft shows several intertwined beasts, a priest riding a horse and a panel of Anglian key-pattern ornament.

Returning to the Kilmartin valley and taking the main road N at Cairnbaan, several standing stones on the left are passed as the bridge over the river Add is crossed. A short distance after the bridge is the minor road to *Kilmichael Glassary* where there is an *inscribed rock*[+] (9) of Bronze Age date (NR/858935). There are cups, cup-and-rings and 'keyhole' figures in a large group (Pl. 17).

At 1·5 km further north along the main road one reaches the farm-road turning left to the *Dunadd*[★+] (10) (NR/837936). This Dark Age fortress (Fig. 20), stands on top of an isolated hill which was once protected on nearly all sides by marshy ground, the Crinan Moss. Dunadd is thought to have been the capital of the Scottish kingdom of Dalriada, founded by colonists from Ireland at about A.D. 500. Excavation in 1904 and again in 1929 confirmed that the site had been occupied in the Dark Age but showed that there had also been an earlier, Iron Age settlement there.

The layout of the drystone fort is sometimes described as nuclear with a central stronghold on the summit of the hill and two outer fortified enclosures on natural terraces lower down—a typical Dark Age plan. One enters the lowest enclosure through a natural gully on the south-east side: the massive outermost wall is well pre-served in part. Above this is the second enclosure, reached origi-nally through a small gateway at the south-west junction of the two walls. The topmost fort, or citadel, is a drop-shaped enclosure at the west end of the summit ridge and measures internally 30·5 m in length by 13·7 m in maximum width. It is possible that this was an Iron Age dun and that the lower enclosures were added in the Dark Age. Immediately in front (north-east) of the citadel is another small enclosure and below this to the north-west is a ravine outside the walls in which a midden had accumulated during the occupation of the site. On the rock ridge in front of these two uppermost enclosures are several rock-carvings. These include a boar allegedly in the Pic-tish style and protected by a glass (Fig. 20), two or three lines of ogham inscription, a hollowed-out basin and a footprint. The boar perhaps dates from A.D. 736 when the Scotic capital was besieged and captured by Fergus, King of the Picts. The footprint and basin probably mark the site of the inauguration of new kings of the Scots

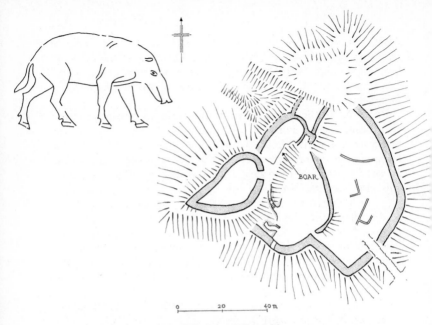

Fig. 20. (*left*) The carving of the boar at Dunadd.
(*right*) Plan of Dunadd Dark Age fortress, Argyllshire, showing the successively higher-walled enclosures with the topmost, pear-shaped dun on the left. The gully in which the Iron Age midden was discovered is immediately NE of this. Scale 1:1615.

who placed their foot in the mark symbolically to affirm that they would walk in the ways of their predecessors (as at Clickhimin, Shetland: p. 280 below).

About 700 m north of the farmroad to Dunadd the minor road to Duntrune Castle turns west from the A816. About 1 km before the castle, on a ridge in a wood on the right of the road, is the *Duntroon vitrified fort*★ (11) (NR/803959). It consists of an oval wall, perhaps 3 m thick, enclosing an area some 43 m by 27 m and surrounded by a concentric outer wall enclosing an area some 91 m by 55 m. There are two more outer walls on the south-west. The vitrified stone is seen best on the inner wall on the north-east and south-west sides. Exploration in 1904 produced early Iron Age artefacts including many saddle querns, thus showing that the fort was probably used in the period before the building of the brochs and duns.

About 2·5 km further down this road, at its end, is the well-preserved *Ardifuir dun*★ (12) (NR/789969). The fort stands on the

Plate 18. Ardifuir dun, Argyll: view from the ridge to the NW.

flat ground of the valley bottom and is in a curious situation in that it is overlooked by the high crag to the west from which missiles can be projected into the interior (Pl. 18). The dun is exactly circular with a wall 3 m thick enclosing a space 19·8 m in diameter. The low platform edged with stone slabs which runs round the interior is probably a secondary addition. The paved entrance passage has door-checks and a small guard cell on the right side. The passage is 1·8 m wide before the checks and 2·7 m behind them; this is much broader than the entrances of brochs—to which Ardifuir has often been compared—and is comparable to that of the Kildonan dun (p. 135). Its width suggests that cattle were taken inside. A short distance to the left of the entrance is a door from the interior to the mural stair. Another broch-like feature is the scarcement on the inside wallface which presumably supported a raised wooden floor but this, and the pronounced batter of the outer wallface, show that the wall can never have been more than 4·5 m to 6 m high. The finds of the 1904 clearance show that Ardifuir dun was probably built in the Iron Age and inhabited also in the Dark Age.

Returning from Ardifuir take the B2025 N and then the minor road E to the main road. A short distance further north the *Bally-meanoch standing stones*★ (13) are visible in a field on the left

(NR/833964); six stones, the tallest 4·3 m high, still stand in an unusual formation of two lines of four and two. Two of the stones in the first line bear cup-and-ring markings as does a fallen outlying stone 18 m north-west of the pair. There is a denuded *henge monument* about 100 m south-west of the stones. It consists of a bank and ditch around a low cairn 21 m in diameter which had two cists in it. One of these yielded an Early Bronze Age beaker.

A few hundred metres further north is the *Dunchraigaig Bronze Age cairn**+ (14), in a copse close to the left of the road (NR/833968). Originally the cairn was more than 30 m in diameter and it still stands 2·1 m high. On the south side is a huge capstone—4·3 m by 2·5 m by 0·37 m thick—resting on the boulder walls of a cist: cremations and inhumations were found in the cist. Two other smaller cists, probably secondary, contained food vessels of the Early Bronze Age.

A short distance further north are the *Baluachraig cup-and-ring markings**+ (15) on a glaciated rock surface not far from the west side of the road (NR/831970). Cups and cup-and-rings are well preserved.

The second turning to the left after Baluachraig leads one to the *Temple Wood stone circle* (16), the *Nether Largie standing stones* (17) and the unique *linear cemetery* of five Neolithic and Bronze Age cairns (18–22). Temple wood circle*+ is beside the road in a copse and originally had 20 stones within a denuded bank of which 13 remain (NR/826979). The circle is 12·2 m in diameter and at the centre there is a cist with a low setting of slabs around it. A pecked spiral carving has recently been discovered on one of the upright stones. In the fields to the south are the five *Nether Largie standing stones*, two pairs and a single one in a line running north-east–south-west (17). The central single stone is ornamented with cup-marks (Pl. 19). It has been suggested that the stones mark the observation points for a prehistoric lunar observatory. In this case the pair of stones at the south end would point north-west to the Temple Wood circle 310 m away and to a notch in the hill slope beyond; at its greatest northerly declination the moon would have set at this notch. Similarly looking along the row to the south-west one could see Bellanoch Hill (except that trees are now in the way) which could have marked the setting of the moon at its extreme southerly declination.

The five cairns of the linear cemetery are a unique phenomenon in Scotland though such lines of Neolithic and Bronze Age barrows are quite common in the Stonehenge area of Wiltshire. Four of the five can be seen from *Nether Largie South**+ (21), not far from the Temple Wood circle (NR/829980). This is the oldest cairn of the group, being of Neolithic age, and when explored in 1864 it yielded cremation burials with Early Neolithic pottery in the segmented main chamber as well as some beaker sherds: the capstones of this chamber are very large. Beaker sherds were also found in some secondary cists in the body of the cairn. Other such cists contained food vessels, confirming the use of the burial mound into the Early Bronze Age. The chamber was probably distorted when the site was reconstructed by the Office of Works and the cairn has been largely robbed. It may have been a long cairn with a forecourt but this latter feature is now hidden.

Nether Largie Mid cairn⋆⁺ (20) lies 450 m towards Kilmartin and was excavated in 1929. It proved to be round, some 32 m in diameter, and has a boulder kerb, traces of which can be seen. Two cists were found, one in the north-west sector and one on the south, and both were empty though apparently undisturbed. The former has side slabs which are carefully grooved to take the end slabs—a technique transferred from woodworking. This cairn seems from its design to be of Early Bronze Age date.

Plate 19.
Temple Wood standing stones, Argyll: the central stone showing the cup-and-ring and cup markings.

Nether Largie North★+ (19) lies 200 m further north and is another Early Bronze Age round cairn (NR/831985). It is 21 m in diameter and still stands 2·7 m high. Excavations in 1930 revealed a large, central, empty cist with a capstone the underside of which is ornamented with cup-marks and representations of flat bronze axes (Fig. 21). An Early Bronze Age date is thus indicated.

The *Glebe cairn*★+ (18) is the most northerly in the linear cemetery and is another round burial mound of the Early Bronze Age 33·5 m in diameter. Exploration in 1864 revealed a central cist 2·3 m long covered by a massive capstone 2·7 m long. An inhumation with a food vessel was found within. The second cist in the south-west sector also produced a food vessel together with a jet necklace.

The *Ri Cruin cairn*★+ (22) is on the same line as the rest of the linear cemetery, 850 m south-south-west of Nether Largie South (NR/825972). It lies in a wood about 100 m west of the farmroad

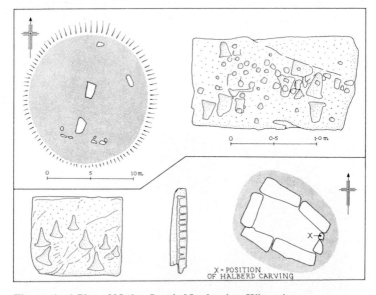

Fig. 21. (*top*) Plan of Nether Largie North cairn, Kilmartin, Argyllshire, showing the position of cists (scale 1:420) and axe carvings on the stone covering the central cist (scale 1:42).
(*bottom*) Plan of the S cist in Ri Cruin cairn, Kilmartin, Argyllshire, with drawings of axe carvings on the end slab and of the upright slab with carvings of a halberd with streamers. Original position of this vanished stone is marked with an X. Scale 1:42.

and is a dilapidated round cairn containing three cists. All of these have grooved side slabs and one end-slab in the south cist still has many carvings of bronze axe-heads (Pl. 20). Another narrow upright slab in this cist, now lost, had a carving of what seems to be a bronze halberd mounted on a shaft with streamers flying (Fig. 21): a cast is in the National Museum in Edinburgh.

There is a *cup-and-ring marked rock* near by at *Ballygowan* (23) (NR/816977). Figures on it include radial grooves, ovals and one horseshoe.

Continuing N towards Oban on the main road *Kilmartin church**+ is reached with its fine collection of Medieval sculptured stones. There is also a Class III *Early Christian cross*+* of slate with short arms which stands to the south (left) of the main entrance path. The front is decorated with Anglian interlace and key-patterns and, at the base, with a plain cross surrounded by four smaller ones of the same type. On the back are key-pattern designs and spirals. There are two more early stones to the south of the cross.

About 6·5 m north of Kilmartin the A816 twists and turns,

Plate 20. Axe carvings at Ri Cruin Bronze Age cairn, Argyll: the W end slab of the large cist.

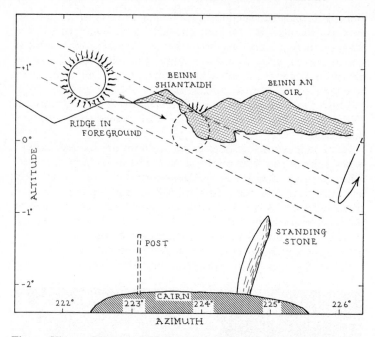

Fig. 22. View to SW from the hill platform, Kintraw, Argyllshire, at sunset on midwinter's day in about 1800 B.C. The standing stone and cairn are in the foreground and the mountains of Jura in the background. At midwinter the upper edge of the setting sun would have just flashed into view again in the col between the two peaks. The curved arrow indicates the direction of the sun's real movement against the background of fixed stars, the straight arrow its daily motion.

descending steeply down to the head of Loch Craignish. About half-way down is the gate to a field on the right in which are the *Kintraw cairns and standing stone*★ with the *hill platform* beyond (24) (NM/830050). The latter is best reached from the bridge at the foot of the hill by following the steep path along the north bank of the stream gorge. The kerbed *cairn*, 14·6 m in diameter, was excavated in 1959–60 by Dr D. D. A. Simpson and a cist was found near the edge: clear traces of a socket for a post were found in the body of the cairn. The standing stone, nearly 4 m high, is close by and is leaning over.

This site has been interpreted as an observatory for the mid-winter solstice of about thirty-eight centuries ago but the natural foresight, Beinn Shiantaidh 45 km away to the south-west on Jura, is not visible from the stone because of the tree-covered ridge a mile in front (Fig. 22). Hence explorations were carried out by the author in 1970 and 1971 on the steep hillside north-east of the field to see whether any artificial platform existed there. The astronomical interpretation required that the initial observations at least must have been taken from up on that slope, in order to see over the ridge. There are two adjacent boulders on the line to Jura which together form a notch and an almost level rubble pavement was found behind these. Various tests confirmed that the structure was almost certainly artificial so Kintraw has produced the first concrete proof through excavation of the Thom astronomical theory. Probably the platform was the primary observation point and the diagram (Fig. 22) shows what should have been seen at midwinter at about 1800 B.C.

At Soroba, 3·5 km from Kintraw down the B8002 on the north shore of Loch Craignish, it is possible to hire a boat from Mr Rogers to visit the Garvellach islands in the Firth of Lorne and the *Early*

Plate 21. Eileach an Naoimh. Early Christian monastic site.

Christian Celtic monastery on *Eileach an Naoimh*[+]. A shorter sea journey, but involving a longer one by road, may be had from Cullipool on Luing or Easdale on Seil: for these places take the A816 N from Kintraw and then the B844 SW (telephone the key-keeper: 085–24–212). The structures consist of a chapel, three quite well-preserved round, drystone beehive cells and a grave. Two of the cells are double with a communicating doorway, their internal diameters being about 4·3 m. The small one is about 1·5 m in internal diameter. Near by is a plain rectangular drystone chapel 6·6 m in length internally; it has a square-headed door in the west end and a small window in the east. A shelf of slate near the window may be an altar. The whole complex looks very like an Irish Celtic Christian monastery (Pl. 21).

Near the church is a low circular wall some 4·9 m in overall diameter containing '*Eithne's Grave*' (Eithne was Columba's mother). The grave is unmarked with two slabs each at the east and west ends, one of which is incised with a cross apparently of 7th-century type. The island is reputed to have been visited often by St. Columba and the beehive cells are typically Irish.

Iona

Iona lies off the south-west tip of the island of Mull and is served by a ferry from Oban (cars are not allowed on to Iona itself). The smaller island is, of course, famous for being the first landing place of the missionary St. Columba who came there from Ireland in A.D. 563, at a time when Irish Scots had already settled in south Argyll (p. 32). He founded a *Celtic monastery*, from which four daughter monasteries were established in Pictland, but few traces of this can now be seen (NM/287245). The bank and ditch of the *vallum* which demarcated its precincts can be traced still along the west side of the modern road (Fig. 23) and part of the remainder of its course can be seen on aerial photographs. Recent excavations have uncovered traces of wooden dwellings in the south-east part of the monastic enclosure and the well just outside the west door of the abbey church is doubtless the original one. A few grave slabs of the 7th and 8th centuries are to be seen just outside St. Columba's shrine to the west of the abbey church and also in the museum.

The remains of *St. Columba's cell* are on top of a hillock known as Tor Abb about 30 m west of the abbey church. On this was a low foundation wall on the artificially levelled and extended top of the hillock and there is a stone base for a wooden cross to the north.

Excavation revealed that the cell contained a clean floor of beach pebbles, a rock-cut bed and stone supports for a seat.

The Celtic monastery was harried by Viking raids from A.D. 803 onwards and not long afterwards the community seems to have abandoned Iona and returned to Ireland. Probably to around this time—early in the 9th century—belong the three almost complete Class III *Early Christian stone high crosses* which still exist on the island. There are fragments of others in the museum. Two of the crosses—St. Martin's and St. Matthew's—stand a short distance

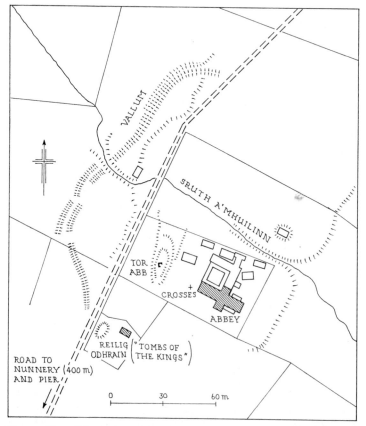

Fig. 23. Plan of the area around the abbey on Iona island, Argyllshire, showing the location of the *vallum* of the Celtic monastery, the Tor Abb, the crosses and Oran's chapel. Scale 1:2070

south-west of the cathedral together with a concrete replica of St.
John's, the original pieces of which are at the Nunnery. *St. Martin's
cross* is the only complete one, a single piece of granite standing 5·1 m
high on its ancient base. It is sculpted in panels, in the Northumbrian
style, on back and front. The front shows the Virgin and Child in
the centre of the cross surrounded by four angels and flanked by
beasts on the arms. At the top of the shaft is shown Daniel in the
lions' den with several figures below him, including a harpist. The
base of the shaft, and the whole of the back of the cross, is ornamented with Celtic spiral work and with interlace patterns and the
lateral arms have slots for wooden extensions.

St. Matthew's is the lower part of the shaft of a sandstone cross still
standing in its original granite base. The front of the shaft shows
the temptation of Adam and Eve above a panel of Anglian key-
pattern ornament. On the back is circular interlace ornament. *St.
John's cross* is of several sections of slate which fit together. The
front of the shaft is decorated with three panels, inside borders of
Anglian interlace work, which are ornamented with raised bosses
and Celtic curvilinear design. The back has more Celtic ornament
and both faces have the 'bird's nest with three eggs' motif which is
characteristic of the Iona group of crosses in which are also included
those on Islay (p. 137) and that at Keills (p. 144). They are all quite
separate from the Pictish cross slabs and show a strong Irish Celtic
tradition. On the other hand the long arms of St. John's have the
slightly concave edges seen on the Anglian Ruthwell cross (p. 42).

The next major episode in the religious history of Iona was the
settlement there in a new monastery by Benedictine monks and
nuns some time between 1156 and 1203 and it is a later version of
the monks' abbey which has recently been restored. Most of the
abbey is in fact later than the 12th century but the nunnery on
the other hand—which stands inland from the jetty—is largely in the
Transitional style of the early 13th century. There is a museum
there and another at the abbey.

St. Oran's chapel stands in the ancient *burial ground*—containing
the 'tombs of the kings'—south-west of the abbey and is dedicated
to Oran, one of Columba's disciples. The original chapel may have
been built by Kenneth MacAlpin, the first King of all Scotland, who
was buried in Iona in the 9th century as were all the later kings until
Malcolm III (1057–93) broke with this tradition. The present
chapel is a late 12th or early 13th-century Romanesque structure, a
simple rectangular building measuring 9·2 m by 4·9 m internally.

The west doorway is round arched and decorated in two orders, though the ornament is much weathered. The high relief of the carving is characteristic of the Irish Romanesque style. No doubt it was the first community of Benedictines which built this chapel.

Isle of Tiree

This flat, sandy island is geologically part of the Outer Hebrides and enjoys exceptional sunshine and winds. It is reached by steamer from Oban. There are a number of Iron Age forts on the island of which the best preserved is *Dun Mor Vaul broch*★ on the north-east coast, 6 km from the pier at Scarinish. Take the road E to Gott bay and then the minor road across the island to Vaul. The broch is 400 m west of the end of the road on a rock knoll at the shore (NM/042493). It was excavated between 1962 and 1964 by the author and produced many finds as well as a long series of stratified occupation levels. The structure is a classic ground-galleried broch with a wall from 3·05 m to 4 m thick enclosing a circular central court 9·8 m in diameter; a scarcement is on the wallface (Fig. 24). The entrance passage faces east and is equipped with door-checks, bar-hole and socket and a round guard cell on the right into which the bar-hole runs. There are three doors from the court to the mural gallery, that in the north-west leading to the stair. Immediately behind the guard cell a fragment of the upper gallery is preserved, with one lintel, and the gallery here was used as a cess pit during the primary occupation of the broch. Directly opposite, on the south-south-west, a short section of gallery is built wider and was inhabited, probably during the construction of the broch.

The main stages in the history of the site were as follows. Phase I was a pre-broch settlement dated by radiocarbon to about 600–300 b.c. A wooden hut with wattle-and-daub walls was on the site of the broch, in a natural depression in the rock. In Phase II the broch was built, perhaps in the middle of the first century b.c., and a new type of pottery with curvilinear ornament was brought to the site. Yet in Phase IIIa, when the broch served as a refuge in times of danger, most of the pottery was the 'native' ware found in the pre-broch levels. It seems probable that a new ruling class had arrived and organised the building of the tower but that most of the local community were aborigines.

In Phase IIIb, perhaps at about a.d. 200, the broch was converted to a dwelling—presumably for the leading family and after it had ceased to be needed as a fort. Soon afterwards the wall was pulled down, the lintels were taken off the entrance passage and mural gallery and a secondary wall built round the interior, blocking up two of the three gallery doors. The broch had become a farm growing crops and herding cattle and it continued to be inhabited for perhaps another century. It was then abandoned and there are one or two signs which suggest that a hostile raid destroyed or dispersed the inhabitants. Thereafter the remains of the broch fell rapidly into ruin with only a few native sherds in the top levels to show the presence of some squatters.

The excavations at Vaul were extremely productive. For the first time in the Western Isles a certain pre-broch settlement was found and the pottery and artefacts of the native population were thus identified. The pottery of the broch-builders was also isolated and its clear links with some late Iron Age wares in southern England suggested where the new ruling group had come from. Many aspects of the social life of the times could be inferred from the abundant evidence, even to such details as that the people who crowded into the broch in times of danger were subjected to firm discipline. A cess pit was in use and the floor level in the court was clean in spite of containing much food refuse.

3. INVERNESS-SHIRE (WEST)

The Glenelg area

Travelling down the A887 from the Great Glen to Kyle of Lochalsh and Skye one can turn off S at Shiel bridge to see four fine Iron Age stone forts. The minor road forks soon after it leaves Shiel bridge and leads to *Caisteal Grugaig broch** (actually in Ross-shire but it is convenient to include it here). The site lies at the end of the narrow right branch to Totaig on the south shore of Loch Shiel: follow the stone footpath for 700 m further (NG/867251). The broch stands on a slope and its interior has been cleared out at some time. The central court is almost circular with a diameter of 9·4 m and the wall is well preserved, up to about 4 m in places, intramural cells and galleries being visible at ground and first-floor level. The broch is particularly interesting in that the rocky floor of the central court slopes sharply, its lowest part being at the lintelled entrance passage. The scarcement ledge is horizontal and thus varies in its height above the floor from 0·7 m to 2·1 m at the entrance. It is thus clear that scarcements did not support a roof, as has sometimes been argued, but must have held a horizontal wooden floor or veranda.

The left branch of the minor road from Shiel bridge goes over the

Plate 22. Dun Telve broch, Inverness-shire, seen from the E.

steep Ratagan Hill to Glenelg. Skye is close by and can be reached by the small car-ferry at Kylerhea. About 1 km south of Glenelg village a minor road turns east into Glen Beag and after 2 km reaches *Dun Telve broch*★+ (Pl. 22) (NG/829172) with its neighbour *Dun Troddan*★+ a short distance further on (NG/834172). Both are solid-based brochs with one part of the wall still standing 10·1 m and 7·6 m high respectively and both show clearly the peculiar hollow-walled construction of their type. Dun Telve is slightly better preserved and has an upper scarcement, presumably a roof-support: its central court is almost exactly circular with a diameter of 9·8 m (12 my). Dun Troddan was found to have a ring of post-holes in its floor when it was excavated in 1920 and these supported the raised wooden floor which is assumed to have rested on the lower scarcements of brochs. Neither site yielded many finds when excavated though a small yellow glass bead of a type possibly derived from southern England came from Dun Troddan.

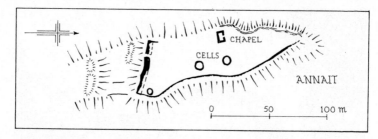

About 2 km further up the glen, beyond the end of the road, stands the broch-like fort *Dun Grugaig*★ on a high conical knoll next to a precipitous drop down to the burn (NG/852159). This is a D-shaped, open-sided fort with a roofed upper gallery preserved on the uphill side. It is in fact a semibroch, one of a small group of forts which has been shown to be the immediate ancestors of the brochs, having the identical high hollow wall and other architectural features seen in the round towers but being much inferior in their design and situation. Thus Glen Beag shows the beginning and the end of the evolution of the broch, Dun Grugaig representing the start and the two brochs the return of the advanced solid-based form from northern Scotland to the area of the genesis of the towers in the west.

Isle of Skye

This island, rich in association with Scotland's highland past, has a wealth of Iron Age forts of many kinds (Fig. 24). For the student of brochs it is of great importance in having both the largest number of towers in the western region and also the most forts from which the brochs could have sprung.

From the ferries from Kyle of Lochalsh one soon reaches Broadford and can turn S there down the A881 to Elgol. This peninsula of Jurassic sandstone has a cliff coastline with promontories very like that of Caithness and there are two well-preserved semibrochs (prototype brochs) to be seen (Fig. 24). *Dun Ringill*★ is about 16 km from Broadford and at Kirkibost a walk of 1 km SE from the road to the shore is needed (NG/562171). It is a well-preserved, D-shaped fort, the open, straight side of the D being formed by the sea-cliff: here the wall was thinner. The inner wall of the upper gallery is preserved as also is a large, finely corbelled mural cell on the south

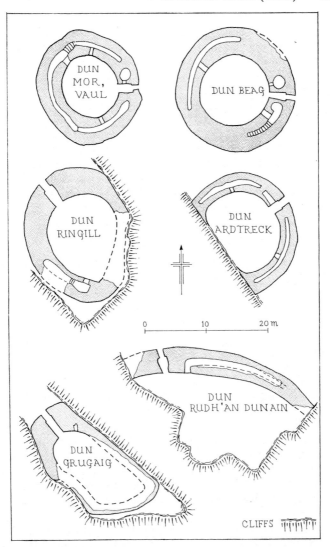

Fig. 24. Plans of five hollow-walled, Iron Age drystone forts on Skye and one (Dun Mor Vaul) on Tiree. Scale 1:590. On the opposite page is Annait, Skye, an Early Christian site within a probable Iron Age fo Scale 1:3130.

side. The entrance passage has been extended inwards with mor-tared masonry, presumably in Medieval times, and the lintels are now over the later part. The original door-checks and bar-hole are visible. Like the very similar Dun Grugaig, Glenelg (p. 162 above), Dun Ringill is a fort whose architecture is of the identical type to, and almost as sophisticated as, that of the brochs but which in design and situation is vastly inferior to them. For this reason alone it can hardly be other than a prototype broch.

Elgol is 5 km further on on the west side of the peninsula and a minor road leads from there to the east coast and then south along it. *Dun Grugaig★* is on a narrow, sheer-sided cliff promontory about 100 m down from the road near its end (NG/535124) (Fig. 24). This fort consists of a short massive wall with a solid base and an upper gallery which bars the neck of the promontory: there are traces of a narrower wall round the sides of the enclosed area. The entrance pas-sage is still partly lintelled with one side of a void preserved over its inner half: door-checks and bar-hole in the broch style are clear. A scarcement is on the inner wallface. Dun Grugaig is the simplest and most primitive form of semibroch and was perhaps among the earliest of the broch class to be built.

Travelling N on the A850 from Broadford one cuts across the bare, stony mountains of Lord MacDonald's Forest (the name is doubtless a MacLeod joke) on the new road to Sligachan. The ferry to Raasay is at Sconser, 3·5 km east of that place. There is a Class II *Pictish symbol stone★* about 200 m north-north-west of Raasay house, north of the pier (NG/546366). It is close to the east side of the road and has at the top a cross of unusual design with the Pictish 'tuning fork' and crescent and V-rod symbols below this.

Dun Borodale★ is an unexcavated broch on a tree-covered knoll about 1 km east of the pier (NG/555364). Take the coastal road S to the right and, after 0·5 km, the minor road E. A track then leads north up over the hill quite near the broch which is invisible until one has reached it. It is interesting in having a central court built round an accurately drawn ellipse with axes of about 8·3 m and 11·6 m (10 by 14 my).

Back on Skye, take the Bracadale road W from Sligachan and then the B8009 to Carbost (which turns off at the head of Loch Harport) to see three sites involving cross-country walking. The two most remote are beyond Glenbrittle, the road to which turns sharply off at Merkadale. A walk of about 5·5 km is needed beyond the road end: follow the track along the coast for about 4 km and then cut S

across the saddle to see the *Rudh an Dunain Neolithic horned cairn*⋆
and *Iron Age semibroch*⋆ in their wild and lonely situation near the
end of the peninsula. The cairn is at the west end of the loch
(NG/393163). It was excavated in 1931–2 and yielded fragments of
human bones, parts of two Neolithic bowls and almost the whole of
a beaker of the Early Bronze Age. The cairn is still 3·4 m high, a
modified round passage grave with a forecourt indented into its
perimeter on the east: this is faced with upright stones with some dry
walling between them. The passage opens from the centre of the
forecourt and four lintels are still in position over it and the antechamber behind. The chamber beyond is formed, like the other
features mentioned, of upright slabs separated by dry walling: it
probably once had a corbelled roof with a capstone.

About 500 m south-east of the cairn is the semibroch, a 'galleried
dun' on its tiny cliff promontory (Fig. 24): the enclosed area is much
reduced in size and great blocks of rock from the cliff can be seen in
the water. The fort is a simple curved wall some 3·7 m thick with the
entrance at the right end and equipped with door-checks. Although
at least 0·6 m of rubble obscures its bases the wall still stands up to

Plate 23. Dun Ardtreck semibroch, Skye, seen from the NE.

2·6 m and is finely built of stone blocks. A ledge scarcement is on the inner wallface and a door to the mural gallery, probably an upper one, is preserved.

Continuing along the west side of Loch Harport, take the left turn to Fiskavaig 4 km beyond Carbost and, after about 1 km, the minor road to the right of this. After another kilometre the right fork leads one to within about 400 m of *Dun Ardtreck** (Pl. 23) which is out of sight to the west on the shore (NG/335357). The site is a D-shaped semibroch in a spectacular, naturally defensive situation on an isolated, terraced knoll with a sheer cliff falling 20 m to the sea. An outer wall with a gateway on the south-east runs along the edge of the top rock terrace. The paved entrance to the semibroch is in the centre of the curved wall and is raised 0·6 m above the external paving: its door-checks are clear but the bar-hole is partly ruined. The wall is built on a rock surface which slopes sharply inland and is 2·8 m thick at base; it encloses an area 13 m long and 10·5 m from entrance to cliff (Fig. 24).

Built ends for the wall were traced at the cliff edge in the author's 1965 excavations which also showed that the galleried wall was founded on an artificial rubble platform revetted by the well-built outer wallface of the fort. A radiocarbon measurement on charcoal in this rubble, laid down at the time of building, gave a date of 55 ± 105 b.c. which was a verification of the early date of the semibrochs deduced on other grounds (p. 28). The excavations also showed that the fort was violently destroyed by fire: broken, partly vitrified pottery was found on the rock floor and the iron door-handle was still lying in the entrance passage, probably after the wooden door had been set on fire and battered in. The semibroch was then demolished and served as a dwelling for several centuries thereafter; a rubble ramp was found piled against the outer end of the entrance passage to make entry easier in this period. Many potsherds and artefacts, including some Roman fragments, were recovered from the deposits of this phase.

Continuing along the A863 to Bracadale the well-preserved *Tungadal souterrain** can be visited if a moorland walk of 2·4 km can be contemplated. Follow the B885 to Portree for 4·7 km and then strike off due SE between the two low hills, keeping to the east side of the gap. The souterrain is visible as a rubbly area on the far slope, about 150 m east of the east end of Loch Duagrich, across the outlet river (there is a ford about 200 m east of the loch, just before it joins the river Tungadal). There are some 6 m of lintelled, dry-walled gallery in a good state of preservation—up to 1 m high—

which can be entered through a gap in the roof; the whole seems to be buried in an extensive artificial cairn of rubble. It is probably of late Iron Age date, belonging perhaps to the 2nd or 3rd centuries A.D. (an alternative approach is to walk 4·4 km along the path up Glen Bracadale from the head of Loch Beag).

On the A863, 2 km beyond the B885 one comes in sight of the ground-galleried *Dun Beag broch** on a rocky knoll 250 m north of the road. Dun Beag, excavated in 1915, is a fine example of a Hebridean broch with a galleried wall 3·5–4·2 m thick surrounding an exactly circular inner court 10·75 m in diameter (13 my) (Fig. 24). The entrance with door-checks is on the east and the door to the mural stair just to its left: on its right is a mural cell opening on to the interior. Opposite the stair door is a raised door to a mural gallery which, though not completely excavated, probably runs the whole way round the wall as at Vaul (p. 159). Because of the unevenness of the underlying rock the mural gallery seems to be on a low rubble foundation as at Dun Ardtreck (p. 166).

In the entrance hall of Dunvegan Castle, 1·5 km south of Dunvegan (NG/247490), is a *Pictish symbol stone** which was found near a well beside the Dun Osdale broch on the opposite side of the sea loch (NG/242464). Though weathered a crescent and V-rod symbol and two concentric circles can still be identified.

About 2 km beyond the castle the minor road crosses a small loch on a causeway. At the far end of this one can strike off just S of W for 1 km into a peninsula with a narrow neck to see the excavated ground-galleried *broch Dun Fiadhairt** just beyond this neck (NG/233505: the symbol on the 1-inch map is 300 m too far northwest). It was cleared of debris in 1914 and, like Dun Beag, stands on a rocky knoll amidst desolate moorland. The entrance, equipped with door-checks and two opposing guard cells, faces west and the door to a dumb-bell-shaped mural cell is at 8 o'clock with the mural stair at 10 o'clock. A ground-level mural gallery occupies the south half of the wall and probably continues to the back of the stair although this last section is still full of rubble. A lintelled door to the gallery opposite the main entrance appears to go right through the wall, an unusual and apparently original feature. The diameter of the court is 9·5 m (11½ my).

Taking the main road (A850) W and then N from Dunvegan one soon reaches the road junction at the Fairy bridge. Continue N down the B886 for 1·5 km and a patch of bright green grass will be seen 300 m to the left (west) of the road. Closer inspection shows that this is part of the level top of a steep-sided, often precipitous long promontory formed by the junction of two rivers on which is *Annait*** (NG/272527: a stream must be crossed). The name is peculiar to the Celtic Church and probably means the first established monastic community in a region. There is a wide natural hollow across the promontory and a massive ruined stone wall on the downstream side of this, 5·5 m thick and with an entrance passage through it, forms the main defence of the promontory (Fig. 24). Another rampart, or forward defence, is on the upstream edge of the hollow and a stone wall runs all the way along the east side of the fortified area for 140 m. Near its north (downstream) end the outer face can be seen standing several courses high. A number of ruined circular structures and some rectangular ones are within the fortified area and the rectangular one furthest north-west seems to be the monastic chapel. Two other such buildings are next to the main cross wall, one overlying it and one outside it, and this may mean that the ecclesiastical settlement is later than the defences. If so the walls may belong to a massive Iron Age fort, one of the largest in Skye.

Further along the A850, just after it passes the head of Loch Snizort Beag 8 km north-west of Portree, is the *Clach Ard Pictish symbol stone*** (NG/421491). Turn up the B8036, left up the minor road after 400 m, and the stone is seen close by on the right after 250 m. It is carved with the crescent and V-rod, double disc and Z-rod and the mirror and comb symbols.

4. THE OUTER HEBRIDES

(*Inverness and Ross*)

The Western Isles of Scotland still provide a dream-like environment unique in Europe. The land is composed of some of the oldest rocks on earth and the rolling or flat terrain is formed of rock, peat bogs, lochs and machair (grass-covered sand dunes). The Gaelic tongue is still in common use here and the people preserve many other aspects of a vanishing world. Iron Age and later brochs and duns abound, particularly on islands in lochs, and standing stones and chambered cairns are also quite common.

Isle of Lewis, Ross and Cromarty

The car-ferry runs from Uig in north Skye to Tarbert in Harris and the A859 towards Stornoway leads to several important sites. The

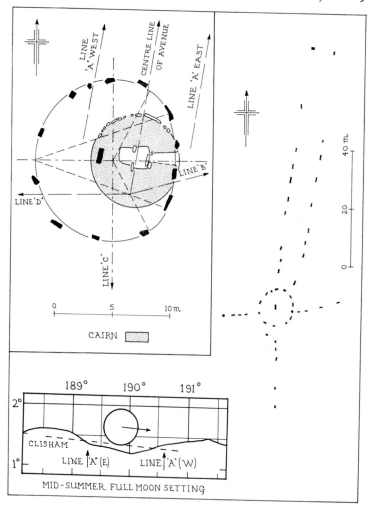

Fig. 25. General plan of the alignments of standing stones at Callanish, Isle of Lewis. Scale 1:1300. The upper inset shows the detail of the central area—the chambered cairn, stone ring and the suggested geometrical constructions incorporated in them. Note how in this plan the central axis of the double avenue and the axes of the E and W lines pass through one of the auxiliary centres of the flattened circle which fits the stone ring. Scale 1:310. The lower inset shows the moon in midsummer setting at its lowest position over Mt. Clisham, which is indicated by the avenue.

first minor road to the left, 9 km before Stornoway, leads to the A858 and to the *Callanish standing stones and chambered cairn**+ on the shores of Loch Roag (NB/213330: signposted). This unique cross-shaped setting of tall, thin stones has often been studied and some kind of astronomical purpose seems certain to have prompted its erection. Yet there must surely be more to this complex site, in which can be included several outlying stone circles, than has so far been discovered. The main features of Callanish itself are as follows (Fig. 25). A central ring is constructed as a geometrical flattened circle the main part of which has a radius of 6·59 m (8 my). A huge stone 4·6 m high is near the centre of this circle in which there is also a round cairn, a Neolithic passage grave, 7·47 m (9 my) in diameter. The north side of the passage of this, built of dry walling, is visible and the chamber is in two compartments separated by transverse slabs. It has been suggested that the cairn was added to the stone circle although this would reverse the usually accepted relative age of such monuments, Early or Middle Neolithic and Early Bronze Age respectively. The careful survey of Thom shows that the two structures are clearly linked geometrically (Fig. 25): the centre of the circle formed by the cairn kerb seems to be exactly on the east–west axis of the flattened circle of standing stones. He also shows that the great central pillar stone is not on the periphery of the cairn as has been claimed but is set within it: this might suggest that the cairn was later. However the solution is not clear and the stones of the flattened circle could well belong to the chambered tomb period and thus be much earlier than others of their class.

Running north from the circle is a double line or avenue of stones: to its east, west and south run single rows. The north avenue, of 19 stones not in pairs, runs for 83 m from the edge of the circle on bearings of 10·6° and 9·2° for the west and east rows respectively. If one moves to the south of the site one can see over the foreground to Mt. Clisham 26 km away in the south to which the double avenue is exactly pointing. Clisham could be a horizon marker for the moon setting at its most southerly mean declination (Fig. 25). The south row of six stones runs exactly north–south on a bearing of 180·1°. A large rock to the south of the site could have been used with the north–south row to judge when various stars passed due north under the celestial pole. The west alignment of four stones points to the two equinoctial sunsets and various other possible alignments have been described by Hawkins and Thom. The axes of four of the five stone rows pass through one point which is one of the auxiliary centres of the flattened circle, which lies within the cairn material (Fig. 25). This would certainly indicate that, if the chambered cairn was built earlier, it was fairly denuded when the stone rows were put up but it is equally if not more likely that the passage grave was added later.

There are two other *stone circles* close by and visible from Callanish. *Cnoc Ceann*★ is an ellipse 1,000 m away to the south-south-east (NB/222326) and *Cnoc Fillibhir Bheag*★ is a double ring 1·3 km to the south-east (NB/226326). There are four others near the head of Loch Roag.

Dun Carloway broch★+ is 10 km further north along the main road from Callanish. The broch is on a rocky knoll 500 m along a minor road which leads west from the A858 about 2 km south of Carloway itself. Part of it still stands about 6·7 m high and shows well the galleried, double wall, a set of voids and the scarcement. The overall diameter is 14·3 m and that of the central court some 7·47 m (9 my). The entrance faces north-west and the massive outermost lintel is still in place: a guard cell opens to the left. There are four doors from the central court to cells and galleries within the wall, that opposite the entrance leading to the mural stair. In 1861 four upper galleries and part of a fifth were still preserved and the wall was then standing 10·4 m high. The structure had evidently already been cleared out before that time but no records of finds survive. In its size and proportions Dun Carloway is almost identical to Dun Dornadilla in Sutherland (p. 221).

North Uist, Inverness-shire

North Uist can be reached by a motor-boat from Rodel, Harris, or by the car-ferry from Uig, Skye, to Lochmaddy. From Rodel two unexcavated *brochs* can be seen with a walk of 14 km there and back. *Dun an Sticir*★ is on an island in a tidal loch less than 1 km from the Newton pier, close to the B893; an artificial causeway leads to it from the shore (NF/89877). It has a secondary rectangular structure inside it. *Dun Torcuill*★ (Pl. 24) is also in a loch and reached by a causeway; it lies about 6 km north-west of Lochmaddy and 400 m north-east of the road (NF/888737). This is still the best preserved broch in North Uist and is now known to have the added rare distinction of an exactly elliptical central court, the long and short axes being slightly under 15 and 14 my respectively and the perimeter being exactly 30 my.

The *Neolithic passage grave of Barpa Langass*★ lies 9 km west of

Lochmaddy, 300 m south of the A867 on the north slope of a hill (NF/838657; a path runs up from the road from the west side). The round mound of stones is clearly visible (Pl. 25) and has a peristalith of stones around its edge some 24 m in diameter. Traces of a funnel-shaped forecourt are apparent on the east side leading to the entrance and this leads to a well-preserved chamber built of seven massive slabs which are surmounted by some dry walling and roofed with three large stone lintels. The chamber still stands 2 m high above an unknown depth of debris on the floor. It was looted shortly before 1911 but some artefacts were recovered soon afterwards from a heap of debris dumped outside. These include fragments of Early Bronze Age beakers and a barbed-and-tanged flint arrowhead of beaker type.

Continue on to the A865 and N towards Sollas. Just before Hosta an untarred but good road leads east up to the summit of South Clettraval hill and 3·4 km along this the *Clettraval chambered cairn and wheelhouse*** are visible on peaty moorland 50 m downhill

Plate 24. Dun Torcuill broch, North Uist, from the NW with the causeway in the foreground.

Plate 25. Barpa Langass Neolithic cairn, North Uist.

(NF/749713). There is a *standing stone** a little to the west. The Neolithic cairn, 29 m long, is well preserved in part, some of the slabs of the segmented chamber and of the south half of the forecourt standing well over 1 m high; the cairn itself shows clearly on the south. The chamber is 10·5 m in length with five compartments, the innermost two being wider than the rest; the tomb may be an example of a hybrid between the passage grave and the 'gallery grave' traditions. The finds made in the excavations of 1934 included decorated Neolithic bowls and some fragments of beaker, the latter showing that the tomb remained in use until the Early Bronze Age.

A major interest of the site lies in the fact that in the Iron Age a wheelhouse farm was built there, perhaps three thousand years after the cairn, and that this was the first of its kind to be systematically excavated (in 1946–8). The main farmhouse, built into the west end of the cairn, is a free-standing, drystone wheelhouse the wall of which is about 2·7 m thick and encloses a circular area some 7·7 m in diameter: there were eight radial stone piers to support the roof and a hearth in the centre. Two of the piers are still visible on the north side but the structure has unhappily been allowed to decay. The door faces west-south-west and traces of the enclosing farmyard wall are apparent about 50 m out in the same direction. Half way towards that on the west is a horseshoe-shaped hut, one of several subsidiary structures within the farmyard of which the largest is the rectangular byre 13 m south-west of the wheelhouse. Although pottery was found of the same kind that appears in Hebridean brochs no trace of grain-growing (quernstones) was noted and the site seems to have been a cattle farm. It was probably built in the 2nd or 3rd century A.D., early in the post-broch period, and inhabited perhaps for a century or so. Clettraval provides a rare chance to see the total layout of an Iron Age farm in much greater detail than usual. (The sad remains of another, once splendid *wheelhouse*★ are still visible on the machair at *Kilpheder*, at the south end of South Uist: NF/732202).

6 · North-east Scotland

(Perthshire, Angus, Aberdeen, Nairn, Moray and eastern Inverness)

This huge zone, stretching from the Firth of Tay to the Moray Firth, is rich in archaeological remains but little systematic study of these has gone forward. The Royal Commission on the Ancient and Historical Monuments of Scotland—the primary source of such detailed field studies—has yet to begin on this area which was the heart of ancient Pictland. The number of early (Class I) symbol stones reflects this.

Plate 26. Dunblane Cathedral, Perthshire: view from the SE showing early square tower.

1. PERTHSHIRE

The road north (1) (A9)

The A9 winds its way through the mountains and moors of Perthshire to Inverness and passes close to a variety of interesting sites. *Dunblane Cathedral**+ (Pl. 26) is 8 km north of Stirling in an attractive setting in the old town and next to the Allan water (NN/782015). The structure is mainly of 13th-century date although the bishopric was re-established by David I in 1150. All that remains of the 12th-century church is the square Romanesque tower which, although differently aligned, has been built into the south wall of the later nave. This tower is six storeys in height of which the lower four are original: it measures 6·9 m square and appears originally to have been freestanding. The doorway, reached from the nave, is about 1 m above the church floor and was probably higher above the ground. This suggests that the tower was for defence as well as for a belfry, like the round towers of Abernethy and Brechin (pp. 183 and 191 below).

At the west end of the nave are two Class III *Early Christian stones*. The largest is an upright cross slab 1·9 m high: the cross shaft is bordered with two beast or serpent heads. On the back is a scene with a jumble of figures including a pair of beasts, a horseman with a spear and a man holding a staff.

(Route continued on p. 178)

The Crieff road (A822 and A85)

Continuing N for 7 km the Crieff road (A822) may be taken as an alternative route to Perth and several interesting sites seen. At 2·8 km from the junction is the well-preserved *Ardoch Roman fort** (Pl. 26) immediately to the east of the road just north of Braco (NN/839099). The site consists of the permanent fort with, north of this, three much larger temporary camps; these last are presumably of different periods since their lines overlap with each other and with the fort. The main fort was excavated in 1896–7 and consists of a turf rampart on a stone base up to 12 m wide and enclosing an area some 67 m east–west by 74 m; this area was originally filled with rectangular barrack buildings of wood and stone. The outer defences consist of a series of parallel ditches fronting the rampart, five on the east and north side: the west and south sides are partly obliterated. The whole system is surrounded by an outer turf rampart. The north defences are wider than elsewhere, having 'ravelins', or broad flat areas, out-

Plate 27. Ardoch Roman fort, Perthshire: the E entrance seen from the NNW.

side the second and third ditches and an extra length of rampart inside the fourth ditch. The east and north entrances are still visible as causeways across the ditch system. The extra width of the north defences is partly explained by the fact that the ground to the east and south of the fort was a deep moss (peat bog) in the 18th century which was subsequently drained; mass attacks on the fort would therefore have been much more difficult from these sides.

The finds made at Ardoch indicate that the fort was occupied during the Flavian (A.D. 80–100) and Antonine periods (p. 29). It was a permanent legionary base set in the partly pacified but hostile area immediately in front of the main frontier as part of the forward defences of that frontier. The Antonine wall lies 29 km to the south and Ardoch was one of a chain of forts, linked by a road system, which extended north-east into Angus (Fig. 3).

Six kilometres beyond Braco is *Muthill church*[*][+]: it lies just north of the sharp corner in the centre of the village of that name (NN/868171). Most of the church is early 15th century but it incorporates another of the earlier, square Norman towers like those at Dunblane, Dunning (p 178, Pl. 28), and St. Andrews (p. 123). As with the others the Muthill tower was once free-standing but has been embedded in the west end of the nave of the later church. It appears to be the original almost to the top. No doubt the tower was a refuge and belfry for the vanished early church on the site.

Continue N through Crieff and take the Perth road (A85). The minor road N to *Fowlis Wester* is reached after 6 km and here is a much-eroded Class II *Pictish cross slab**+, 4 m high, standing in the village square (NN/928241). Though much weathered this red sandstone monument is unique in that the arms of the cross project slightly from the slab. The fine scene of horsemen, animals, foot-soldiers and Pictish symbols on the back is almost obliterated.

There is another, much finer Class II *cross slab** inside the church, standing on the north side of the choir. It was found in 1931 during the restoration of the church, embedded in the north wall. The freestone slab stands 1·6 m high and is carved on one face only. The design shows a wheel cross standing on an upright rectangular base and both are finely carved and ornamented with key, interlace and spiral patterns. Flanking the top arm of the cross on the left is a peculiar animal with a ring or tusk in its mouth with a rare illustration of a sword and a probable round shield beside it. On the right is a similar beast apparently eating a small human figure. On each side of the shaft of the cross is a seated figure, presumably a cleric, wearing embroidered vestments and on a throne; the left one has a tree behind him and a staff with nine buds growing from it in front. Two similarly robed standing figures are on the left of the base.

The road north (2) (Strathtay and Glen Garry)

Taking the A9 north-east of Dunblane a Class I *Pictish symbol stone** is encountered in a field just south of the road 2·4 km beyond *Blackford* (NN/924097). On it is a bird (a goose?) with the head turned back (Fig. 4: 17) and a rectangular grid representing a double-sided comb. (The detour SE into Fife from this point is described on p. 182 below: those from Perth NE into Angus on p. 184ff.)

Just beyond Auchterarder the B8062 turns north-east to *Dunning* where there is another *church* (Pl. 28) with at its west end a *square tower* of the Norman type already seen at Dunblane. In this case the tower and the rectangular church were built as a unit, probably early in the 13th century, and the tower is therefore a late example of the type. The doorway leading into it from the nave has a fine, elaborately decorated Gothic pointed arch—mounted on round Romanesque columns—which shows how late the structure is

despite the Norman character of its architecture. The tower is built
in three unequal stages and stands nearly 23 m high to the ridge; the
stepped roof gables are late. The rest of the church is much altered
but the early, round-arched north doorway is still partly visible from
the outside, half-hidden by an external stair.

At 600 m north of the village on the B934 are the fragmentary
remains of a *Roman camp* of Agricolan date (about A.D. 80): a length
of the ditch, leading to an obliterated entrance, approaches the west
side of the road just inside *Kincladie Wood* (NO/023152). The low,
wooded hill of Duncrub is 1·6 km north-north-west of this camp,
1·5 km along the B9141 from Dunning, and it has recently been
persuasively argued that this hill, rather than one north of the river
Tay (p. 204), was the site of the decisive *battle of Mons Craupius* at
which the Roman governor Agricola defeated a British force under
the chieftain Calgacus (Pl. 29). The name Duncrub could, it seems,
be derived from Mons Craupius. Tacitus describes how a legion in

Plate 28. Dunning church, Perthshire, from the
WSW showing the square tower.

Plate 29. Hill of Duncrub, near Dunning, Perthshire: view from the bridge over the river Earn at Forteviot.

reserve watched the battle from in front of a Roman camp, which could be that at Kincladie Wood (*cladhaidh*, 'ditchy place'). The subsequent rout of the Britons put Agricola in a commanding position which he was not allowed to follow up (p. 30).

Nineteen kilometres north of Perth is the 15th-century Dunkeld Cathedral in a fine situation on the north bank of the Tay. The name of the town may mean the 'dun (fort) of the Caledonians', the major proto-Pictish tribe of the area in Roman times. The famous *Inchtuthill Roman fort* is 10 km south-east of Dunkeld along the A984 to Coupar Angus (NO/125397). It has recently been excavated by the late Professor Ian Richmond and a spectacular find was an enormous hoard of nearly 1 million iron nails, weighing about 12 tons, which was deliberately buried by the Romans when the fort was evacuated at about A.D. 100.

Continuing N towards Pitlochry there is a damaged Class II *Pictish symbol stone* in the churchyard at *Logierait* (NO/967521): turn down the A827 to Aberfeldy for 1 km. On the front is a cross ornamented with interlace work with bosses in the angles of the arms and, on the back, a damaged scene showing a horseman with spear and shield over a serpent and rod symbol.

If a detour to Loch Tay is contemplated the *Croftmoraig stone circle***** can be visited (NN/797473). Take the B846 at Aberfeldy for 5 km and the circle is close beside the road on the south, at the entrance to a farm. The site was excavated in 1965 and three phases in its history were reconstructed. In Phase I there was a penannular or horseshoe-shaped setting of wooden posts, some 7–7·9 m in diameter. This may well have been a timber house of some kind, analogous to those found in Woodhenge and Durrington walls in southern England. In Phase II these posts were dismantled and an oval of standing stones (the present inner ring) was erected together with an arch of three more just outside this on the south-south-east. The stone bank around the site seems to belong to this phase and presumably makes the site a monument of the well-known henge type. There is a cup-marked stone in the south-south-west part of this bank. The stones of this circle have been claimed to lie on an ellipse with major and minor axes 11 and 8 my. In Phase III the present outer stone circle was added, incorporating the arc of the previous phase, and two outliers were added 5 m to the east and, in the view of the excavators, imply a change in the axis of the site from north-east–south-west (post setting and stone oval) to north-west–south-east. It has been suggested that the outliers indicate a solar observation point but they are close and inaccurate. The pottery discovered suggests that Phase I and the start of Phase II fell in the Early Neolithic period, in the 4th millennium B.C. The Phase III circle is difficult to date, but, by analogy, probably belongs to the Early Bronze Age.

The *Balnacraig Iron Age dun* is 6 km further west (NN/748476): take the minor road to Fortingall after 2·5 km and the farmroad N to Balnacraig 0·5 km before that village. The dun is 300 m north-north-west of the farm at the top of a steep hill and is well preserved, both wallfaces being completely visible and standing up to four courses high. The interior measures 17·7 m by 19·8 m and the wall is from 2·4 m to 4 m thick.

Returning E towards the A9 take the minor road N along the west bank of the river Tummel 0·5 km before the bridge for 5·5 km to see the fine Class II *Dunfallandy Pictish stone***+** (NN/946565). The stone stands just outside the churchyard south of Dunfallandy hotel (signposted) but was originally in a disused chapel near Killiecrankie. The front face is sculpted with a cross decorated with spiral bosses and patterns of interlace ornament. Flanking the cross are various animals and beasts including (bottom left) an animal swallowing or disgorging a man, possibly a depiction of Jonah. Two angels are on the right. On the back is a scene flanked by two fish-tailed serpents containing two enthroned men with a cross between them (probably clergymen), a horseman (another cleric?), two 'elephant' symbols, a double disc, two crescent and V-rods, a pair of pincers, a hammer (or axe) and possibly an anvil. The stone at St. Madoes (p. 184) shows three cowled horsemen with the same three symbols.

A short distance to the north the river can be crossed to return to the A9 at Pitlochry and 5 km further north the B8019 turns west to Loch Tummel and the Queen's view (Victoria's). The remains of an *Iron Age dun** can be seen 400 m from the viewpoint (NN/863602): take the first forest path to the left (or right) and then the first path right (or left) to circle round above the dun which stands in the cleared space below a power line. The first course of the wall, 3·05 m thick, is preserved for several stretches and the internal diameter is about 17 m.

The village of Calvine is 14 m further north on the A9 and the Class I *Struan Pictish Stone* is near by (NN/808654). Take the B847 across the river and down Glen Errochty for 600 m where minor roads to the left and left again lead to Struan church on the south bank of the river Garry. The stone is at the church and is ornamented with the double disc and Z-rod and the fragment of another symbol.

(Route continued on p. 205)

Perth to Fife (A90)

The A90 south-east from Perth leads through Bridge of Earn to the A913 and so to Newburgh and the sites in north Fife (p. 122). About 1 km before Abernethy a minor road turns south-east to Strathmiglo and curves south round the base of the ridge on the east end of which stands the *Castle Law* (Abernethy) *hillfort* (NO/183153). This stone-walled fort, measuring internally some 15·5 by 41·5 m, was explored between 1896 and 1898 and the inner wallface was found to contain sockets for timber beams which ran into the wall. This was the first direct evidence for timber-framed stone walls the burning of which is now known to produce vitrified stone (p. 27). The site is also interesting in that it produced several datable Iron Age finds—such as a bronze spiral finger ring and an early type of La Tène fibula (safety pin)—by which the site was assigned a date in the 2nd or 3rd century B.C. The discovery through radiocarbon dating that such timber-laced forts can be as early as the 8th century b.c. well illustrates the limitations of dating the construction of sites by the artefacts used by their occupants.

In *Abernethy* itself is the famous *round tower*★+ (Pl. 30) with a Class I *Pictish stone*★+ beside it (NO/191165). The stone is a broken granite slab incised with part of a crescent and V-rod with, above this, a 'tuning fork' symbol flanked by a hammer and an anvil (?). The round tower—one of two remaining in Scotland (p. 191)—is 22 m high and is usually dated to the 11th century, having Romanesque windows to the belfry. However the lowest 12 courses are of hard grey freestone, less weathered than the softer, yellowish freestone above. The tower may therefore have been rebuilt in the 11th century on an older foundation. The diameter at the base is 4·6 m and the wall is 1·1 m thick there. The doorway is on the north side and raised 0·6 m above the present ground-level: the steps in front of it are modern. The interior had six wooden floors resting on stone scarcements and access to the upper floors was by removable wooden

Plate 30. Abernethy round tower, Perthshire:
view from the WSW.

ladders. Round towers are Irish in origin, devised in the 9th century by ecclesiastical communities as refuges against Viking raids. Those at Abernethy and Brechin appear to reflect the return of Irish clergy to Pictland in the later 9th century, after a period during which contacts with Ireland were severed by the Viking raids.

(Route continued on p. 122)

The Dundee road (A85)

Eight kilometres east of Perth on the Dundee road (A85) is Glencarse where the B958 turns south. The fine Class II *St. Madoes Pictish stone* is in the churchyard, under cover, just north of the road and about 400 m from the junction (NO/197212). On the front is a fine cross decorated with interlace and key-patterns and with spiral bosses in the centre: it is surrounded by various fabulous beasts some of which are biting themselves and each other. On the back are three cloaked horsemen, presumably clerics, the lowest one having a book satchel slung over his shoulder. Below these figures are the crescent and V-rod and double disc and Z-rod symbols. The details of the horse trappings are exceptionally clear.

A minor road turns north 11 km further north-east to *Rossie Priory* where, within the old church, there is another finely carved Class II *Pictish stone*, distinguished by having a cross carved on both faces (NO/292308). The cross on the front is filled with interlace and key-pattern ornament and flanked by fabulous beasts, including a bird-headed man with an axe, human-headed animals and a creature like a cow (Fig. 4: 23). On the back is the second cross on the bottom arm and shaft of which are three horsemen, with two more to the left. There is also an angel, various beasts and a crescent and V-rod symbol.

(Route continued below, p. 185)

Perth to Kirriemuir (A94 and A926)

Near the A94 at Coupar Angus is the well-preserved *Pitcur souterrain* (actually in Angus: NO/253374). Take the A923 SE of the town for 4 km; the site is in a field on the north side of the road opposite the farm. The main passage is some 58 m long and a side passage 18 m long leads off this. About a quarter of the main passage retains the roofing lintels.

North of the A926, in the porch of the church at the north end of *Alyth*, is a Class II *Pictish stone* (NO/244487). There is a simple cross, decorated with interlace, on the front and part of a double disc and Z-rod symbol on the back.

The B952 can be taken E from the Alyth stone and, after 2 km, the minor road forking right (east) past Bruceton farm which is 2·8 km from the junction. The Class I *Bruceton Pictish stone* is in a field south of this minor road and is an irregular monolith carved with an arch or horseshoe symbol with, below it, the elephant symbol. This stone can also be reached from the A926 1 km east of Ruthven.

The *Meigle museum**+ is on the A94 7 km north-east of Coupar Angus and contains an important collection of *Pictish stones* which should not be missed (NO/287446).

(Route continued on p. 188)

2. ANGUS

Two routes are described NE from Perth through Angus, the first along the north shore of the Firth of Tay to Dundee and Arbroath and the second, the inland route (A94), through Coupar Angus, Forfar and Brechin.

Dundee and the Firth of Tay

Immediately north and east of Dundee are a number of interesting sites of Iron Age and later date. At *Balluderon*, 7·5 km north-north-west of Dundee, is a broken Class II *Pictish stone* (NO/375375). Take the minor road through Downfield and Kirkton of Strathmartine. Just over 2 km due north of the latter village is the stone, 200 m west of the road. Only the lower part of the cross is preserved, with a horseman on it, and below is an 'elephant' symbol, another horseman and a serpent and Z-rod (Fig. 4: 13 and 8).

Take the minor road E a little further north to Balgray where is the *Tealing souterrain*+ (NO/413382). Alternatively the A929 to Forfar passes 1 km east of Balgray 8 km from the city. The souterrain consists of a stone-lined passageway sunk into a trench in the ground and about 24·3 m long. The covering lintel stones have been removed so the passage is open to the air. There is a cup-and-ring marked stone built into the passage wall just inside the doorway (see Ardestie below).

Continue E from Dundee along the A92 and turn up the B962 for 300 m where the *Ardestie souterrain**+ is found a short distance west of the road (NO/502344). This site, with Carlungie (below), was excavated in 1949–51 and the usual long, paved, sunken passageway was uncovered; this is still 23 m long but incomplete and the roofing slabs have disappeared. The foundations of contemporary huts were uncovered near by on the surface showing that the souterrain was not itself a dwelling: more probably it was a cattle byre (a drain runs down the centre of its passage under the paving) and storage place. The finds suggest that the site was occupied during the first three centuries A.D. and evidence was found that the surface huts were still in occupation after the souterrain was in ruins. This probably makes the latest inhabitants the earliest Picts and this site and Carlungie are two of the few known which link the Iron Age with the Pictish period.

Laws Hill★ with its *vitrified fort* and *broch*, is a short distance north-west and is reached by minor roads (NO/493349). The stone walls of the hillfort can be seen in part, the site having been extensively but unskillfully explored in the middle of the 19th century and the exposed walls probably partly restored. The fort is oval in plan, measuring some 120 m by 60 m and with a block-faced wall 9 m thick. There are outer defences at the ends. Vitrified stone was noticed in the wall core so the fort wall was timber-framed and could be as early as the 8th to 6th centuries B.C. What appear to be the foundations of a broch—probably built, as at Torwoodlee (p. 86), when the hillfort was in ruins—are also visible. The interior of this is 10·6 m in diameter and the wall is 4·9 m thick. The entrance passage is on the south-east.

At the cross-roads north-east of Laws Hill take the minor road E for 1·5 km to see the *Carlungie souterrain*★+ (Pl. 31), south of the road (NO/511359). This site is very similar to Ardestie (above) and was excavated at the same time. The souterrain is 42·6 m long, has a main entrance and three subsidiary ones and eight huts were found on the surface near by.

Continuing E along the A92 to Arbroath one can visit the ruins of the 12th-century *Arbroath Abbey*+ (NO/644414): the A92 to Montrose passes it and an excellent guide-book is available (p. 290). There is a fine collection of *Early Christian Pictish stones* in a cottage museum at *St. Vigeans*, 1 km north of Arbroath (NO/639429). The minor road which runs due north of the town, west of the railway, leads to the village. The 32 sculptured stones have been found at various times in the adjacent church of St. Vigeans, dedicated to the Irish St. Fechin who presumably founded the Early Christian settlement there in the 7th century.

One of the most interesting is the *Drosten stone*, which is an up-

Plate 31. Carlungie souterrain, Angus, seen from the SE.

right cross slab with an inscription in late 9th-century letters at the base of one of the narrow sides. It reads: DROSTEN/IPEUORET/ETTFOR/ CUS/ which presumably reads 'Drosten ipe Uoret ett Forcus' and refers to three named Picts. The meaning of 'ipe' is unknown; 'et' is the Latin 'and'. The front of the stone has a cross ornamented with interlace patterns flanked by beasts; there is also foliage ornamentation, particularly characteristic of Northumbrian art. On the back of the stone is a stag hunt at the top, the double disc and Z-rod (with interlace on the discs), a crescent and a mirror and comb together with various fantastic beasts and a bowman at the base. It has been suggested that the three symbols represent the three named persons commemorated on the stone.

Stone number 7 is also particularly interesting, a massive cross slab, damaged and reshaped in some later re-use. The ornamentation on the cross and base shows a classic mixture of Celtic curvilinear decoration (base of the shaft) and Anglian interlace motifs. The cross is flanked on the left by two standing clerics carrying staffs, one also having a book satchel. There seem to be two more above them. On the right is a scene with two seated figures, probably St. Paul and St. Antony breaking bread in the desert.

Strathmore (A94 and A926)

Continuing E along the A926 from Alyth the *Airlie souterrain* can be visited: it is the most complete of the accessible structures of its class in the area (NO/305515). Take the minor road N 2 km east of the bridge at Ruthven and turn left for 400 m at the cross-roads at Kirkton of Airlie. The souterrain is on a ridge at the west end of the second field west of the farmhouse. The main passage is 20·4 m long but the entrance is not excavated. The roof is intact except for one lintel which has been removed for access and on the underside of one of the lintels are cup-marks and grooves.

If continuing along the A926 visit the *Kirriemuir Pictish stones* in the cemetery on the north of that town (NO/386545): take the minor road to Northmuir due north from the town centre and the cemetery road turns east after 400 m. Two Class II and two Class III stones are here: the two Class II cross slabs have interlace ornament and human figures and number 2 has the double disc and Z-rod on the back above two mounted spearmen.

Travelling E on the A94 three *Pictish stones* can be seen before reaching Forfar. At *Eassie* churchyard, 15 km from Coupar Angus, is a Class II *cross slab*[+] (NO/353475). On the front is a Celtic cross richly ornamented with interlace pattern, flanked by angels, a spearman with a shield, a stag, a beast and a hound. On the back is a scene with three clerics (?) carrying staffs, a potted plant, and three cows below. The elephant and double disc and Z-rod symbols are at the top.

In the garden of *Glamis Manse* on the main road at the east end of the village, is a fine Class II *Pictish stone* (NO/386467). It might be a converted Class I stone since it is incised on the back with a fish, a serpent and a mirror symbol and carved in relief on the front. On the latter face is a fine cross with interlace ornament flanked by the beast head and triple-disc symbols, two men with axes with a hanging cauldron above them (apparently cooking two humans), and at the top a beast and a centaur holding two axes.

The exceptionally fine Class II *St. Orland's stone*[+] should be seen: take the A928 N from Glamis for 2·3 km and then the farmroad E immediately after the railway bridge. This goes under the railway again and the stone is then found in a field near the railway 700 m east of this bridge. The rectangular pillar stands 2·2 m high with a great carved wheel cross on the front heavily ornamented with spirals and interlace patterns: fish monsters flank this. The back is framed by two snake-like monsters and has the crescent and V-rod and

double disc and Z-rod symbols at the top. Below these is a deliberately cut-out recess and then two pairs of horsemen with a boat
underneath.

Continuing E to Forfar one may visit *Restenneth Priory*+, 2 km
east of the town on the B9133, which has a 13th-century choir but
also a much earlier square tower, of the kind already described at
Dunblane and St. Andrews. This tower has been incorporated into
the later priory church and measures 4·8 m by 4·7 m at the base: it
stands 13·7 m high without its 15th-century spire. It is particularly
interesting in having several different kinds of masonry visible in it.
The lowest and oldest part, up to about 3 m, contains the narrow south
door with a round arch cut from a single great block of stone: it has
been suggested that it was the porch of the stone church built for
the Pictish King Nechton at about A.D. 710 by masons sent from
Wearmouth and, if so, it is of outstanding historical interest. Later
this porch was heightened into a tower, still in pre-Norman times
judging from the character of the masonry.

At 3·5 km south-east of Forfar on the A958 a minor road turns
east to *Dunnichen* where there is a fine Class I *Pictish stone*+ in the
garden of Dunnichen House (NO/508488). Incised on one face are,
from top to bottom, the flower symbol (Fig. 4: 12), the double disc
and Z-rod and the mirror and comb. The double disc is particularly
interesting in being ornamented with the ancient Celtic curvilinear
motif.

Follow the A94 N and NE of Forfar for about 7 km to Finavon
and then take the minor road running south over the hill towards
Aberlemno. This climbs up and after 2·4 km passes immediately
south of the hill on which is the *Finavon vitrified hillfort*★
(NO/507557). The tumbled and grass-grown remains of the great
vitrified stone wall enclose an approximately rectangular area on top
of the hill about 150 m by up to 36 m: the north rampart still stands
over 2 m high in places and there seems to be a hornwork at the east
end. Excavations in 1933–5 exposed a dry well in the east part which
is still open. The excavator suggested that the evident failure of the
fort-builders to find water here resulted in the west end being
extended over lower ground to enclose a good well. Traces of hearths
and wooden huts, as well as thick, gritty pottery, were found at
that time.

In 1966 a trench was dug by the author against the south rampart
to obtain charcoal for C-14 dating. Carbonised planks, probably the
floors of huts, were found and a date in the early 6th century b.c.

Plate 32. Class II Pictish stone in Aberlemno churchyard, Angus: left, the front face; right, the rear face.

obtained (8th–6th centuries B.C.). This was the first vitrified fort to be so dated and the result was unexpectedly early (p. 27).

Continue NE along this minor road down to the B9134 and turn left along it to *Aberlemno* where there are three *Pictish stones**. A particularly fine sandstone Class II *cross slab*+ (number 2) stands in the churchyard (NO/523555). On the front face (Pl. 32) is a cross carved in relief, decorated with spirals in the centre and interlace ornament. This is flanked by intricately intertwined beasts including seahorses (bottom right). The back shows Pictish horse and foot soldiers in a battle scene, below the rectangle and Z-rod and triple disc symbols; the weapons and armour are clearly seen and this is one of the best preserved of the Class II stones.

At 300 m further north-east from the side road leading to the church are the other two stones in the field south of the road (NO/523559). Number 1 is a fine *Class I stone* (Pl. 33) incised on one face with the serpent, double disc and Z-rod and mirror and comb symbols. A short distance south-west of it is number 3, next to the road: it is a rectangular sandstone Class II *cross slab*, somewhat weathered, with a wheel cross on the front flanked by interlace ornament and two angels. The other figures are damaged. On the back is a hunting scene under the crescent and V-rod and double disc and Z-rod symbols.

Continue along the B9134 to *Brechin* to see the 13th-century cathedral and the earlier *round tower* beside it: take the side road S from the A94 just after entering the west end of the town (NO/ 596601). The tower is incorporated in the south-west corner of the nave but was once free-standing, like that at Abernethy. It stands 26·5 m high to the base of the conical roof and, like its Irish prototypes, tapers slightly as it rises and has the door set 2 m up from the ground. This door is particularly interesting in that it has all the features of the Irish originals—narrow aperture, inclined jambs made of single stones of the full breadth of the wall and capped by a similar stone carved into an arch. The sill is also monolithic. The carved decoration too is typically Irish. On either side of the doorway is depicted a bishop; the one on the left holds a normal crozier

Plate 33.
Class I Pictish stone at the roadside at Aberlemno, Angus.

but the one on the right has the Irish T-shaped version. The interior is divided into seven unequal storeys which were reached by wooden ladders. A date early in the 11th century is usually suggested and, since Brechin is reported to have been destroyed by the Danes in 1012, the need for it is clear.

The 13th-century *Maison Dieu chapel*[+] can also be visited in the centre of Brechin (NO/598604).

Take the minor road NNW from Brechin and the left turn after 2 km. This is followed NW for 6 km till it runs between two hills on which are two very large, unexcavated *Iron Age hillforts**. The *White Caterthun*[+], on the west hill, is the more spectacular: a sign-posted path leads 800 m up to it from the road (NO/548660). Two enormous, concentric ruined stone walls—the debris of which spreads over 30 m—enclose an oval area on the hilltop about 150 m by 67 m. The inner of the two walls may have been 12 m thick, the outer one perhaps 6 m. The regular plan of this main wall suggests that it may be an unburnt example of a timber-framed wall. The entrance is on the south-east.

A short distance outside the walls is a low rampart with an internal quarry ditch and there are two more ramparts from 30 m to 70 m further out. No doubt the fortifications are of more than one period but without systematic excavation no further deductions are possible.

The *Brown Caterthun*[+] is on the opposite hill and shows six concentric lines of fortifications (NO/555668). The innermost is a ruined stone wall enclosing an area about 60 m by 80 m with an entrance on the north. Outside is a massive rampart, possibly a ruined wall, with nine entrances, and two more ramparts, with a ditch between, just outside this: they also have nine entrances. Two more ramparts, with eight entrances, are further out, the last enclosing an area 300 m by 275 m.

3. ABERDEENSHIRE

The Upper Dee valley (A93)

If one is travelling to Aberdeen by way of the Perth–Blairgowrie–Braemar road (A93) there are a number of sites to be visited as one emerges from the mountains into the Dee valley.

About 3 km after Ballater is the Class I *Tullich Pictish stone* next to the ruined church: this lies just south of the main road, between it and the railway, 600 m east of the junction with the B972

(NO/390975). A nearly rectangular slab of blue slate 1·8 m high is carved with the double disc and Z-rod, the elephant and mirror symbols. The stone was dressed and re-used as a window lintel in the north wall of the church so the ends of two of the symbols have vanished.

Aboyne Castle is 14 km further east and in the grounds is a broken Class II *Pictish stone* (NO/521992). It stands on rough ground about 100 m from the west gate (leading off the B9094), between the drive and the walled garden. This fragment of a cross slab is of considerable interest because of the presence of two lines of an ogham inscription as well as a Pictish mirror symbol. Ogham (Fig. 26) is a

b l f s n h d t c q m g ng z r a o u e i

Fig. 26. The Scottish ogham alphabet. In the earlier Irish form the vowels are depicted by notches rather than lines.

system of writing which was developed in Ireland and which the Picts probably learned from the Scots of Dalriada. The Pictish ogham inscriptions seem to be of 8th-century type and to record personal names.

Continue along the B9094 NW from Aboyne for 5·5 km to see the *Tomnaverie recumbent stone circle*[+], 700 m south-east of Tarland and on the edge of a disused quarry south of the road (NJ/488035). It consists of an outer ring 17 m in diameter and an inner one 8·5 m. The huge recumbent stone on the south-west is 3·3 m long. The purpose of the recumbent stone in this type of circle—more or less confined to Aberdeenshire—is obscure but the monument probably dates to the Early Bronze Age.

From Tarland the most southerly minor road can be followed 5 km NW (taking the right fork) to *Migvie* to see a Class II *Pictish stone* in the churchyard there (NJ/437069). On the front of the irregular slab is carved a cross ornamented with plait-work; on the left side of the top arm is a double disc and Z-rod and, on the right, a horseshoe and V-rod. On the left of the shaft is a pair of shears with a horseman on the right and another on the back. The stone looks like a transitional form between Classes I and II.

At 2·5 km north-east of Tarland is the *Late Iron Age Culsh souterrain*[+] close to the south side of the A974 (NJ/505055). The sunken passageway is still roofed with heavy stone lintels and may be entered.

Continue E for 5 km and take the minor road SE to Lumphanan where there are the remains of a *Norman motte*, the *Peel Bog of Lumphanan*[+], 1 km along the minor road south-west of the village (NJ/577037). The word 'peel' is derived from the Medieval Latin *palus*, a stake, a reference to the timber tower and palisade with which this unusually broad and low, 12th-century Norman earthwork was once crowned. There is no bailey because of the large size of the top of the motte. The mound was defended by a wet ditch and there are traces of masonry on the top, suggesting that the original timber castle was replaced by stone defences. Lumphanan is reputed to be where Macbeth was finally defeated in 1057 but of course the earthwork was not there then.

Approaching Aberdeen from the W on the A974 two sites may be visited. The *Barmkin of Echt* is a large *hillfort* with multiple defences 2 km north-west of Echt (NJ/725070). Take the B977 N at that village and, after 800 m, a farmroad W which runs round the southwest flank of the hill. The innermost defence is a ruined stone wall enclosing a circular space about 112 m in diameter; there are two entrances. About 3–12 m outside this is a second concentric wall, its entrances in line with the inner ones. About 3 m outside this are three concentric ramparts enclosing an area some 150 m in diameter. There are five entrances through this system, three of which face the unbroken inner walls. Several phases of fortification are doubtless represented.

Four kilometres east towards Aberdeen take the B9125 S to see the *Cullerlie stone circle*[+] (NJ/785043). After 300 m there is a left fork and the circle is 1 km along this in a field on the east side. It consists of eight stones the centres of which lie almost exactly on a true circle 10·2 m (just over 12 my) in diameter: there are no apparent outliers. The site was excavated in 1934 and it was found then that a level, burnt floor lay all over the area of the circle, apparently the result of the lighting of many fires. At a later time eight small ring cairns had been placed on this burnt layer and these evidently covered fire pits in which human remains had been burnt. This circle has thus provided useful information about the primary and secondary use of such sites: in most such cases where a sequence has been established the burials have been found to have been added later so that the primary function of the circles is likely to have been used for ceremonial of a different kind (p. 26).

Ballater to Huntly (A97)

If cutting N from the Upper Dee valley towards Huntly or Elgin five sites may be visited. The *Migvie Pictish stone*, already described (p. 193), is more conveniently reached from the A97 by following the minor road N at Newkirk 3 km north of the junction with the A974.

The B973 to Strathdon turns west 8 km further north and the fine *Norman motte* called the *Doune of Invernochty* is close beside this road 4 km from the junction (NJ/351129). The foundations of stone buildings are visible.

Kildrummy Castle+, 11 km further north on the main road, dates to the 13th century and was the seat of the Earls of Mar (NJ/455164). It is the most complete castle of its period in Scotland and a guide-book is available.

The B9002 turns west 8·5 km further north and *St. Mary's church+*, *Auchindoir*, may be visited 800 m along this (NJ/477246). Apart from lacking a roof the church is almost complete. It is rect-angular in plan, measuring 15·25 m by 5·9 m internally. Although details of the building have been altered at later times there is a particularly fine, original doorway on the south. This preserves the Romanesque round arch but the details of ornamentation are of the Transitional style: a date late in the 12th or early in the 13th century seems indicated. The elaborate sacrament house in the north wall near the east end was put in (with the east doorway in the south wall) in 1557, doubtless when the church was altered for Presbyterian use.

Rhynie is 3 km further north and the *Tap o' Noth vitrified hillfort* overlooks the village from the high hill of that name 2·5 km to the north-west (NJ/485293). Follow the A941 W for 2 km and there at Howtown a farmtrack winds its way north-west up past the west flank of the hill. The fort is defended by a stone wall perhaps 6 m or more thick and enclosing an area 102 m by 32 m: there are numer-ous lumps of vitrification, indicating a fierce fire inside the timber-framed wall. Near the south end is a depression which may be a well and the remains of an outwork wall in the form of a row of boulders is visible lower down on the north and east sides of the hill.

From here one can travel N on the A97 to see *Huntly Castle* (below) or NW to Elgin and the north coast (p. 201 below).

North-west from Aberdeen (A96)

The A96 north-west from Aberdeen to Huntly, Elgin and Inverness passes close to many ancient monuments including a large number of fine Pictish stones. First make a detour for 4 km up the A947 to

Dyce to see two granite *Pictish stones*, one Class I and one Class II. They stand inside the ruined St. Fergus's church, 800 m north-west of the village, and are reached by the minor road to Pitmedden from its centre. The Class I stone is incised with the elephant and double disc and Z-rod symbols. The Class II stone is beside it and is sculpted on one face only with a Celtic cross ornamented with a central boss of spiral work and elsewhere with interlace. Beside and below the shaft are the crescent and V-rod, mirror case, double disc and Z-rod and the triple ring symbols.

The minor road can be followed round to the S to rejoin the A96. At Blackburn a detour for 1·2 km N up the B979 brings one to a minor road which is followed for 1 km NW to the Class I *Kinnellar Pictish stone* in the church near Kirkton (NJ/822145). The stone is inside the porch on the north side of the church and the keys are kept at Kirkton farm. The granite slab is incised with a crescent and V-rod symbol with, above this, a disc containing three smaller circles the centres of which are dots forming an equilateral triangle.

The minor road runs on north-west for 3 km to the centre of *Kintore* where there is another granite Class I *Pictish stone* in the churchyard. It is unusual in being decorated on both faces, one side having the fish and triple disc and bar symbols (Fig. 4: 16 and 3) and the other the crescent and V-rod and elephant. Two other Class I stones were found here and are now in the National Museum in Edinburgh.

Continuing up the A96 for 4 km one finds, on the southern outskirts of Inverurie and not far from the east side of the road, the *Broomend of Crichie henge and stone circle* (NJ/779196). This is a Class II henge, with two opposed entrances aligned north–south and a ditch with an external bank enclosing a circular area 33·5 m in diameter. Within the henge there was once a circle of six standing stones but only two of these remain. The Class I *Pictish symbol stone* which stands with them was set there in the 19th century: it used to stand 50 m to the north-east and is incised with the elephant and crescent and V-rod symbols. Digging in 1885 revealed several cremation burials within the stone circle as well as Bronze Age artefacts like a perforated stone hammer and cinerary urns. There was a sunken cist grave in the centre containing an inhumed skeleton, presumably of the Early Bronze Age. Two beaker burials were found not far away in 1866.

There was a larger stone circle, apparently consisting of three concentric rings of stones, 50 m north of the henge but this has completely vanished. Moreover the 18th-century reports describe an

Plate 34. Bass of Inverurie Norman motte, Aberdeenshire.

avenue of standing stones 200 m long which ran from the large circle to the smaller one and beyond it to the south. One presumed member of this avenue stands 175 m south of the henge. This complex of sites—stone circles, an avenue and Early Bronze Age graves—was clearly once of some importance and it is a pity that so little is left.

One kilometre further north take the B993 E for 500 m to see the *Bass of Inverurie*, a splendidly preserved *Norman motte* next to the river (Pl. 34) (NJ/781206). Close by is an old church near which there were four Class I *Pictish stones*, one of which is incised with a fine trotting horse (Fig. 4: 21).

At the northern outskirts of Inverurie a farmroad turns west from the A96 to *Brandsbutt farm* and to an interesting Class I *Pictish stone[+]* 100 m west of the farm (NJ/760225). The stone has been reassembled from fragments and is incised with the crescent and V-rod and serpent and Z-rod symbols and also with a line of ogham writing, doubtless contemporary with the symbols. The inscription has been translated as IRATADDOARENS . . ., hardly an improvement on the original.

The minor road leading west from the A96 400 m north-west of its junction with the A981 leads, after 4 km, to the farm road south-east to *Easter Aquhorthies* and to the *recumbent stone circle*+ of that name half-way along it and to the west (NJ/733208) (Pl. 35). Nine stones stand in an almost exact circle 19·52 m in diameter (24 my), but the recumbent stone on the south side lies slightly within this perimeter, together with its two flanking stones. The site has not been excavated.

A short distance further north a minor road turns north-east to join the B9001 which passes west of Daviot after 6 km. The *Loanhead of Daviot recumbent stone circle*+ is at the east side of a wood 600 m north of the village (NJ/748288). The site was excavated in 1934 and consists of a ring of nine stones on a circle 20·5 m in diameter (25 my). One of these flanks the recumbent stone on the south but the other flanker is set within the ring. About 1·5 m within the circle is a ring of stones which enclosed a central clear area 3·7 m in diameter: the site could be a ring cairn like the much clearer examples at Clava described below (p. 205). To the south-east of the main circle an annular bed of stones was found which in fact circumscribed an ellipse the long axis of which is orientated towards the midwinter sunrise position on the horizon. There are five outlying standing stones to the west and south-east of the main circle.

Plate 35. Easter Aquhorthies stone circle, Aberdeenshire, seen from the E.

The excavation revealed beaker sherds in various parts of the site, probably indicating that the circle, and perhaps the ring cairn, were constructed in the Early Bronze Age by these influential newcomers (p. 25). Several minor cairns had been piled up around the standing stones and one of these covered a cist containing a small incense cup of the Middle Bronze Age. There was also Late Bronze Age and Iron Age pottery though the nature of this secondary use of the site is not clear: it may be that the centre of the ring cairn, where a hearth was in use at this time, was used as a small dwelling. It is possible, though not certain, that the stone circle with its astronomical potential was the earliest structure and, if so, the cairns would represent secondary funerary uses of the site.

The A96 can be rejoined at Pitcaple by minor roads SW from Daviot. The fine Class II *Pictish Maiden stone*[+] is 2 km further west and can be reached by the minor road south of Pitcaple through Chapel of Garrioch: the stone is 1·5 m west of that village and close to the road (NJ/703247). This is the best-known cross slab in Aberdeenshire and has, on the front, five panels of sculpture around the carved cross the ornament of which has been defaced. In the top panel is a man and a fish monster, perhaps Jonah and the whale and, in the bottom one, some spiral ornamentation. The sides of the slab are finely ornamented with interlace and knotwork patterns and the back, divided into four panels, shows (from top to bottom) beasts, the notched rectangle and Z-rod (Fig. 4: 5), the 'elephant' and the mirror and comb symbols. The comb is a double-sided one of which composite bone examples are known in Scotland from about the 4th century A.D. onwards.

The Class I *Logie Elphinstone symbol stone* is not far away, in the grounds of Logie (NJ/705259). The drive leaves the A96 2·4 km west of Pitcaple: immediately after crossing the river turn E for about 500 m. At the top of this pointed monolith is an ogham inscription cut in a circle: under this is a crescent and V-rod symbol with a double disc and Z-rod below that. There are traces of a double disc symbol which has apparently been erased to make way for the others.

Newton House is on the A96 5 km north-west of its junction with the A979 and in the grounds, close to the east side of the house, are a Class I *Pictish stone* (Pl. 36) and an *ogham stone* (NJ/662298 approx.). The former has the double disc (without the Z-rod) and the serpent and Z-rod symbols: it was moved to the house early in the 19th century from its original site about 1·5 km to the south. The ogham stone is next to it and is famous for its bilingual inscriptions, neither of which has been satisfactorily deciphered. The other text consists of six horizontal lines of debased Roman cursive script.

A little further west take the B992 SW to Insch from where a minor road leads NNW and then W for 3 km to the Class I *Picardy stone*[+] on Mireton farm (NJ/610303). This undressed standing monolith has incised on it the double disc and Z-rod, serpent and Z-rod and mirror symbols. The symbols are well preserved because of the hardness of the black whinstone.

If the minor road due west from the centre of Insch is taken for 1·5 km—to the point at which it turns north-west—the footpath to the near-by hilltop can be followed to see the *Dunnideer vitrified hill-fort* (NJ/613281). The vitrified wall encloses an oblong area some 27 m by 67 m and there may be a well near the west end. There are traces of two outer ramparts further down the hill but these seem to be only partly completed, being largely defined only by marker trenches. It seems possible that the enlargement of the hillfort began after the burning of the timber-framed wall but direct evidence is lacking.

Plate 36.
Class I Pictish stone at
Newton, Aberdeenshire.

By following the A979 for 12 km the A97 to Huntly is joined and the Tap o' Noth vitrified hillfort, described earlier (p. 195) can be quickly reached by turning south to Rhynie. The splendid *Huntly Castle*+, seat of the Gordons, lies north of the town, close to the river Deveron (NJ/532407). The remains of the *Norman motte*, the predecessor of the later stone constructions, can be seen at the site.

4. NAIRN AND MORAY

There are several interesting sites west and north of Elgin which can be easily reached either from Inverness or from Aberdeen and Huntly (A96). The 13th-century *Elgin Cathedral*★+ is situated on the north-east outskirts of the town and—though it was burned in 1390, vandalised in the 17th century and suffered a collapse of the tower into the nave in 1711—it still remains one of the finest fragments of Medieval architecture in Scotland. A guide-booklet is available. Standing in the nave is a fine Class II granite *Pictish cross slab*★ the designs on which, though the stone is somewhat blackened and defaced, are quite well preserved. It was found lying flat near St. Giles church in 1823 during street repairs. On the front there is the cross on a large rectangular base; the interlace ornament on it is much defaced. Flanking it are figures probably representing the four Evangelists and below the base are four intertwined beasts. The back shows, from the top, an unknown figure or symbol, the double disc and Z-rod, and crescent and V-rod symbols and a hunting scene with four horsemen (one with a hawk), hounds and a stag.

Take the B9012 W from the northern outskirts of Elgin (from the A941 to Lossiemouth) to see *Duffus Castle*★+ (NJ/189673). The B9135 turns north-east 1·7 km before Duffus and runs close to the castle which is a rare example of a 12th-century Norman motte and bailey earthwork subsequently fortified with stone (in the late 13th or early 14th century). The great motte has sunk under the weight of the added stonework causing the latter to split and partially to collapse (Pl. 37). The whole site is surrounded by a ditch or moat enclosing about 0·03 km². This was not defensive but served to mark the boundary of the lord's land. The bailey is defended by a bank, now surmounted by the later stone wall but originally no doubt defended by a strong wooden palisade. The motte is in the north-west corner of the bailey, separated from it by a wide, deep ditch so that the lord's wooden castle on top could be defended if the bailey was overrun. The Norman family de Moravia, or Moray,

Plate 37. Duffus Castle, Morayshire: the keep from the SW.

built the castle in the middle of the 12th century. A leaflet describing the stone castle is available.

Continue on the B9012 through Duffus to *Burghead* where there are the remains of a massive *Late Iron Age or Pictish stone promontory fort* and an *Early Christian well*+ (NJ/110692). The fort was systematically quarried early in the 19th century and only a little is now left but it was planned in the 1740s by General Roy. This plan shows that there were three ramparts—presumably ruined stone walls—which ran for about 240 m across the neck of the promontory to enclose an area to the seaward some 300 m long. Explorations later in the 19th century showed that one of the walls was some 7·3 m thick and was still standing about 5 m high. Wooden beams projected from the core through the inner face and were apparently fastened with massive iron nails to planks running horizontally (but not vertically) inside the core. Burghead thus seemed to be a unique example in Britain of the *murus gallicus*, a specialised form of timber-framed rampart devised by the Gauls in the 1st century B.C. to withstand Roman siege tactics.

However more skilful excavations in 1966 failed to find any iron nails or indeed any internal timber-framing at all: the beams apparently only projected from sockets in the wall into the fort interior,

Plate 38. Sueno's stone, Elgin, Morayshire: view of the rear face.

presumably to support a wall walk. Radiocarbon measurements on charred wood from the wall gave dates in the 4th or 5th century a.d., strongly suggesting that the fort was a Pictish stronghold, the only one so far known. Stone slabs carved with Pictish motifs, including several Class I examples with the famous bull (Fig. 4: 24), have been found on the site. The old idea that Agricola's Roman army sacked this stronghold and fought the battle of Mons Craupius near by now seems doubly unlikely (p. 179).

The *well* is unique in Scotland, a rock-cut chamber at the base of a crag, about 4·9 m square and 3·7 m high. In the floor is a rock-cut basin 3 m square and 1·2 m deep. From Roy's plan it seems that this chamber lies on the line of one of the fort walls and that there-fore it was constructed at a later time, when the defences were out of use. It has been suggested that it was an Early Christian baptistry.

Take the B9089 SW to Kinloss and the B9011 to Forres on the main road. The Class III cross slab known as *Sueno's stone**+ is on the outskirts of the town beside this B road (Pl. 38) (NJ/047595). This is one of the most remarkable Dark Age sculptured stones in Britain, if not in Europe, and even more remarkable is the fact that no systematic analysis of it has been published. The sandstone pillar, now much weathered at the top, stands 7 m high and is sculptured on all four faces. The front has a tall wheel cross on a rectangular base, the shaft ornamented with interlace work: below the base is a blurred scene with five men. The back has a unique scene in four panels showing (from top to bottom): (1) an eroded scene and nine men on horseback in three rows; (2) many armed foot soldiers and horsemen in five rows, including a row of decapitated bodies next to an object which looks remarkably like a broch, and scenes of combat; (3) a sort of canopy or tent over some decapitated bodies; (4) some sort of procession. The edges of the stone show Anglian foliage and interlaced beasts and a date for the whole stone in the 9th or 10th century seems likely from this and other signs.

It has been persuasively argued that Sueno's stone is a Pictish memorial, or cenotaph, commemorating a great victory—depicted on the back—over the Norsemen; the identity of the enemy is sugges-ted by the traditional name of the stone. It is quite possible that there was a well-preserved broch on or near the battlefield which was shown on the stone. Indeed 46 km away to the north-west as the crow flies, on the south shore of the Dornoch Firth (NH/657867), there was a broch which still had tower-like proportions 450 years ago; Dun Alascaig was described as having a bell-shaped appearance (like Mousa) in 1520. The broch is now completely destroyed, only a triangular stone entrance lintel in the grass indicating what it was. Perhaps the presumed defeat of Sueno took place there.

Continuing W on the A96 one can see a fine Class II *Pictish stone* in the grounds of *Brodie Castle* (NH/985576). Take the minor road NE towards Dyke and the stone is about 50 m from this, near the lodge at the north-east corner of the grounds. On the front is a cross with interlace ornament with badly defaced pairs of beasts flanking it. On each side of the front is an ogham inscription. On the back is a simple panel with a pair of fish monsters with spiral tails at the top, an elephant symbol below and a double disc and Z-rod at the base ornamented with double spirals. On the raised borders of the panel are two more ogham inscriptions.

5. INVERNESS-SHIRE (EAST)

The main road north (3) (A9)

Approaching Inverness from the S turn E along the B851 6 km before the town past Culloden battlefield to see the fine group of three *chambered cairns* at *Balnuaran of Clava**+ (NH/756443: Pl. 39, Fig. 27). Turn SE along a minor road just before the junction with the B9006 and then left (SW) once over the river. There are three cairns in a row, each surrounded by a stone circle. The *south-west cairn* is encountered first: the road actually runs through the surrounding stone circle. The cairn is a passage grave bordered by a kerb of upright boulders 16 m in diameter and with an oval central chamber 3·5 m by 4 m. The entrance passage faces south-west and there are cup-marks on the foundation stone of the chamber wall just to its left. The surrounding circle has 10 stones remaining out of a probable original total of 12, some of which have been re-set, and its diameter is 31·6 m (38 my). There are cup-marks on the second stone west of the entrance. The chamber was explored in about 1828 and calcined bones and fragments of two pots were found (now lost) which, from the contemporary description, might have been Late Bronze Age ware.

The centre cairn is a *ring cairn* with no passage to the chamber. Otherwise it is similar in size and proportions to the one just described. Nine standing stones surround it and lie on an exact circle 38 my in diameter. Three of these stones are connected with the cairn by low, artificial banks of rubble. During the excavation of 1857 only a few flint flakes were found in the central chamber.

The *north-east cairn* is another passage grave but here the surrounding stone circle of 11 stones is in fact a geometrically constructed egg-shape, the base being a circle of radius 19 my and the other part being drawn on the base of a Pythagorean triangle with sides 6, 8 and 10 my (Fig. 27). The boulder kerb of the cairn is 16·8 m in diameter and a stone on the north side is decorated with cup-marks and one cup-and-ring. The enclosed chamber is 3·8 m across and its walls overhang slightly, suggesting that it was once

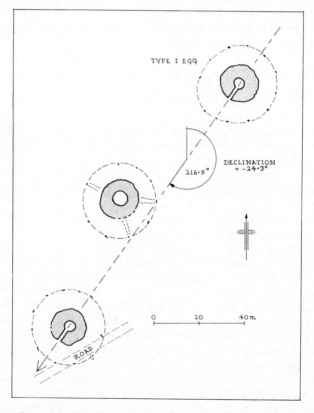

Fig. 27. Plan of the three cairns at Balnuaran of Clava, Inverness-shire. The two entrance passages are on the same line which points to a spot on the horizon having a declination of —24·3°, suitable for a prehistoric midwinter sunset. Scale 1:1600.

Plate 39. Cairns at Balnuaran of Clava, Inverness-shire, seen from the SW.

completely roofed with a drystone corbelled dome. Only a 'few bones' were found in the chamber in 1858.

A recent integrated plan of the site made by Professor A. Thom strongly suggests that the two passage graves at least were laid out as a unit (Fig. 27). Not only are the passages aligned in exactly the same direction (216·5°) but they are also on the same line which passes through two of the stones of the circle round the ring cairn. That this line points to the setting position of the midwinter sun can hardly be fortuitous. The Clava group provides a fascinating hint of links between the geometry and astronomy of the stone circles of the early 2nd millennium B.C. with the Neolithic passage graves of an earlier epoch.

On leaving Inverness on the N road the fine *Craig Phadrig vitrified fort** on its dominant hilltop may be visited (NH/640453). Immediately after crossing the Caledonian Canal take the minor road SW along it for 500 m, then turn right to Leachkin. A track winds up the tree-covered hill from the road. The fort overlooks the narrows between the Beauly Firth and the Moray Firth and is matched by the Ord of Kessock hillfort on the opposite side. New excavations took place at the fort in 1971 and 1972 so the fort should be reasonably clear of vegetation. A massive turf-covered vitrified rampart—a ruined drystone wall—encloses a rectangular area 30 m across by 80 m long. An outer rampart, also vitrified, is visible in many places up to 23 m outside the inner wall. Both walls were dated by radiocarbon after the recent excavations; the former was probably built in the 4th century b.c. and the latter at the same time. Presumably the destruction and vitrification of both was also simultaneous.

The hillfort has often been thought to be a Pictish capital but the date of the walls is far too early for that. However traces of a Dark Age occupation inside the ruins were found, most notably in the form of a piece of clay mould for part of a bronze hanging bowl perhaps dating to the 7th century A.D. Whether this indicates only the presence of a workshop producing these luxury objects, or of a bowl craftsman at the court of a Pictish king or chief, is not clear.

Seventeen kilometres beyond Inverness is the 13th-century *Beauly Priory**⁺ in the centre of Beauly (NH/528466). Only the aisle-less church remains above ground. The site is of interest in being one of only three priories, all founded in 1230, of the French Valliscaulian order in Britain: the other two were Pluscarden in Moray and Ardchattan in Argyll. A guide-pamphlet is available.

The Great Glen (A82)

From the centre of Inverness the A862 may be taken SW for a short distance and then the minor road to Essich. This leads after 2·5 km to the Class I *Pictish Boar stone**+ beside the road (NH/657413). Unhappily this has been defaced by initial-cutting and has consequently been surrounded by a wire cage: the fine boar incised on it is thus hard to see (Fig. 4: 24).

Soon after crossing the river Ness in the centre of the town the A82 leads south-west straight down the Great Glen 25 km to Drumnadrochit and to *Urquhart Castle**+ near by (Pl. 40). On this site there are the remains of a *vitrified fort* of the Late Bronze or Early Iron Age, a *Norman motte* (probably largely a natural rock) and a 14th-century *stone castle*, the latter being one of the largest in Scotland. A guide-booklet is available. If contemplating a detour W up Glen Urquhart on the A831 the *Corrimony chambered cairn*+ may be visited, 13 km from Drumnadrochit at the junction with the A82 (NH/383303). The minor road to Corrimony passes close to the cairn which was excavated in 1952 by Professor S. Piggott and is

Plate 40. Urquhart Castle, Inverness-shire: view from the tower looking SSW.

another passage grave of the Clava type surrounded by a stone circle. The central chamber and its passage are not now accessible but the former is a broken-down, corbelled cell 3·7 m in diameter and the passage is 7 m long: both features are built of dry walling on top of massive blocks. The stain of a crouched inhumation burial was found in the sand of the floor. The kerb of the cairn is of slabs on edge and forms an oval from 13·7 m to 15·3 m across. Some of the 11 stones of the surrounding circle have been re-set in modern times: in particular the two south of the entrance are composite and may include lintels taken from the passage.

7 · Northern Scotland

(Ross-shire, Sutherland and Caithness)

The three northernmost counties of the Scottish mainland show some striking contrasts in their terrain. Ross and Sutherland are wild and mountainous: the modern roads, and the archaeological sites, tend to follow the long straths between the hills or to be on the few flat areas on the east coast. Caithness is quite different—a grey-green, flat and rolling plain with large numbers of sites scattered all over it. Sutherland and Caithness nevertheless tend to be similar in having close archaeological links with the northern islands at several periods: they are famous in particular for their Neolithic chambered cairns and Iron Age brochs, two kinds of structures common in the island or Atlantic zone of Scotland.

1. ROSS-SHIRE

The main road north (4) (A9)

Just across the county border is the *Muir of Ord henge monument*, one of three of its type—with two entrances—in Scotland (NH/527497). It stands on the golf course 0·5 km south of Muir of Ord and has been utilised as a green. Turn down the minor road to the S where the Ullapool road leaves the A9: the henge is on 'Castle Hill' about 400 m south-east of the road. In this type of Late Neolithic ceremonial structure the central area was marked off by a circular ditch, interrupted by two causeways, with a bank outside this. No doubt spectators sat on the bank to witness the ceremonies within. This henge has a diameter of about 34 m from crest to crest of the bank and the ditch, which has been partly filled in in modern times, is still elsewhere 1·2 m deep.

If making a detour into the Black Isle along the A832 a Class II *Pictish stone* can be seen at *Rosemarkie* 1·5 km north-east of Fortrose (NH/737576). It has been broken and repaired and now stands against the wall of the church: although the upper end of the slab is broken off it still stands 2·6 m high. The front face has a very elaborate interlace pattern surrounding a cross with equal arms. On the back are three elaborately carved crescent and V-rod symbols with the double disc and Z-rod between the two lower ones. There are also two mirrors below the bottom crescent and a comb above it. Below is a cross panel with elaborate interlace. The sides of the slab are also carved.

The fragmentary remains of *Fortrose Cathedral* are in the centre of the town in an open space. All that is left is the south aisle of the nave which looks rather like a complete church on its own, and the undercroft of the chapter house. Although the cathedral was probably founded in the 13th century the aisle in fact probably belongs to the late 14th.

Further north on the A9 one reaches *Dingwall* where there is a Class I (pre-Christian) *Pictish Stone** (NH/548589). It stands just inside the gate of Dingwall church which is a short distance north of where the A9 turns north in the middle of the town. The stone was found serving as a lintel in the church during restorations in 1880 and is carved on both faces. On one side is a double disc and Z-rod with two crescents and V-rods below. The other face has a crescent and V-rod with three circles above. There are also six cup-marks on this face, suggesting that an old prehistoric standing stone may have been re-used in Pictish times.

A detour W from Dingwall along the A834 to Contin leads one to another Class I *Pictish stone** at Strathpeffer, known as 'Clachan Tiompan' or the 'standing stone' (NH/485585). It stands in a field to the north of the road and is reached by a wide footpath a little inside the 30 m.p.h. zone. The field gate is 50 m up the footpath on the right. The stone is of hard gneiss and the sculpture, consisting of a horseshoe symbol with a fine eagle below it, is well preserved.

If one takes the minor road leading south-east from the north end of Strathpeffer one can visit the *vitrified fort* on the hill of *Knockfarril* (NH/505585). The fort encloses a roughly rectangular area some 130 m by 38 m with an extensive outer rampart running along for half of the circuit. A unique and so far uncomprehended feature is a heavily vitrified wall which projects outwards from each of the narrow ends of the fort as if to bisect it down its long axis. The date of the structure is not known but a vitrified (timber-framed) wall could be as old as the 8th century B.C. (p. 27).

Follow the A9 N past Tain to *Edderton* where there are two

Pictish stones, one of Class I (NH/708850) and one Class III (NH/719842). The former is about 300 m from the main road in a field to the left (north) of the minor road which turns south in the middle of the village. It is a tall, pointed stone decorated on one face with a fish and a double disc and Z-rod.

The Class III stone is in the churchyard at the south-east end of the village. One side is carved with a cross on an arched base under which is a horseman. There are two more horsemen with shields and spears, hidden under the ground. The back is entirely occupied by a large cross with a ring connecting the arms. The stone is probably later than A.D. 850 and a cross on both faces is very unusual (*route continued on p. 215*).

Loch Broom, Wester Ross

Travelling NW to Ullapool along the A835 one can visit two important fortified sites on the south shore of Loch Broom. At the bottom of the hill leading down to the head of the loch is a minor road turning left (south-west) to Loggie. Stop 1 km before the end of this and a stone fort can be seen 100 m south of the road on top of a sheer-faced rocky bluff on the mountain slope (NH/149901). *Dun an Ruigh Ruaidh*★ is one of the small class of broch-like structures which, while having the true hollow, galleried broch wall, are yet not totally enclosed round towers. They have been called semibrochs and are almost certainly ancestral to the brochs. Rhiroy was excavated in 1968 by the author and proved to be a semibroch, even though its wall runs round as a flattened circle next to the low cliff. The wall near the cliff is narrower and lacks a gallery so that the true broch high wall is only found on the other sides where it stands up to 2·9 m. The entrance is on the south-east, equipped with the usual door-checks. At 8 o'clock is the door, now filled, to the mural cell and to the stair which leads to the upper gallery, well preserved and lintelled on the south-west arc: the base of the wall here is solid. A fine ledge scarcement runs round the inner wallface and the foundations of a doorway leading on to this can be seen to the right of the stair door.

Excavations showed that the semibroch originally had an internal ring of massive wooden posts which supported a raised floor on the scarcement. This was dismantled when the fort was turned into a dwelling and part of the upper wall pulled down: at this time the entrance passage was unlintelled. Occupation debris accumulated as a thick black layer in the interior but artefacts were few. Later the weakened structure underwent a sudden further collapse, shattering a complete quern on the floor, and occupation ceased except in the still accessible mural cell. The semibroch is likely to have been built in the 3rd or 2nd century B.C.

Carry on till the end of the road at Loggie and a pathway north-west over rocky ground soon brings one in sight of a long, isolated rock ridge at the narrowest point of Loch Broom, with Ullapool visible across the water. This is *Dun Lagaidh** (Fig. 28), a three-

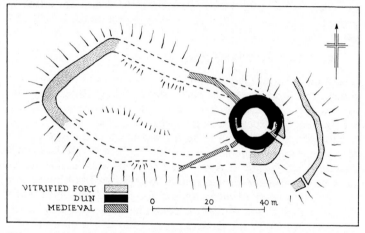

VITRIFIED FORT
DUN
MEDIEVAL

0   20   40 m

Fig. 28. Plan of Dun Lagaidh, Ross and Cromarty, showing the three phases of fortification. The doorways and other intramural features discovered during recent excavations are now re-buried. Scale 1:1250.

period fortified site of considerable interest which was excavated in 1967 and 1968 by the author (NH/143913). The earliest structure is a *vitrified hillfort* which, from radiocarbon dates, could have been built somewhere between the 8th and 6th centuries B.C. It has been extensively robbed of stone by the builders of the later forts but there is a good stretch, with some exposed vitrified stone, at the west end. The massive timber-framed wall, 4·3 m thick, encloses an area about 78 m long and up to 27 m wide. Its east end contains the narrow main gate, only 1·2 m wide, which is now buried: it is imme-diately east of the dun wall which partly overlies the foundations of the hillfort wall here. Further east, along the easy approach, there are what look like banks and ditches but in fact the outer defence here consists of a single timber-framed wall or hornwork, now vitrified, 2·4 m thick. It has a narrow gateway at the extreme south end, almost at the cliff edge. Few finds were made in the hillfort which another radiocarbon date showed was destroyed at an early stage in its existence.

A massive, round, solid-walled drystone dun was later built on the ruins of the east end of the hillfort. Its entrance, with two sets of door-checks and a guard cell, faces east and there is a mural stair on the west side. Many finds were made on the dun floor, including an iron bridle bit and fragments of a beaten bronze vessel, and they suggest that this was the fortified residence of an Iron Age chief. It is possible that he had come north from Argyllshire where such duns are common. The fine masonry of the dun, built of Torridonian sandstone, contrasts strikingly with that of the Rhiroy semibroch which is of Moine schist.

The dun was abandoned but rebuilt again in Medieval times. Mortared masonry was used to heighten the walls, to block up the old entrance and to build two radial walls from the dun on the west side. The south one of these had a gateway in it and the whole had become a simple castle and bailey. The entrance into the dun at this time was down the mural stair. A hoard of silver pennies of the early 13th century gave precision to the end of the third phase of fortification of the site. Dun Lagaidh well illustrates how a naturally strong site—situated in a strategic position at the narrowest point of the longest sea-loch in north-west Scotland—was repeatedly used as a fortress over a period of perhaps nearly two thousand years.

2. SUTHERLAND

The main road north (5) (A9)

One enters Sutherland at the head of the Dornoch Firth at Bonar bridge and thereafter the road runs east for several kilometres. A *standing stone**, 3·4 m tall and known as Clach à Charra, is next to the south side of the road at Ospisdale House (NH/716895) and 6 km further east one can make a detour along the A949 to see the 13th century *Dornoch Cathedral**.

Following the A9 N along the coast through Golspie one may be able to visit the museum in Dunrobin Castle where there is housed a collection of Pictish stones found locally. About 2 km east of the castle the road crosses the railway and immediately to the right, just before the bridge, is the *Carn Liath broch*⋆ (NC/871013). The broch was crudely cleared out in the middle of the 19th century and tidied up in 1972 so the remains are now clear and well worth a visit. As was usual in these early excavations only the interior was emptied of debris, the outer wallface being left largely undisturbed and buried; thus the broch gives the impression of being a cylindrical crater mostly below ground-level. The entrance passage faces east; it is partly lintelled and equipped with door-checks, bar-hole and a guard cell on the right. The inner wall stands up to 3·6 m high in places but is largely concealed by a thick secondary facing which was presumably added in the Iron Age when the broch ceased to be a fort and was partly dismantled. The mural stair is well preserved at 10 o'clock and there are two deep, stone-lined pits in the floor, one of which was presumably a well: it is 2·4 m deep. Many outbuildings are visible outside the broch and these too presumably date to the peaceful period following the use of the site as a fort.

Carn Liath is a solid-based broch with a wall which is thick in relation to its overall diameter of about 21 m. Its design and dimensions are very similar to those of the Torwood broch in Stirlingshire (p. 116) and this suggests that some of the brochs in the southern mainland may be the work of builders from Sutherland.

About 2 km further north a minor road turns north-west to Loch Brora through Doll and on the hills on its south side are two Iron Age defence works worth a visit. The road from Doll crosses the river Brora at a ford and just before this is the track to be taken along the south side of the river, through a Forestry Commission plantation and on to a private road. About 600 m beyond the end of the plantation strike left uphill to the hillfort of *Duchary rock* (NC/850050). There is another track which gets closer to the fort; this leaves the minor road shortly before the ford. The site is in a spectacular situation with extensive views, standing as it does on a high rocky knoll of great natural strength. The easiest approach is from the north-west and here the wall is best preserved, being composed now of a line of tumbled stones, some of great size. Stretches of the inner and outer faces can be seen, indicating that the wall is about 3·7 m thick. The entrance passage can be seen on the north-west and is lined with upright slabs. A second entrance only 1·2 m wide can be seen on the east side. The enclosed area measures some 238 m by 55 m and is unexcavated and featureless.

If one travels further up the road on the south side of the loch, to a point 2·4 km from the end of the Forestry plantation, one may visit the *Carrol broch*★ which was excavated in the 19th century (Craig Carril: NC/846065). The site looks like a low cairn from a distance and is about 400 m to the south of the road and up the sloping moorland (follow the burn up). However when one reaches it one finds the interior excavated and the wall standing about 3·5 m high. The lintelled entrance passage is on the east-south-east and is complete. There are two sets of door-checks with a well-preserved corbelled guard chamber opening to the right behind the outer door-checks: its low door contrasts with its high, domed roof. A scarcement of the ledge type is preserved on the inside wallface and the mural stair is at 9 o'clock: the door leading to it is raised more than a metre above the floor. An extremely long stair-foot guard cell runs anti-clockwise for 5·8 m. An outer wall surrounds the broch and there are signs of a gateway in it in line with the broch entrance.

Five kilometres north of Brora is the second excavated *broch* on the raised beach, *Kintradwell*★ (NC/929081). It is visible from the road as a low line of reddish masonry just beside the railway and was cleared out shortly before 1870. It yielded a remarkable number of rotary quernstones as well as some late burials in the wall chambers, one of which had with it an iron spear blade. There is the usual entrance passage, partly lintelled, with two sets of door-checks and a guard cell; a mural stair is preserved at 9 o'clock. A well 2·1 m deep is in the interior with a flight of steps leading down into it.

The Strath of Kildonan

The valley of the river Helmsdale (A897) is full of archaeological remains, mostly of the less spectacular kind of which there is space to describe briefly only four sites.

On the moorland above *Kilphedir* is a group of *hut circles*★ and *field clearance cairns* four of which were excavated by Dr H. Fairhurst during the 1960s (NC/989194). One can either follow the left bank of the burn N from the road bridge at Kilphedir for 1 km or start along the farm track 100 m west of the bridge. There is a group of five stone hut circles surrounded by traces of field walls and cultivation plots. The site is now in desolate peaty moorland but the excavations showed that the peat had grown since some of the huts were built so that the terrain was probably much different when the settlement was occupied. The most massive hut circle proved to have a thick stone wall revetted with boulders around the interior, a long entrance passage, a central hearth and signs of a cellar or souterrain within the wall. The wooden superstructure had evidently caught fire at the end of the use of the hut and masses of charcoal was found on the floor. A number of radiocarbon dates for this charcoal gave an average age in about the middle of the first century b.c. but this presumably dates the construction or repair of the roof rather than the fire (p. 22).

The other hut circles, less massively built, appear to belong to an earlier phase of the Iron Age judging by the pottery recovered. These huts consisted of low banks of stones for the wall foundation—up to 11 m in diameter—with holes in the floor for an inner ring of roof-supporting posts. There was a central hearth in each. A radiocarbon date for Hut 3 fell in the late 5th century b.c. The small cairns proved to be heaps of stones cleared from the cultivated plots.

This Iron Age settlement is one of the few of its kind to have been systematically examined and dated. There are hundreds of such hut circles on the Sutherland moors.

A walk of 1 km to the SE across the burn brings one to the *Kilpheir broch*★ (NC/995188). This unexcavated structure is on top of a knoll, a huge mass of rubble in which a few structural features can yet be seen. The entrance is on the north-west with three lintels in position: door-checks can be seen. The mural gallery, with a door to the central court, is visible at 12 o'clock. The broch is worth visiting for its formidable outer defences. These consist of a deep ditch completely surrounding the knoll, with a massive rampart within this. A short forework, consisting of a second bank and ditch, is on the south-west where the approach from the hut circle settlement is across flatter ground.

Continuing along the A897 for 11 km to Kildonan Lodge one can visit the complex of *standing stones, stone rows, stone circles* and *cairns*, on and near *Learable Hill*. About 1 km after the lodge and telephone box one can cross the river and railway to Learable farm and the structures begin about 600 m north-west of the house. The *stone rows* (NC/892234) are here and it has been suggested that they were set out for an astronomical purpose: the hilly horizon to the east is sharp and clear. There are the remains of five parallel stone rows pointing almost due east and indicating a possible marker for the sunrise at the equinoxes. A few metres to the north are two interesting rows of single stones which may also point to astronomically significant notches on the east horizon. There is an isolated *standing stone* 1·6 m high about 35 m south of the first rows mentioned; it has been incised with a cross. About 30 m south-east of this is a fan-shaped setting of stone rows (see Mid Clyth, p. 226

below) and there are numerous cairns dotted over the hillside. The area was clearly of considerable importance to the erectors of standing stones.

About 120 m west of the cross-marked standing stone mentioned is a *stone circle* with five uprights still in position.

At a distance of 6 km further up the main road is the *Kinbrace burn chambered cairn* (NC/875282). It is 150 m east of the road (which should be left 200 m before the bridge over the burn), standing on a level spot in rising moorland. The cairn is much disturbed but traces of a horned forecourt are visible in the north side. The chamber was excavated in the 19th century and consists of three compartments, the largest in the centre, separated by projecting stone slabs. Traces of the dry-walled entrance passage can be seen leading off towards the east. Presumably the cairn dates to the 4th or 3rd millennium B.C. (route continued on p. 222).

The north coast (A836)

If one is travelling W from Thurso along the north coast road, on the A836, there are several sites in Sutherland which can conveniently be seen. For a stimulating walk along a deep river valley a visit to the *Armadale burn broch*★ can be recommended (NC/800625). About 5 km west of Strathy the main road crosses the Armadale burn: the old road bridge stands next to the new one and provides a convenient parking space. One follows the burn upstream along whichever bank is convenient (wellingtons are advisable). The broch is on a high, steep conical summit overlooking the river valley from its western side and about 1·5 km south of the road. It is full of rubble but the wallfaces are visible, as is the entrance passage on the south-east. As one would expect from the cramped situation the interior is small, only 7·2 m in diameter.

Brochs like this one, situated in wild moorland far from modern habitations, are numerous in the highlands of Sutherland and present a problem. Where did their owners live? In this case the nearest cultivable land is nearly 2 km away towards the sea and, if one supposes that the Iron Age population cultivated the same fields, their refuge could not have been reached quickly in an emergency. Probably its hidden situation more than made up for the inconvenience of access to this broch.

Further west, just before reaching Bettyhill, one can see the *Early Christian cross slab* at Farr standing in its original position in the churchyard and outside the east end of the church (NC/714623). The easiest way to reach the site is to leave the main road as it starts to go down to Bettyhill, just before the bridge over the Clachan burn (300 m west of the power line). The old church is about 200 m down the burn and on its north side. This monument, sometimes known as the Red Priest's stone, is one of the relatively few Class III stones, i.e., it is an elaborately decorated cross slab but without any Pictish symbols on it. It probably dates to the period immediately after Pictland ceased to be an independent kingdom in about A.D. 850 (p. 33). The stone stands 2·3 m high and is sculptured in relief on only one face. This has a main central panel, containing a large wheel cross with curved interlace ornament on and surrounding it and the remains of a spiral-ornamented, circular boss in the centre. Above and below this are two more panels filled with straight, geometrical interlace ornament. There are two birds with intertwined necks in the semicircular cross base; the latter feature illustrates the Irish influence on the monument.

Just after Bettyhill the main road crosses the river Naver but a side road to Skelpick turns south down Strathnaver just before the bridge. There are two *Neolithic chambered cairns* at *Coille na Borgie*, immediately east of the minor road and 1·2 km from the junction (NC/715590). They are only 10 m apart and the south one is the better preserved; its edge is clear in places, being marked here and there by a peristalith of upright stones up to 0·76 m high. The cairn has horns at both ends of its 72 m length; the north end, with the chamber, is considerably wider than the other and there are six large upright stones marking the line of the façade. The passage and chamber are aligned about 10° away from the long axis of the cairn which suggests that the tomb was originally in a small round cairn, and that the long horned one was added later. The chamber is in three sections with portal stones at the entrance and two pairs of projecting side slabs to hold up the roof. Two lintels remain in position. The chamber was cleared out in the 19th century but no significant finds were made.

Coille na Borgie North was probably also a double-horned long cairn but has been badly robbed and only the tops of three of the side stones of the chamber are now visible above the rubble.

An unexcavated broch, *Allt an Duin**, is 1·5 km further south: go due E up from the road for 800 m just before the bridge over the Skelpick burn (NC/723575). The broch is on a high, steep, conical rocky knoll overlooking the fertile Strathnaver. Most of the features are obscured by rubble but the entrance is on the north-west and a very large triangular rock lying in front of it was probably the front lintel. This was an ingenious device to divert the weight of the high outer wallface on to the sides of the passage. The lintels behind, one of which is apparent, were flat indicating the presence of a void or chamber above the passage. A ledge-type scarcement can be seen on the inner wallface.

The *Skelpick long horned cairn* is about 900 m south of the bridge mentioned, and about 300 m east of the road, but the Skelpick burn must be crossed (NC/722567). Alternatively one may walk along the slope from the broch just described. The cairn is 59 m long with horns at both ends. The burial chamber is at the north end and consists of two polygonal chambers with two lintels still in position: again the axis of this is set several degrees away from the long axis of the cairn. The passage leads directly to the centre of the façade. The inner chamber was excavated in about 1867 but no finds were reported.

Loch Hope

If travelling W towards Cape Wrath it is worth making a detour for 16 km down the single-track road along Loch Hope to see *Dun Dornadilla**+ (NC/457451). This broch stands beside the road and the river and is one of the rare ones still standing in part to a considerable height, in this case to 6·7 m over the entrance passage. The rest of the wall is only about 2·4 m high. The broch is 14·5 m in diameter and the wall seems to be 3·5 m thick. The inner half of the high section of double wall has fallen and the outer half is shored up with a modern buttress. A massive triangular lintel is in position over the entrance. The interior is full of debris and the top of a tall, corbelled mural cell is visible at about 2 o'clock. In its size, proportions and surviving height Dun Dornadilla is strikingly similar to Dun Carloway on Lewis (p. 171).

3. CAITHNESS

The flat and fertile plain of Caithness provides a striking contrast with the mountainous moorland of Sutherland. Like Orkney (Chapter 10), the underlying rock is Old Red Sandstone which splits readily into the flat flagstones which provided prehistoric man with such excellent building material. The archaeological sites in the county are numerous and the Neolithic chambered cairns are particularly fine: there are many excavated brochs too but, unlike the cairns, none has yet been laid out for inspection by the Department of the Environment.

The main road north (6) (A9)

At about 7 km north of Helmsdale the new road curves round above the *Ousedale burn* and the *broch*★ of that name (ND/072188). There is a large rubble parking space on the seaward side of the road at this point and the broch is about 600 m below the road, overlooking the valley of the burn. Like many another only its interior has been excavated (in 1891) so it is not obvious from a distance. The main entrance, with many lintels in position, is on the south-west and is equipped with two sets of door-checks. Brochs with double-doors— the most advanced and efficient form of defence in these structures— are almost unknown outside Sutherland and Caithness and this is one of the reasons for believing that the massive, solid-based brochs of this area were among the latest and most sophisticated to be built. There is a guard cell on the right. The mural stair at 9 o'clock and another cell at 7 o'clock are visible but otherwise the wall base appears to be solid. The scarcement ledge is visible, but not near the entrance where there is a buttress of recent masonry. Much of the upper part of the broch in this sector seems to have been reconstructed, presumably in 1891. The internal wallface follows very closely a circle 6·66 m in diameter.

Continuing N to Dunbeath one can take a pleasant walk of a little under 1 km to see the *Dunbeath broch*★ (ND/155305). Next to the north side of the road bridge is a paved footpath running along the Dunbeath water, at the top of which a car can be parked. Continue along this path and cross a flimsy-looking suspension footbridge to the broch, which is in a good defensive position on a knoll between two converging streams and under an isolated clump of trees. This solid-based broch was excavated in about 1870 but no plan or report was published. The wall still stands over 3 m high in places but the entrance area is badly ruined: trees are growing inside and no doubt the number of growth rings in the trunk of the largest would approximately date the clearance of the interior. A long curved guard cell opens from the right side of the entrance, which has two sets of door-checks (above). A corbelled mural cell is at 1 o'clock but there is no sign of the stairway.

About 5 km further north is Latheron where there are several sites of interest. At the whitewashed Latheron Mains Farm, on the east of the road just south of the junction with the A895, there is a fragment of a *Pictish symbol stone** built into the south wall of the farmhouse (ND/198334): the crescent and V-rod symbol can be clearly seen. The permission of the farmer, Mr McGregor, should naturally be sought before inspecting this stone. A very fine symbol stone, complete with ogham inscription, was found some years ago in a farm wall at Latheron and is now in the National Museum in Edinburgh.

Immediately behind the post office at the road junction is a massive, rectangular *standing stone** 3·4 m high from which there is a good view to the south-east across the sea and perhaps, in fine weather, to a horizon marker on Kinnaird's Head in Aberdeenshire (ND/200337). Another small *stone* stands about 100 m to the north.

A detour of 9 km N along the A895 from Latheron to Thurso takes one past Loch Rangag on the left. On its west shore is the *Rangag broch** the mound of an unexcavated structure standing on a short promontory (ND/179416). A minor road turns off south-east 1 km further north and soon passes close to Loch Stemster. Close to the north of the road and just beyond the loch is the remarkable and unique setting of the *Loch Stemster standing stones** (ND/190416). Thirty-six flat, thin stones and snapped-off stumps can be seen arranged in a U-shape with parallel sides and one open end. All the slabs are aligned with their long sides at right angles to the perimeter of the setting. In fine weather the conspicuous Mt. Morven is visible in the south over the near-by ridge and seems to be indicated by some of the stones. It may well be an astronomical foresight.

At *Rangag*, 2 km north of the junction, a massive *standing stone** is close to the road on the east, just north of the house (ND/176449): it is rectangular in section and about 2·9 m high. There is another flat-sided *stone* about 800 m to the east-north-east on top of a ridge which in fine weather may be discovered to be indicating some distant peak in the south-west (ND/184452).

Returning to the main road, 1 km north-east of Latheron there is an old overgrown cart road running straight north-north-west between drystone walls. Follow this for about 1·5 km to its end (one can drive to the first gate) and then strike off to the north-east for about 400 m to see the *Wag of Forse** (ND/205352). Alternatively go up the A895 to Upper Latheron and cut across to the east. This unique site, visible from afar as a spread of grey stones among the grass, was excavated in 1939 and 1946 by Dr A. O. Curle who revealed two main phases of building. The first structure on the site was a massive, circular drystone enclosure with an internal diameter of 14 m and a wall 1·2 m thick. This building was interpreted by the excavator as a cattlefold but is perhaps more likely to have been a defensive structure, a round dun in fact. It has a much thicker wall immediately around the entrance passage, on the north, which recalls the 'blockhouse' forts of Shetland (p. 269 below). Within this entrance section, which still has one lintel in position over the passage, there are the remains of a stair to the wallhead on the left as well as a passage or guard chamber leading off from the right side. The stair presumably gave access to a look-out point as well as allowing defenders to get to the wallhead. On the west side the inside face of the wall is again enlarged to accommodate a mural cell. If the structure is a dun it is unique although the stair in the entrance section has analogies in the Keiss brochs (p. 228 below). There are traces of a turf wall with an outer ditch surrounding the settlement; it may be an outer defence, or stockyard, for the dun.

At a later stage several long, rectangular stone buildings were erected on the site and one of them partly overlies the dun which, one may suppose, was largely demolished for building material at this time. The best preserved of these long-houses is to the south-west of the dun and several members of the double row of internal standing stone pillars can still be seen. These presumably supported the roof. These long-houses are of particular interest (there are similar ones at the broch of Yarrows, p. 227 below) because the great majority of Iron Age dwellings discovered in Britain are round. On the other hand wooden Iron Age long-houses with internal rows of roof-posts are common in northern Europe—in Denmark for example. It is quite possible that at Forse we have a rare fragment of evidence for the arrival in north-east Scotland of prehistoric settlers direct from the continent, an influx of people who may have laid the foundations of the Pictish nation of proto-historic times (p. 31). Certainly the dun appears to be earlier than the Caithness brochs and to have contributed some elements of its architecture to them. The few finds made at Forse include none of the novel items which are associated with the brochs.

There is a green mound, an unexcavated *broch*, 200 m away to the north-east.

Travelling past Lybster one can make a detour of 8 km up the minor road to Watten, which leaves the A9 at West Clyth. This brings one to the *Grey cairns of Camster**+, a remarkable and well-preserved pair of excavated Neolithic burial mounds (ND/260443).

Camster Round is reached first, only 100 m west of the road: the passage and chamber have been repaired and consolidated and can be entered. The cairn is 18 m in diameter and was edged with dry walling. The lintelled entrance passage on the east is 6·1 m long and only 1·1 m high at the outer end; it decreases to 0·76 m at the inner end. The chamber consists of a lintelled, rectangular antechamber 1·1 m high with portal slabs separating it from the passage. Another pair of portal slabs separates it from the main chamber which is a fine, round corbelled structure 3·05 m high and 2·3 m long. The rear part is separated off by projecting slabs. The excavations of 1865 discovered a thick layer of black earth, charcoal and ashes which contained burnt bones, four or five broken pots (now lost) and several flint implements. The remains of several human skeletons were found including two which had been placed in the entrance passage when this was finally filled with stones and blocked.

Plate 41. Camster Long Neolithic cairn, Caithness: view of the forecourt after restoration.

Camster long cairn is 200 m north of the round cairn and is currently being re-excavated, consolidated and restored by Dr J. X. W. P. Corcoran for the Department of the Environment. By the time this book appears it may be accessible to visitors. It is a double-horned long cairn of the well-known type and was first excavated in 1866. Fragments of human bones were found at that time in the south-west chamber but no artefacts. The recent work has re-exposed the massive horned façade at the wide north-eastern end of the cairn, which measures 69·5 m in overall length. The horns in fact consist of flat, stepped projections and the upper steps continue across the façade for a total length of 19·8 m as a wide ledge (Pl. 41). One wonders whether ceremonies took place on this elevated 'stage' at this enormous structure which, like many similar ones, was surely the Neolithic equivalent of a cathedral (p. 25).

Two chambers are visible, one just behind the façade just described and one half-way along the cairn. The former was a tall corbelled cell with an antechamber divided by portal stones from the main compartment; the latter has a rear segment defined by a pair of projecting slabs. Both open on to the long, south-east side of the cairn and both appeared originally to have been inside small, separate round cairns which were later incorporated into the huge double-horned cairn. In the north-eastern chamber a kink in the entrance passage probably marks the junction between the two cairns. This change in architecture, visible at many sites, must surely reflect an important religious change in Neolithic times (p. 25).

Four kilometres further north-east on the A9 one reaches the side road leading to the stone rows known as the *Hill o' many stanes**+ at Mid Clyth, 600 m from the main road (ND/295384: signposted). Though not visually spectacular the site could be an extremely important relic of a prehistoric astronomical observatory if the interpretation put on them by Professor Thom is correct. Along the southern slope of a low hill are 22 rows of at least 200 low slabs arranged in a slightly fan-shaped pattern which is only traceable by careful surveying. The highest stones are less than 1 m and all are packed with smaller stones round their bases.

There is a fallen standing stone 2·7 m long 46 m away from the rows on the near-by ridge to the west and it has been suggested that it was positioned so that from it one could observe the moon rising at its most southerly declination (the lunar 'solstice') behind Durn Hill 80 km away in Banffshire (on a bearing of 159°). It has been shown that fan-shaped rows of stones could theoretically have been used to work out the maximum declination of the moon setting or rising behind a notch: a succession of daily observations of this phenomenon would not—unlike at the equivalent solar sites—necessarily pinpoint the extreme position of the moon because of the relative rapidity with which its real position changes against the background of the horizon and the fixed stars. The stone rows could have been a form of grid against which the successive observations were plotted and the extreme position of the moon discovered by extrapolation.

Further north at *Bruan* there is a huge mound, the debris of an unexcavated *broch*★ surrounded by a ditch and wall (ND/310394). A farmroad turns north 1·5 km further north at the post office at Ulbster and leads to Loch Watenan. The excavated horned chambered cairn of *Garrywhin*+ (or Cairn of Get) is on moorland 500 m west of the loch (ND/313411). The cairn, including the horns at both ends, is only 24 m long and the passage to the burial chamber leads in from the south end. The chamber consists of a rectangular outer compartment and a round main one, separated by large stone slabs. The tomb seems originally to have been in a small round cairn and the horned structure to have been added later. Some Neolithic leaf-shaped arrowheads and many potsherds were found when the chamber was cleared in 1866.

There is a track leading west to an abandoned farm 3 km further north and from there one can climb 600 m due west to the *Yarrows standing stones*★ on top of the ridge (ND/316432: there are some wire fences to cross). Both stones are flat-sided slabs and from them there are views of distant hills which might include astronomical foresights indicated by the orientation of the stones. The tallest stone is to the north and stands 2·5 m high.

If one takes the by-road NW to Thrumster 1·5 km further north, the farmroad on the left of that, 600 m from the main road, will eventually lead to the South Yarrows farm beside the loch and to the *broch of Yarrows*★ (ND/308435). It was excavated in 1866–7 by Dr J. Anderson and stands, surrounded by a waterlogged ditch, on a blunt promontory below the farm. This broch is probably an early form (p. 251): a stretch of lintelled ground-level gallery, un-noted by the excavator, is in the north-eastern arc and most of the rest of the wall contains galleries or long cells at ground-level. The mural stair is preserved and the door at its foot is probably a secondary one, pushed through the wall when the settlement outside was being built. The primary door seems to be that on the east. A secondary wall was added to the interior at some stage, the usual sign of the conversion of a broch into a dwelling and the destruction of its high wall. The outbuildings are interesting in that they appear to include the same long, pillared stone houses that are so well seen at Forse (p. 223 above).

At 300 m just south-west of the farm are the two massive excavated *Neolithic long cairns*, 300 m apart, of *South Yarrows* (ND/304431). Both are double-horned cairns, the southern one being the larger and 73 m long: parts of the facing wall, or peristalith, of the latter are visible. Both cairns have compartmented chambers at their east ends and both were excavated in 1865. No doubt these cairns too have been enlarged from small primary round ones but no evidence of this has been looked for. The south cairn has a second chamber half-way along it.

A minor road turns east 1 km before the outskirts of Wick and leads to the *Castle of Old Wick**+ (signposted: ND/369489). The structure, a single rectangular stone tower, stands at the landward end of a narrow cliff promontory about 100 m long of the type used for defence works in Caithness over many centuries. There are traces of stone buildings on the promontory behind the tower which measures about 9·5 m by 7 m overall with walls 2·1 m thick. The main door was probably on the first of the three floors, in the north-east wall, and was reached by an external wooden stair: there are no openings at ground-level. There was no internal vaulted ceiling: the beam holes for an intermediate floor and scarcements for two upper floors can be seen in the interior wallfaces. The tower is one of the oldest stone castles on the Scottish mainland and probably dates to the 12th century.

Just north of the town, behind the churchyard, is the *Keiss West broch**, excavated late in the 19th century (ND/349615). The interior of this solid-based broch is almost an exact circle 11·67 m (14 my) in diameter and, as at Yarrows (p. 227), there are two entrances. The east door seems to have been pushed through the wall after the broch was converted to a dwelling and the north-west entrance to have been the primary one. This last has a feature very rare in brochs, a stair running from up the west side of the passage which recalls the design of the dun at Forse. It is probable that Keiss West shows how an imported fort plan was modified by the pre-existing local traditions seen at Forse (p. 223 above).

Along the road from Wick to John o'Groats much of the coast is a vertical cliff with many inlets and there are excavated brochs on several of the resulting sheer-sided promontories. *Nybster**, 2·5 km north of Keiss, is well preserved although it is nothing now but a featureless ring of thick walling with an entrance passage (ND/370632). It can be identified by the ornate, tower-like structure which was built at the time of the excavation in 1898. Like other Caithness brochs Nybster is very accurately designed and built: the interior wallface is close to an exact circle 6·4 m in diameter (8 my). In its small size and extremely thick wall base (4.7 m) the proportions of this broch are very close to those of Mousa in Shetland (p. 272). A massive and thick drystone promontory wall protects the broch and could well be an earlier promontory fort.

*Skirza Head broch** is reached by the by-road turning east just north of Freswick: the site is 200 m south-east of the end of this road (ND/394684). This again is a small, thick-walled, solid-based broch built precisely round a circle 6·62 m in diameter, or almost exactly 8 my. There is a secondary wall of uneven thickness inside the broch.

West of Thurso (A836)

Travelling W towards Sutherland along the A836 from Thurso one can see several interesting sites. At 7 km west of the town there is a side road to Crosskirk and, after a walk, *St. Mary's chapel**+ (ND/025701: signposted). This simple, rectangular roofless chapel, not far from the cliff edge, probably dates from the 12th century and is the oldest ecclesiastical building in Caithness. It consists of a nave 5·4 m long inside with a later chancel, on old foundations, at the east end. The doorway is Irish in style with slightly converging jambs, like those of the round towers (pp. 183 and 191). The site was possibly a religious one at an earlier date: a Pictish symbol stone is said to have been found in the near-by broch (now demolished) on the edge of the cliff and evidence of occupation as late as the 8th century was found during the recent excavation of the latter in 1966, 1969 and 1970 by Dr H. Fairhurst.

Almost immediately the main road crosses the Forss water and 3·5 km further west a minor road leads south through Achreamie to Shebster. At 1·5 km south of the Achreamie road junction, at the end of the wood, a track leads west towards the *Cnoc Freiceadain chambered cairn*+ which is about 300 m from the road (ND/013654). There are, in fact, two long cairns here, at right angles to one another and only 120 m apart. Cnoc Freiceadain is 67 m long with the horns at the narrower, north-east end. The wider south-west end looks like a round cairn: if there were any horns here they cannot now be seen. There are signs of slabs in the body of the cairn which may be the remains of chambers. The other cairn, *Na Tri Shean*, is further to the south and on the crest of the hill with a splendid view over Caithness and Orkney. This huge double-horned cairn, 71 m long, appears to be undisturbed. Two large slabs at the south-east end may be the tipped-up lintels of a chamber.

Continue on to Shebster and turn west back to the main road. Half a kilometre before the junction is *Achvarasdal House*, a Church of Scotland Eventide Home, at the end of a long driveway with a *broch*★ in the wood immediately in front of it (ND/983647). This solid-based broch was cleared out some time ago but no records survive of the operation. The entrance, with door-checks, is on the east-south-east and there are signs of a blocked-up door to a guard cell behind the right check. An interior door, probably to the mural stair, is at 3 o'clock. The interior wallface follows very closely a circle 10·072 m (almost exactly 12 my) in diameter. There are traces of outbuildings which have not been excavated.

One kilometre further west is the village of *Reay* and in the churchyard on the north side of the road is a reconstructed fragment of the old church. Set into the west wall of this is a Class III *cross slab* (lacking Pictish symbols) of grey sandstone 1·9 m high. The upper half has sculptured in relief a cross with square-ended arms carved with interlace ornament—key pattern on the arms and circular knotwork on the shaft. It stands on a massive base which occupies the whole width of the stone and is also carved with key-pattern interlace. The slab was used as an 18th-century gravestone for one Robert McKay whose name is carved on the top arm of the cross. Presumably the stone was set up in the latter part of the 9th century, after the Pictish kingdom had ceased to be.

(Route continued on p. 219 above)

8 · The Orkney Isles

The Orkney Isles are an archaeologist's paradise. A great variety of ancient stone structures have been consolidated and put on display by the Department of the Environment and the architecture of the buildings themselves is often spectacular owing to the nature of the local stone which was available as building material. The Old Red Sandstone of Orkney and Caithness splits into large, flat flags which are ideal for drystone masonry. The islands are particularly rich in Neolithic chambered tombs and in Early Christian and Medieval church sites. They are low lying and fertile and their modern environment is peaceful and civilised.

Car-ferries run to Orkney mainland from Scrabster, near Thurso, and from Aberdeen. It is advisable to write in advance to the Tourist Information Office in Kirkwall, and ask for a list of the sailing schedules of the local inter-island ferries. In this way one can plan in advance how to visit the outlying islands within one's allotted time; some of the most important monuments are on the smaller islands. Alternatively Loganair run short flights from Kirkwall to the larger islands. It is useful to carry a torch when exploring the Neolithic cairns and earth-houses and to be dressed in clothes the staining of which will not be regretted.

Hoy island

Inquire at Stromness for a boat to Hoy on which is the *Dwarfie stane*[+], an apparently prehistoric rock-cut tomb unique in northern Europe (HY/244005). A walk of about 4·5 km from the pier at Linksness is required, first S along the B9049 and B9047 and then taking the right fork along the minor road for 2 km. The chamber is in a huge, fallen rectangular block of sandstone about 500 m south-east of the road and surrounded by barren moors. In the vertical west face of the stone is a rectangular opening 0·7 m high, and slightly greater in width and a passage of similar dimensions leads back into the rock for 2–3 m. A shaped block of stone lying on the ground in front once closed the opening. Inside the rock the plan of the tomb is roughly T-shaped with a cell excavated on either side of the central passage. The roof of the one on the north (left) is now broken and the cell seems to be unfinished, being smaller and more unevenly cut than the other one. The cell on the right has a curious 'pillow' or ledge of un-cut rock at its inner end. Both cells are separated from the passage by kerbs of uncut rock 30 cm high and their floors are 18 cm higher than that of the passage.

It has been argued that this rock-cut opening is a tomb of Neo-lithic age: its features closely resemble in rock those built into the Maes Howe passage grave (p. 235). Even if this is true, the question of whether the Dwarfie stane also illustrates the translation of the idea of the rock-cut tomb from the Mediterranean to the Orkneys, as has also been claimed, is not so clear.

Mainland: Stromness to Kirkwall

Travelling from the car-ferry at Stromness to Kirkwall on the A965 one passes close to several important sites. The first is the *Unstan chambered cairn*[+], which stands on a low promontory on the south side of the Loch of Stenness (HY/283117). It is reached by a farmroad which turns north from the main road just east of the junction with the A964. This is a well-known example of the Neo-lithic stalled cairns, which are confined to Orkney and Caithness and which provide an excellent illustration of how variations on a well-known structural tradition arise because of the availability of unusually good building material. Enormous stone flags were set at right angles into the walls of the long central burial chamber to form a series of pairs of opposing stalls. The round cairn itself is slightly oval, measuring from 13·7 m to 13·1 m in diameter, and was evi-dently built in at least two concentric rings of stonework, each edged with an upright face of masonry.

A narrow passage about 4·3 m long enters the cairn from the north-east and meets the side wall of the main chamber at right angles: the chamber itself is 6·6 m in length and slightly boat-shaped so that its greatest width is 1·9 m at the centre: it is divided into five facing pairs of compartments by the projecting upright stone slabs already mentioned and its walls are some 1·8 m high. Presumably the chamber was once roofed with flat flags: the alternative, a long dry-stone barrel-vault, seems a high technical achievement for Neolithic engineers but it may have been possible. The two end pairs of compartments are kerbed and may have been two-storeyed, and a side chamber opens from the centre of the west wall.

The finds made in this cairn in 1884 are unusual and of some interest. Both burnt and unburnt human bones were found in the floor deposit as well as many flint arrowheads and other tools together with sherds of an unusual pottery style. The vessels were broad, shallow bowls often with vertical walls and with close-hatched incised decoration. Fragments of at least 22 vessels were identified, and later some of the sherds proved to have on them the impressions of grains of barley similar to that still grown on Orkney. Unstan may be regarded as a locally evolved type of passage grave in which the central chamber has been elongated laterally. A date in the 4th or early 3rd millennium B.C. seems very probable.

Further along the main road the B9055 turns north along the narrow isthmus and bridge between the Lochs of Stenness and Harray. Along this road are three famous groups of standing stones.

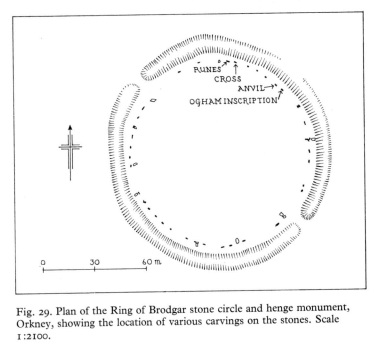

Fig. 29. Plan of the Ring of Brodgar stone circle and henge monument, Orkney, showing the location of various carvings on the stones. Scale 1:2100.

Plate 42. Ring of Brodgar stone circle, Orkney.

The *stones of Stenness**+ are reached first; they lie on the east side of the road 0·5 km from the main road (HY/306125). The site was originally a henge monument but the surrounding bank and ditch are now hardly traceable. Within these are four great monoliths, the tallest of which is 5·3 m high. The table-like structure in the centre of the site is an entirely fanciful modern construction, dating from 1906. What may be an outlier from this site, which must surely be a ruined circle, is visible just to the south end of the bridge of Brodgar. This is a single huge monolith 5·6 m high and is known locally as the Watch stone.

Just over 1 km further north-west is the *Ring of Brodgar**+ (Pl. 42; Fig. 29), another henge monument containing one of the most complete, largest and most spectacular stone circles in Scotland (HY/294134). The ditch and bank of the henge structure are well preserved, the former being about 9·2 m in breadth and with an average depth of about 1·8 m. There are two causeways across the ditch, on the north-west and south-east, leading to two entrances through the bank which encloses an area some 113 m in diameter. Brodgar is thus a Class II henge.

There are now 27 stones standing around the circle and stumps of at least 13 more can be identified: if they were all as equally spaced as the surviving ones an original total of 60 would be indicated. Thom has recently surveyed the site and found that an exact circle 125 my in diameter runs neatly through the stones, which are set with their flat faces along the circumference. He also believes that the west cliff of Hoy, visible in the south-west, was a lunar foresight to be used from the circle.

Counting the stones clockwise from the north-west entrance, numbers 3, 4, 8 and 9 are of interest in that they have carvings on them. Number 3 has a runic inscription on it (undeciphered), number 4 has a cross, number 8 an anvil carved on one face and number 9 an ogham inscription.

Just over 1 km further east along the main road from the junction mentioned earlier is the famous passage grave *Maes Howe*[*][+] clearly visible as a green, bowl-shaped mound 200 m north of the road (HY/318128). Nothing quite like this monument is known anywhere else. The mound is some 4·6 m high and 35 m in diameter and it is surrounded by a broad ditch which lies from 15 m to 21 m from its base. The ditch itself has a greatest depth of 1·8 m and averages 13·7 m in width.

The entrance into the mound is on the south-west and consists of a lintelled megalithic and drystone passage 11 m long, slightly restored at the outer end but otherwise original. There are checks for a door— a unique feature—at 2 m from the outside. For the last 5·6 m both walls and roof of the passage are composed of three huge single blocks of stone of that length, 1·32 m wide and 18 cm thick. The tall central chamber (Pl. 43) is 4·6 m square and built so that each corner is a projecting square pier or buttress the purpose of which was to help support the corbelled roof. Each pier is faced with a massive upright slab. The original walling stands 3·8 m high before giving way to the modern roof which covers the hole made by the excavations of 1861 and the plundering of earlier times (below).

Three side chambers lead off the central space, each 1·07 m high and reached by a small raised rectangular opening which has been closed by a block of stone; the three blocks now lie on the floor in front of the openings. The structure is thus what is termed a cruciform passage grave, and may be assumed to have been the burial vault or mausoleum of some powerful Neolithic Orkney family.

The standard of workmanship in Maes Howe is extremely high. The largest of the many orthostats used weighs 4 tons and often the

Plate 43. Maes Howe passage grave, Orkney: the interior of the chamber.

joints are so well made that a knife blade can hardly be inserted into the cracks. The great slabs are accurately levelled and plumbed and signs of dressing are apparent on many of them. Structures like Maes Howe—remote geographically from the rest of Europe but yet exhibiting skill and enterprise of an extremely high order—are at the focus of the current discussions about the effect of foreign influence on the megalithic structures of Neolithic Britain and Europe. Is Maes Howe likely to have been a local invention—a form of Neolithic tomb perfected in Orkney after generations of practice—or did the skill and motivation which lies behind its construction come from the outside? Again, was it just a tomb or also a temple? (p. 24.)

In the 12th century the passage grave was broken into several times by Norwegian crusaders who left runic inscriptions recording their exploits on several stones in the chamber. For example, about 1 m from the floor on the east edge of the slab forming the south face of the north-west buttress is an inscription (continued on the west face of the north-east buttress about 0·3 m from the floor) which has been translated as: 'It is true what I say, that treasure was carried off in the course of three nights. Treasure was carried off before the crusaders broke into the howe.'

Again, on the lowest stones immediately west of the south side chamber is another: 'This howe was built a long time before Lothbók's. His sons were bold; scarcely ever were there such tall men of their hands. Crusaders broke into Maes Howe. Hlíf, the Earl's maidservant, carved. Away to the north-west is a great treasure hidden. A long time ago was a great treasure hidden here. Lucky will be he who can find the great fortune. Hákon single-handed bore treasure from this howe.'

There is also a carved figure of a dragon on the face of the north-east buttress. This has been dated to the 12th century on the basis of comparisons with similar carvings in Norway.

The *chambered cairn* on *Cuween Hill**+ can be visited next, standing as it does overlooking the Bay of Firth south of Finstown. Take the minor road to Kirkwall which forks south from the A965 at 0·5 km east of Finstown and the route to the cairn is signposted (HY/364128). Cuween Hill is another round cairn, some 16·8 m in diameter, with a rectangular central chamber off which four side chambers open. The entrance passage is 5·3 m in length but only 0·71 m wide and 0·81 m high, being thus suitable for negotiation only by active people. The four side chambers are corbelled, as at Maes Howe, and the one on the west has an annexe opening off its north end. The cairn was broken into in 1901 and some fragmentary human remains were found; it had probably been looted at some earlier time.

A short distance further east along the main Kirkwall road turn north to *Rennibster earth house*⋆⁺ (HY/397127). This souterrain is in the farmyard and is reached by a trap-door over the main chamber. The structure consists of a low, lintelled, narrow sloping entrance passage 3·5 m long which was reached by a vertical shaft without steps. The main chamber, which originally of course was reached only by way of this passage, is approximately hexagonal in plan, some 3·3 m long with a maximum width of 2·6 m. The walls of the pit are partly lined with dry walling and partly with slabs on edge and the roof consists of overlapping flat slabs supported by four up-right monolithic pillars. There are five shelves, or aumbries, in the corners of the wall. No datable finds were made in the earth house but the passage was found to be full of a deposit of black earth mixed with huge quantities of shells. The chamber contained none of this but there were human bones and skulls on the floor, four of the latter having been placed side by side against the base of one of the pillars.

Evidently this souterrain had been used as a burial chamber at the end of its period of use and the passage then served as a midden pit. Such structures are assumed to have been refuges originally and to date from the latter part of the Iron Age—probably in the 2nd–4th centuries A.D.—but such a date for the Orkney ones depends on evidence from elsewhere (p. 185).

The fourth of the chambered cairns on the Kirkwall road is on the north-west slope of *Wideford Hill*⋆⁺ and is reached from either the major or minor road to Kirkwall (signposted: HY/409122). Again the cairn is round and built in three concentric rings of stonework, the outer face of each being a vertical built wall. The overall diameter is 12·8 m. Presumably these built features, like those in other cairns, were intended to be seen from the outside and were not turfed over; it may therefore be assumed that Neolithic Orkney was dotted with neatly shaped, dome-shaped stone buildings rather than featureless green mounds. The central chamber is reached by a passage from the west 5·34 m long, only 0·6 m high and slightly less in width. The contrast between this and the tall corbelled chamber, 3·1 m long and rising to 2·51 m at its capstone, is very striking. There are three side chambers with low doors at floor-level.

The cairn had evidently been ransacked before it was entered in 1849 and no human remains were found.

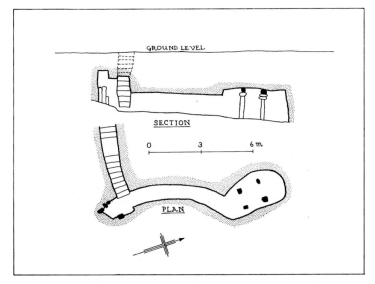

GROUND LEVEL

SECTION

0   3   6 m

PLAN

Fig. 30. Plan and elevation of the Grainbank souterrain, Orkney, showing the steps at the left end and the pillared, flag-roofed chamber at the right. Scale 1:210.

The second *earth house* on display is *Grainbank*⋆+, just west of Kirkwall (HY/442117), and is not a visit for those with claustrophobic tendencies (Fig. 30). The site is now surrounded by buildings and is reached by following the side road which leads north along the shore from the main road at 300 m west of the town, and turning W again after 200 m. The souterrain consists of a chamber dug out of the ground, lined with drystone walling and roofed with flat lintels supported by four orthostatic pillars. The chamber is about 3·7 m long by 1·9 m wide with a maximum height of 1·68 m. No relics of any kind were found within the structure in 1857 when it was opened up and explored, although a large quantity of bones, shells and ashes were found on top of it.

The chamber is entered only by a sloping, curved passage 7·9 m long, 0·76 m wide and only 0·9 m high. A trench has been cut in the passage floor to make it easier to crawl down. A flight of steps, of which the top part has been restored, leads down to this passage.

No doubt it was to souterrains such as this one that the *Historia Norvegiae* of about A.D. 1200 referred when it described the Orkney

Picts as doing wonders in the morning and evening, building towns (brochs?), but losing their strength completely at midday and hiding through fear in little underground houses.

Kirkwall itself has one of the finest and most complete Medieval buildings in Scotland in *St. Magnus's Cathedral**⁺ in Broad Street (Fig. 31) (HY/449109). It was founded by Earl Rognvald in 1137 and dedicated to his kinsman St. Magnus who had been murdered on Egilsay twenty years earlier (p. 256). Although it is the largest and most ambitious structure built during the Norse occupation of the Orkneys its design and construction are—like those of Dunfermline (p. 120)—held to be the responsibility of masons of the Durham School, who were brought in for the purpose.

The original design was for a cruciform Romanesque church with an aisled nave having eight bays, two transepts each with an apsidiole on the east, and a choir of three bays with a central apse at the east end. Originally, too, there was to have been a cloister against the south wall of the nave but only the lowest courses of this were laid. The choir and transepts were completed in the round-arched Romanesque style by about 1150 but there was then a pause in

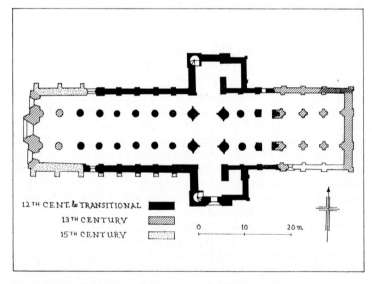

12ᵀᴴ CENT. & TRANSITIONAL

13ᵀᴴ CENTURY

15ᵀᴴ CENTURY

0   10   20 m

Fig. 31. Plan of St. Magnus's Cathedral, Kirkwall, Orkney, showing the Romanesque, Gothic and later architecture. Scale 1:785.

building activity for some reason so that when work started again it was in the Transitional style. The original apsidioles on the transepts were replaced by chapels in the new style and the crossing was reconstructed: its four pillars are thus Transitional in date while the adjacent ones on either side are Romanesque. The nave as far west as the sixth bay is mid and late 12th century and the rest is 13th-century Gothic. Originally the nave was to have had a light roof of wood and slate but in fact a stone vault was constructed over it when the time came in the 13th century. The pointed arches of this are unusual in springing from the sill level of the clerestorey. The second pillar from the west in the north arcade is leaning because of the unforeseen stress of the stone roof. The choir was extended east also in the 13th century, the pair of long piers between the third and fourth bays marking the point where the original apse had been. The original choir had a wooden roof so high Gothic vaults were built over the Romanesque bays.

The crossing tower was completed in the 14th century and in the 15th century the west end of the nave was completed. Earlier there had been a temporary gable at the east end of the sixth bay. No significant damage was suffered by the cathedral during the Reformation but it fell somewhat into decay through neglect. In 1903 a thorough restoration was carried out.

On the outside wall of the north side of the nave the junction between Romanesque and Transitional styles is clearly seen between the round-arched aisle windows of the first three bays and the pointed-arched windows of the nave higher up. The contrast between the two styles can be seen on other parts of the exterior and give an indication of the height that the different parts of the building reached in the first phase of construction. The north doorway of the nave is particularly fine, dating from 1190-1200: the innermost of the three orders of the arch is modern. The three bays east of the transepts are the oldest parts of the cathedral and the exterior of the north and south sides of the choir again show the junction of Romanesque and Gothic work.

The interior of the cathedral has an austere and impressive appearance, partly because of the mellow colour of the stone. It is well to note, however, that in Medieval times the stone surfaces were covered with painted decoration in various colours. The contrast between the round arches and simple drum pillars of the Romanesque and Transitional periods—built in block-faced ashlar masonry—and the elaborate 13th-century Gothic piers in the choir with pointed arches and built with carved stone facings—is again very striking.

Two wall burials were found early in the 19th century, one in the broad pier in the north arcade of the choir and one in the corresponding south pier; they were 2·6 m and 2·8 m above the floor respectively. The bones were examined and those in the south pillar were deduced to be the remains of St. Magnus and those in the north of St. Rognvald.

Deerness peninsula

There is an *Early Christian monastic site* at *Deerness*+ at the east tip of Orkney mainland (HY/596088). Take the A960 SE of Kirkwall (the airport road) and on to the Deerness peninsula. The B9050 leads to Skaill from where a minor road leads 3 km north along the shore to the site. The buildings stand on a cliff promontory up to 30 m high, known as the Brough of Deerness, with only a narrow, steep track connecting it with the land. Traces of the stone-faced rampart which defended the site are apparent: near the west end there is a 2 m stretch which still stands 0·76 m high. The area enclosed by this rampart and the cliff measures some 129 m north–south by 73 m on average from east–west.

Nineteen rectangular buildings can be seen under the turf grouped around a stone chapel near the centre. The chapel has walls 1·2 m thick which enclose an area 5·2 m by 3 m and they have been pointed with lime mortar. A series of circular hut foundations on the south-east part of the site may be older than the monastic settlement.

It is possible that the Brough of Deerness is one of the foundations established by the 7th- and 8th-century missions from the Irish Church to Orkney. There is a famous passage in the *Historia Norvegiae* which describes the Orkneys as being originally inhabited by 'Peti et Papae', i.e. Picts and monks (Irish-Scottish priests); it is further explained that the latter were so called because they wore white robes. This then was the impression of the Orkney people received by the first Scandinavian visitors in the 8th century and doubtless there were white-robed 'Papae' at Deerness until they were driven out or destroyed by the Scandinavians.

Burray and South Ronaldsay islands

Taking the A961 S of Kirkwall to St. Mary's one crosses, by way of two small islands, to the island of Burray on the Churchill barriers—ramparts of concrete blocks erected during the Second World War. The rusting remains of the Kaiser's ironclads of the First World War can still be seen half submerged close by. The *east broch of Burray*★ is still an impressive ruin, even though it has been excavated and almost filled up again through further dilapidation (HY/490988). Turn E off the main road to Northfield farm 0·5 km after reaching Burray. The broch is on the shore 300 m north-east of the farm buildings—a great green, cratered mound which seems to stand on an artificial platform. Few structural details are now to be seen though the wall still stands high under the rubble.

There is another broch on South Ronaldsay, the *Howe of Hoxa*★ (HY/425939). Take the main road to St. Margaret's Hope and then the B9043 to its end; there turn sharp right (N) and right again and follow the green track down to the shore. The broch is on a low knoll near by. It is of some historical interest in that it was one of the first brochs to be excavated in modern times (in 1848). However it was then 'conserved' with lime mortar and various strange additions— such as a flagpole and platform, and a doorway—were added which tend to obscure the original appearance. The base of the inside wall face is original however and is an exact circle in plan, 9·96 m (11 my) in diameter. The outer wallface is not exposed anywhere.

The north mainland

There are three major archaeological sites and one minor one on the west and north coasts of the mainland of Orkney which can be visited by following the coast road right round. Starting from Stromness and going N it is worth visiting the *broch of Borwick*★ for the spectacular cliff scenery on that part of the coast (HY/224167).

Continuing N up the B9056 to the Bay of Skaill one reaches *Skara Brae*★⁺ situated among the sandhills close to the shore (HY/231188) (Pl. 44; Fig. 32). This is one of the most famous prehistoric settlements in Europe both because of its remarkable state of preservation and because many of the interior furnishings of the huts, made of perishable wood elsewhere, were here constructed of durable stone flags. The village has been overwhelmed by a natural catastrophe, probably in the shape of a storm which set the sand dunes moving to bury the huts. That this catastrophe was a sudden event is shown by evidence of the hasty abandonment of the village by its occupants. One woman, in fleeing from Hut 7, broke her necklace of animal teeth the beads of which were found scattered along the passageway. Thus the settlement was not sacked by a hostile raid but remained intact for three thousand years under the sand until exposed by the spade of the modern excavator.

Plate 44. Skara Brae, Orkney: the interior of Hut no. 1.

The village consists of a cluster of drystone, above ground, huts linked by many covered passageways; the outer faces of the hut walls were plastered thickly with clay where they were exposed. However the settlement was gradually submerged under its own midden and eventually became almost subterranean. The individual huts of the latest village are six in number, with two more smaller chambers. These dwellings are roughly rectangular in plan with rounded corners, varying in size from 6·1 m by 6·4 m to 3·97 m by 4·3 m. The walls still stand up to 2·4 m in height and tend to corbel inwards at the corners. There is no evidence that the chambers were covered with beehive stone domes, however, and roofs of turf or skins, resting on rafters of wood or whalebone, are more likely.

Hut 7, on the south side, is probably the best preserved and a description of it will give an idea of the settlement as a whole (Fig. 32). It is now covered with a glass roof. The doorway leads into it from a passage on the north and this entrance is paved with flat stones and equipped with a bar-hole in the wall. This hole held a wooden beam which kept the door shut but, oddly, the bar was controlled from an external cell, not from inside the hut: it is as if Hut 7 was a place of confinement. There is a square hearth in the centre of the floor with a cubical stone seat next to it. On the right of the door is an enclosed working dais on which were found in 1928 a large whalebone basin, a stone mortar and two cooking pots filled with animal bones. A tiny whalebone dish containing red pigment was set in the floor in the left front corner and two stone mortars were in the left rear corner. Two rectangular stone beds, edged with upright slabs, are on opposite sides of the hearth: they probably contained skins and mattresses of heather. The top edge of the front slab of the right bed has a series of deeply cut notches in it, possibly decorative or perhaps a tally of some kind. Against the rear wall is the remarkable stone 'dresser', similar to another in Hut 1. It consists of two shelves made of flat flagstones separated by three short pillars and standing on three longer ones.

There is a small beehive cell in the wall in the right rear corner: on examination it was found to contain a small hoard of beads and a broken pot. (In Hut 5 a comparable mural cell has a drain leading

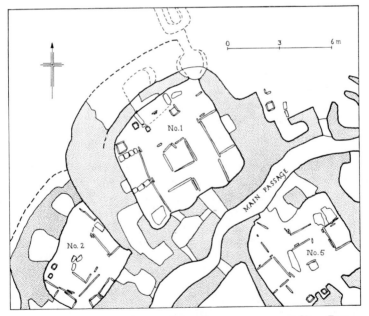

Fig. 32. Plan of Hut 1 and parts of the adjacent structures at Skara Brae, Orkney, showing the various slab-built structures inside the rooms. Scale 1:210.

away from it under the wall and it doubtless served as a latrine.) In the floor is a sunk tank which probably held sea water to keep shell-fish fresh. The long stone beside the hearth is a roof pillar which fell before the sand blew in in the final disaster: it broke a pot in its fall. Under the right bed is a stone slab level with the floor which projects under the wall. Below this slab were found the skeletons of two old women interred on their sides in the crouched position. No doubt they were put there for ritual reasons when the hut was built.

The economy of the villagers of Skara Brae seems to have depended entirely on cattle breeding and sea-food. No clear traces of agriculture were found in the excavations of 1927–30 but vast quantities of bones of cattle and sheep were recovered. The bones of young cattle were most common, suggesting that autumn slaughtering was practised: this custom was due to the difficulty of feeding the whole herd over the winter. No evidence of fishing was found. Tools were of stone and chert, clothes doubtless of skins and ornamentation may have included body painting (the red pigment) and necklaces of bone beads. The pottery used at the site is known as grooved ware and is found in Late Neolithic contexts in southern and eastern England. A similar village was found at Rinyo on Rousay island in 1937, with the same pottery, and it also yielded some sherds of beaker pottery. So Skara Brae was probably inhabited in the Late Neolithic period and at the beginning of the Bronze Age, at the same time in fact that the great stone circles and standing stones were being erected and used.

Nine kilometres north of Skara Brae is an important site of the Early Christian and Norse periods—the tidal islet of the *Brough of Birsay*[+] (NY/239285). Follow the A966 W to its end at the shore and from there a minor road and a track leads N along the shore to the site. On the promontory the main buildings (Fig. 33) are a church (known locally as Peter Kirk), built in about the middle of the 11th century during the Norse period, and several rooms thought to be a Bishop's Palace which date to the early 12th century. That there was an earlier Celtic monastery on the same site is shown by the dis-covery of the ruins of a small church under the Norse 'church' and of an earlier burial ground under the Norse one. Parts of a surround-ing precinct wall, typical of Celtic monasteries, have also been traced. The cemetery has yielded a broken Pictish stone, a copy of which is on the site (the original is in the National Museum in Edinburgh), an early cross and a piece of an ogham inscription. These finds show that the site was already occupied in the 7th or

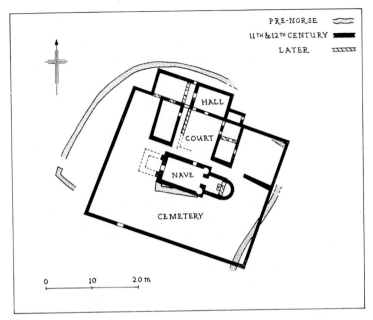

PRE-NORSE

11TH & 12TH CENTURY

LATER

HALL

COURT

NAVE

CEMETERY

0   10   20 m

Fig. 33. Plan of the ecclesiastical buildings at Brough of Birsay, Orkney, showing the location of the Pictish structures, the 11th-century church and the 12th-century Bishop's Palace. Scale 1:785.

early 8th century. Lastly a settlement of Norse homes was found about 60 m away from the chapel to the east and these lay on top of the ruins of the great hall of a Norse earl.

The Norse church—a cathedral as it is sometimes called—consists of a rectangular nave and a chancel or choir with a semicircular apse at the east end (see Dunfermline, p. 120). There are foundations for a tower at the west end but this does not seem to have been built. The nave measures internally 8·8 m by 4·9 m and the building is constructed of flagstones set in lime mortar and plastered inside and out. The chancel arch is a later addition as are the two altar recesses in the east corners of the nave and the screen wall separating off the chancel apse. One of the rune-inscribed stones was built into the outer wall of the chancel, behind the large aumbry in the north wall.

Two graves were found in the centre of the nave and one may have originally been that of St. Magnus himself before his remains were taken to his cathedral in Kirkwall about twenty years after his death.

The second grave could be of Earl Thorfinn the Mighty, who is described in the *Orkneyinga Saga* as having settled down on Birsay (after a life of raiding and travelling) to govern the islands and to have built a fine church there. This would have been some time after 1050.

The later buildings north of the church were at first thought to be the domestic buildings of a monastery and to be partly contemporary with the church, both being then assigned to the mid 12th century. Dr C. A. R. Radford, however, put forward the identification of the church as that built by the 11th-century Earl Thorfinn, described above, and of the other buildings as the palace built for Bishop William who is supposed to have held the See of Orkney (which included Shetland) for sixty years. He died in 1168 and was the first bishop to live in the islands. The buildings north of the church on Birsay are thus likely to have been built as his palace early in the 12th century: they are set over the old boundary wall surrounding the church. The door in the north wall of the nave was cut at this time to give direct access to the palace.

The palace is laid out with four large rooms or halls around three sides of a square, the church being on the fourth side. More buildings, only partly explored, lie to the north. The west room probably contained the bishop's private apartments on the vanished first floor, including his camera or audience chamber. The main hall was on the north side, divided in two by a passageway. The west half of this may have been the ante-chamber where people waited before seeing the bishop. Originally there was a doorway from it to the west range and another out to the courtyard beyond it but these are now blocked up.

The cemetery lies around the church, within its rectangular boundary wall. On the south and east of the church are the later Norse graves but lower down is an earlier series of Pictish graves marked by slabs set on edge. Many of these are now exposed and they are found all round the church including the west side. The famous broken Pictish gravestone, decorated with three men holding shields and spears, was found near a triple grave on the south side. Traces of the curved boundary wall of this Pictish cemetery of the Celtic Church have been found under the later wall (Fig. 33).

East of the church site is a large complex of Norse homes which have been partly explored and there are several isolated similar dwellings on the slope above the church. In the former group the latest dwellings are a number of small rectangular rooms with stone and turf walls and paved floors; it seems likely that these are contemporary with the Bishop's Palace and were the homes of his staff. Under these dwellings is a rectangular hall the masonry of which is superior to that of the buildings just described. It is not yet completely uncovered but seems to consist of a number of long rooms running east–west including one with a raised dais. Objects of the 11th century were found in this building which seems almost certain to have been the residence of Earl Thorfinn the Mighty himself. Remains of a bath house have been found near the cliff edge and there is an earlier large dwelling, belonging no doubt to previous earls.

Travelling E again for 13 km from Birsay take the N by-road at Georth (shortly after the junction with the B9057) to see the *Gurness broch**+* on Aiker Ness (HY/383268). A walk of about 1 km is needed to reach the site. This is one of the two Orkney brochs under Guardianship and it is protected by impressive outer defence works. Gurness is a ground-galleried broch but the basal gallery has been blocked up in ancient times and only partly re-opened (see Midhowe broch, p. 251, for comments on this feature). The site was extensively excavated during the 1930s but no detailed report was published. The floor inside the broch is the secondary one, the original floor being lower down. The interior is filled with secondary structures built with huge flags of sandstone; presumably these belong to the same period as the mass of secondary dwellings which surround the broch. The broch has the usual features—a narrow entrance passage with checks for a door, two guard cells (which connect with the mural gallery) and a stairway in the wall at about 9 o'clock which begins at the level of the first-floor gallery. Hence a removable wooden ladder would have been needed to reach it from the central court, an extra defensive feature. The remains of an upper gallery are visible on the wallhead and a ledge or scarcement runs round the inside wallface at a height of about 3·8 m above the primary floor. This feature is usually supposed to have supported a wooden upper floor (p. 160).

The outer defences apparently consisted originally of a formidable series of three, stone-lined, rock-cut ditches in front of a wall. Half of these defences have been destroyed by the sea but enough remains to show that a massive causeway crossed the ditches in line with the broch entrance. At a later date the outer wall was modified and built with projecting bastions, a feature without parallel elsewhere in Iron Age Britain. This is likely to be a post-broch feature and is coeval with the secondary settlement that had grown up round the ruined tower. A very large quantity of Iron Age material, dating from the 2nd and 3rd centuries A.D. but not later, was recovered from the site.

At a later stage a 'courtyard house'—analogous to those at Jarlshof in Shetland (p. 262)—was built on the ruins of the outbuildings and later still a Viking long-house.

Rousay island

Mr Tom Sinclair (tel.: Rousay 6) will ferry people across to Rousay from Sandwick 1 km west of the Gurness broch. Mr Magnus Flaws (tel.: Wyre 203) will arrange for motor-boat trips to Rousay, Egilsay, Wyre and Eynhallow islands. On landing, one can choose to walk W to the broch and chambered cairn at Midhowe or E to a series of chambered cairns: the distance is about 3 km to the former and much less to the first of the latter.

The Midhowe stalled cairn*+ is down by the shore and under a huge shed with raised gangways from which one can see the structure clearly (Fig. 34) (HY/372306). The cairn, built of stone flags and edged with dry walling in a herringbone pattern, is 32·6 m long and

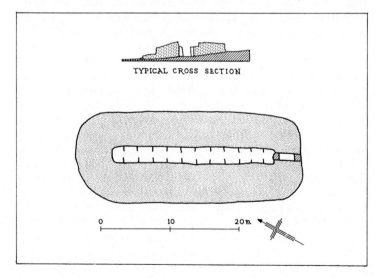

Fig. 34. Plan and cross section of the Midhowe stalled cairn, Rousay island, Orkney. Scale 1:525.

12·9 m wide. The burial chamber is a long room running down the centre of the mound and is split into 12 compartments by pairs of opposing slabs projecting from the sides. This chamber is 23·2 m long and 2–3 m wide on average. The entrance to the tomb is from the south end.

Of the open-sided cells created by the dividing slabs, the tallest of which stands to 2·3 m, nearly all those on the east side have a stone platform or bench in them. During excavation human bones were found on most of these benches, often disarticulated and collected together in groups. The remains of 23 persons were found and of these, six were adolescents and two children. Other relics were few

*The Midhowe broch**+ is close by and is the second of the Orkney brochs under Guardianship (HY/371308). Like the Gurness broch, which it much resembles (p. 249), it is a ground-galleried structure close to the shore, defended by massive outworks and containing and surrounded by a cluster of later domestic structures. In this case the outer defence is a broad and thick wall up to 5·8 m wide over the wallhead: there is an entrance through this at the south end. In front of this is a wide shallow ditch with stone-faced sides and a flat, paved base: another deeper ditch is immediately behind the wall. It is more than likely that this forework and its ditches were a promontory fort before the broch was built but further stratigraphical digging would be needed to check this possibility.

The broch itself has a well-preserved entrance with several lintels in position in front of the door-checks. There are gaps between these through which a spear could have been thrust at attackers in front of the door from the void or chamber above the passage. This was reached from the interior. There are two opposed guard cells, one of which connects with the ground-level gallery. As at Gurness this had been filled up in Iron Age times because it was collapsing: the curvature of the distorted gallery is well seen on the seaward side where the wall core is lower. This is one of the reasons for thinking that ground-galleried brochs were an early form (imported from the Hebrides) which soon gave way in Orkney to the more massive and stable solid-based brochs.

The door to the mural stair is raised 1·75 m above the secondary floor of the central court and the scarcement ledge—for the upper wooden floor—is 3·66 m above the same floor: it was probably reached from the mural stair and galleries by way of an opening which is still visible, though now converted into a secondary cell on the wallhead.

The broch is full of secondary chambers made of huge flagstones and was surrounded by similar ones which overlay the filled-in inner ditch. Most of these last have now been removed. Probably the tower was demolished when it was no longer needed and the stone from the upper walls was used to build the open village surrounding it. Many artefacts of 2nd and 3rd century date were found during the excavations in the 1930s and probably belong in the main to this secondary occupation.

There are good reasons for thinking that the Orkney brochs were built by, or for, Celtic chieftains who had not long arrived from southern England. The Roman writer Orosius describes how the chieftains of Orkney made formal submission to the Emperor Claudius when he invaded Britain in A.D. 43. Such a manœuvre was a familiar device among the tribes of Gaul to get the help, or at least the neutrality, of Rome in inter-tribal quarrels and the fact that Orkney chiefs practised this sophisticated diplomacy implies that they were well versed in southern ways. In A.D. 43 they can only have been the owners of the brochs.

Walking E from the ferry and phone box one soon reaches the *Neolithic chambered cairn* known as the *Knowe of Yarso*[+] (HY/403281). About 0·5 km from the phone box strike N up the hill for 0·5 km to the cairn. Alternatively follow the path N from the ferry for 0·5 km and then turn E along the slope of the hill. The rectangular cairn stands at the edge of a precipitous natural terrace and is 15·25 m in length by 7·8 m wide: it is edged with dry walling, the courses of which are laid slanting. The entrance passage, 3·97 m long, is in the narrow east end, and leads to the long, stalled burial chamber which runs down the long axis of the mound for 7·35 m. Three pairs of projecting slabs divide this chamber into four compartments. There is a ledge or scarcement in the wall of the innermost compartment which suggests that it was two storeyed.

When the cairn was excavated in the 1930s the bones of 20 adults and one adolescent were found. Seventeen of these individuals were represented only by skulls, 15 of which were placed side by side along the foot of the wall. The tomb had evidently been in use for a long time and the skeletons had been rearranged. There were also bones of red deer, some sheep and a dog. Some pottery, probably of Early Bronze Age date was found, as well as four arrowheads and over 60 scrapers and other implements of flint. Some of the animal bones were charred and the state of the stonework inside showed that fires had been lit in various parts of the chamber.

Plate 45. Blackhammer Neolithic cairn, Rousay, Orkney; view of the stalled chamber.

The *Blackhammer stalled cairn*[+] (Pl. 45) is 1 km further east and a few metres north of the road (HY/414276). The cairn is rectangular, 22 m long and with a maximum breadth of 8·2 m: it is built in two concentric parts, the outer part or casing, 1·3 m thick, now being reduced nearly everywhere to less than 0·76 m in height. The courses of this outer facing are laid tilted first one way and then the other. The wall of the inner casing is plain. The entrance passage leads in from the middle of the south long side and was presumably once lintelled over; it had been carefully blocked at the outer end with a wall whose face was laid to match the tilted slabs of the primary wall.

The central chamber is 12·3 m long and divided into seven compartments or stalls by six pairs of projecting stone slabs. Three of the slabs have been removed by a later activity which probably also left two blocks of secondary masonry in the chamber. Fragmentary remains of two human skeletons were found in the 1936 excavations, one of which was in the entrance passage. No doubt the later activity referred to had removed many other remains. A large piece of a pot of Unstan type was also found and a fine flint knife with it.

The last of the four stalled cairns laid out for inspection on Rousay is *Taversoe Tuack*[+], again close to the north side of the road and about 1·2 km east of Blackhammer (HY/426276). This is in some ways the most remarkable of the four in being two-storeyed, inside a round cairn and also in having near it what must be the only known example of a Neolithic earth house. The situation of the site is spectacular, being 217 ft above the sea in a spot with a fine view, and it was this situation which led to its discovery in 1898 when the landowner started to build a sheltered seat there.

The lower burial chamber is sunk into the ground with its entrance passage, also partly subterranean, on the south. Both features were more or less intact when found and are roofed with stone lintels. The lower chamber is at right angles to the passage and is approximately rectangular, measuring some 3·7 m by 1·5 m wide. It is divided into four compartments with the usual upright slabs, but these project only from the rear wall. When the lower chamber was excavated in 1937 fragments of several skeletons were found together with a perforated hammer of granite and some potsherds of the decorated Unstan ware.

The upper chamber was presumably built at the same time as the lower one and most of its floor is on the roofing lintels of the latter. Little but the lowest courses of the walls now remains. The passage approached at ground-level from the north, from exactly the opposite direction to the lower one. The line of the passage continues beyond the centre of the cairn as a small recess and the chamber opens from either side in the middle; the plan thus has the appearance of a cross with fat, bulbous arms of unequal size and thickness. Slabs project from the walls at several points but not far enough to make the chamber an irregular stalled cairn. There is now a trapdoor from the upper chamber into the lower. Both chambers had originally been covered by a circular cairn about 9·2 m in diameter.

The line of the entrance to the lower chamber was found, on excavation in 1937, to be continued outwards as a shallow trench or drain for some 6 m. Near the end of this a small roughly oval underground chamber was found, only 1·5 m long and 0·93 m wide; the dug-out walls were neatly lined with drystone masonry from which four upright slabs projected at intervals and the flat roof was of stone lintels and only 1 m above the floor. Two Neolithic pots were found in the chamber so its resemblance to the much later souterrains is probably fortuitous.

Wyre island

This island and Egilsay (below) can be reached by boat by arrangement with Mr Magnus Flaws (tel.: Wyre 203). On it is one of the oldest stone castles in Scotland, known as *Cobbie Row's Castle*[+]

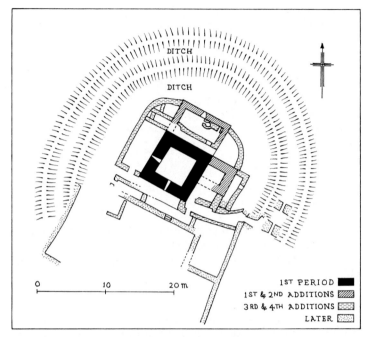

Fig. 35. Plan of the 12th-century Cobbie Row's Castle, Wyre island, Orkney, showing the primary and later masonry. Scale 1:525.

(HY/442264: Fig. 35). In the *Orkneyinga Saga* it is recorded that 'At that time [about 1150] there lived in Wyre in the Orkneys a Norwegian called Kolbein Hruga, a most mighty man. He had a good stone castle built there: that was a safe stronghold.' Cobbie Row is almost certainly the local dialectic derivative of the name of the builder. The castle stands on the summit of a ridge and is minute compared with the Medieval strongholds of the Scottish mainland; the whole fortified area is only 38 m across while the castle itself is a keep 7·9 m square with walls 1·7 m thick; they still stand up to 2·4 m high. There is a scarcement on the inner face 1·99 m above the floor which supported the wooden first floor. The masonry, of flat stones, is laid in hard lime mortar. No door is in the existing masonry and it must have been on the vanished first floor level, presumably being reached by a wooden ladder (see Wick Castle, p. 228). The ground-level storey, the floor of which is rock, must have been the cellar and reached by a trapdoor. A well or tank 1·2 m deep has been excavated in the rock and there are two narrow slit windows in the walls.

Later buildings have been added round the tower within the massive series of primary outer defences. The latter consist, from the inside out, of a strong but crudely built wall, a bank, a ditch nearly 2 m deep and an outer bank. These defences are destroyed on the south side by a later extension outwards of the central area. The original tower with its outer defences strongly resembles a broch in its small size but is perhaps unlikely to have fulfilled a similar function (p. 159).

Close to Cobbie Row's Castle is *St. Mary's chapel*, one of several well-preserved 12th-century churches in Orkney. It consists of a rectangular nave and a narrower chancel and has been somewhat restored since it was first surveyed in 1866. The entrance at the west of the nave has a semicircular Romanesque arch as also has the door to the chancel. It has been suggested that the church may have been built by Kolbein Hruga or by his son, Bjarni, who became Bishop of Orkney at about 1190.

Egilsay island

The famous Earl Thorfinn the Mighty died in about 1065 and his two sons, Paul and Erlend, ruled the islands peacefully for some years. However King Magnus of Norway exiled these two towards the end of the century but after his death Earl Hakon, son of Paul, re-established his rule. Magnus, the son of Erlend, also claimed a share in the Orkney inheritance and the dispute became a feud which culminated with the murder of Magnus by Hakon's men on Egilsay in about 1117. He was buried in Birsay church but was later canonised after miracles had been persistently reported at his tomb: in other words his defeated party was re-asserting itself against Hakon. His body was taken to Kirkwall in about 1135 and St. Magnus's Cathedral was built and dedicated to him (p. 240).

St. Magnus's church+ on Egilsay is the most impressive of its kind in Orkney and its tall round tower is a landmark over a wide area (Pl. 46) (HY/466304). In plan the church is rectangular with a nave 9·2 m long, a narrower chancel and the round tower at the west end; the latter is 3 m in diameter internally at the base and still rises to a height of 14·9 m. The chancel is 4·6 m long. The masonry is lime mortared and plastered internally and is of a low standard compared with the prehistoric work seen everywhere in Orkney. It has been

Plate 46. St. Magnus's church, Egilsay, Orkney.

suggested that the walls may have been built within wooden shutter-
ing, held apart by short timbers, and that the many put-log holes in
the walls are the remains of this. There are two round-arched entrances into the church, the north one of which is blocked. There are
checks for the door in each and the one on the south side has a bar-
hole, a feature reminiscent of Iron Age brochs. Two of the lintelled
windows in the south wall are later insertions but the two round-
arched ones facing each other are original. The tower contained at
least three upper floors and there was an upper storey over the
chancel reached by a round-arched doorway over the chancel arch.

The local name for this chamber over the chancel was the 'Grief
House' and it has been suggested that this word derived from the
Old Norse *grið* (peace or sanctuary) implying that it was a refuge or
sanctuary for fugitives. The bar-hole behind the south door may be
significant in this respect. It is unlikely that this church was built
when Earl Magnus was killed on Egilsay so he presumably took unsuccessful sanctuary in its vanished predecessor.

17

Eynhallow island

The *Orkneyinga Saga* mentioned 'Eyin-helga' or 'holy island' under the year 1155 and implies in another place that 'Hellis-ey' (probably the same place) was occupied by monks. The ruins of the 12th-century *Eynhallow church*+ and the near-by domestic buildings which stand at the south of the island were once identified as a Cistercian monastery but this has been shown to be incorrect: the domestic buildings are now known to be much later (HY/359289). The church consists of a rectangular nave, a narrower chancel and a porch at the west end. It has been much altered with later masonry but the earliest parts date from about 1200. The church was modified and reconstructed as part of the domestic settlement when this was built and was only discovered to be a church when the settlement was evacuated in the mid 19th century. No doubt the church was that of a monastic community but the original domestic buildings do not yet seem to have been traced and doubtless will not be without excavation.

There is a *standing stone* 1·6 m high south of the church and a few metres above high-water mark (HY/359287 approx.).

Westray and Papa Westray islands

These islands are reached by steamer from Kirkwall (p. 231 above). On Westray there are two early churches (as well as the mid 16th-century Noltland Castle+) and on Papa Westray is a Neolithic cairn and some domestic buildings which date to Early Neolithic times. The 12th-century *Westside church*+, or *Cross Kirk*, is in a graveyard at Tuquoy 5 km due south of Pierowall and close to the shore (HY/455432). The building consists of a nave and a chancel with square ends. The original length of the nave was 5·7 m but this has been more than doubled at a much later period: it is now 14·2 m long internally. The 12th-century walls are better preserved, standing up to 2·5 m high. The round-arched, 12th-century door is on the south side of the nave: it has no door-checks, unlike the later one further west. The chancel arch is preserved and stands 1·86 m high: the chancel itself was originally roofed with a barrel vault.

At *Knap of Howar*+, on Papa Westray, are the remains of two drystone dwellings which until 1973 were thought to be of Iron Age date (NY/483519). New excavations in that year by Dr Anna Ritchie showed them to be much earlier and to be probably the oldest known standing stone houses in north-west Europe. The site is on the west shore of the island, 600 m west of Holland house and it was first explored in the mid 1930s. The two houses lie side by side and are approximately rectangular; the larger one measures about 9·5 m with the greatest width being 4·8 m while the smaller is 7·8 m long and only 3·4 m wide. Both buildings are divided internally into compartments by projecting slabs and by the shape of the walls, the large buildings into two equal halves and the smaller into three areas. The stone slabs which stand up to 1·8 m high doubtless supported a roof of timber and turf. Each building has an entrance passage at the north-west narrow end, the sides of which are checked for a door. There are several aumbries or cupboards in the wall of the smaller (north) building and, at its east end, a series of recesses or stalls in the wall flanked by projecting stone slabs. The outer parts of the two adjacent houses are joined by a connecting passage.

The first excavations produced badly made flint implements, potsherds, bone awls and both rotary and saddle querns. The rotary querns suggested an Iron Age date for the site but the new excavations in the S house revealed Neolithic pottery and obtained material for radiocarbon dating both from food refuse inside the dwelling and from the midden which surrounded and underlay it. These dates when converted to calendar years, show clearly that the house was inhabited between about 3500 and 3100 B.C., at the time the Neolithic chambered tombs were being built. Knap of Howar has thus suddenly become the only well preserved Early Neolithic stone house in Britain and is consequently of great importance and interest.

On the highest point of the tiny island of *Holm of Papa Westray*[+] is the *chambered cairn* of that name (HY/283117). The size of this massive tomb is in sharp contrast with the islet on which it stands, which does not seem to have been inhabited in historical times. The cairn is a rectangle with rounded short ends, and in 1849 when it was cleared out it measured 35 m in length, about 16·7 m in width and up to 3 m in height. It seems likely that the rubble of the cairn itself was retained by a low casing wall 5·5 m thick but this was only traced on either side of the lintelled entrance passage. This entrance, 5·5 m long, is in the middle of the east long side and is at right angles to a long chamber down the centre of the mound. The entrance is now closed and access to the chamber is gained by trapdoors in its concrete roof.

The burial chamber is 20 m long overall and has an average width of 1·53 m. It is divided into three sections by two cross walls with low doorways in them and opening off it are no less than 12 side chambers, two of which have a double or 'dumb-bell' plan. Each of these side chambers is a corbelled, beehive cell within the rubble of the cairn with doorways from 0·61 m to 0·5 m high leading into them at ground-level. No relics were found in the tomb when it was excavated.

The plan of this cairn, as of several others on Orkney, suggests that is is essentially an example of a passage grave—the basic idea of which was presumably imported—which has undergone local development. The central chamber could have been enlarged laterally and the side chambers are seen in simpler forms like Maes Howe (p. 235). A similar lateral enlargement of passage graves is seen in Denmark.

9 · The Shetland Isles

These islands, the most northerly outpost of Britain, present a striking contrast to Orkney. They are bleaker and less fertile with larger areas of bog and moor, a coast which is split with many narrow inlets, or voes, and larger areas of higher ground and hilly country. Consequently there are more opportunities for obtaining solitude and spectacular scenery.

In spite of its remoteness Shetland was comparatively densely populated from Neolithic times onwards and there are abundant archaeological remains of all periods: brochs and Neolithic cairns are particularly common. Two extremely important Iron Age sites—Jarlshof and Clickhimin—have been excavated and the former also has the most complete Norse settlement known in Britain. The best-built and most completely preserved broch is to be found on the island of Mousa.

The Dunrossness peninsula

The islands are reached by boat from Aberdeen or Orkney to Lerwick or by air from Glasgow and stations north to the south tip of the islands. If arriving by air it is convenient to visit *Jarlshof**+ a little over 1 km south-east of the airport buildings (HU/399096). Follow the A970 along the shore of the bay and the site is signposted thereafter (Fig. 36, Pl. 47). Jarlshof stands on the edge of the beach and was originally exposed by a great storm in 1897: a sea-wall has been constructed to secure the remains. Since then the site has been excavated by Dr A. O. Curle and Professor V. G. Childe in the 1930s and in the early 1950s by Mr J. R. C. Hamilton, who produced the final report. In general there are seven major phases of occupation all of which are represented by substantial stone buildings. These phases are two successive open villages of the Late

Bronze and Early Iron Ages; a broch; a post-broch wheelhouse settlement; a village of Viking longhouses; a Medieval farmstead and, finally, the late 16th-century laird's house which was christened 'Jarlshof' by Sir Walter Scott in *The Pirate*. The explanation of this long history of almost continuous settlement is doubtless to be seen in the fine harbour provided by the shallow West Voe on the east shore of which the site is, by the good arable and grazing land close by, with freshwater springs, as well perhaps as by the presence of near-by Sumburgh Head itself which would have been suitable as a look-out point and as a land-mark for sailors.

When entering the site, follow the path along the shore, past the broch to the early villages next to the site museum. The earlier of these settlements is a cluster of courtyard houses but an even older series of midden deposits was found below this, probably dating to the early 2nd millennium B.C. A remarkable find from these levels was a decorated bone plaque, unique in Britain but very similar to stone plaques commonly found in the megalithic tombs of the Portuguese copper age. It provides a rare and undervalued demonstration of the hidden influence of travellers of some kind on the archaeology of Atlantic Britain (p. 232).

The four '*courtyard houses*' revealed by excavation are presumably only a part of a larger settlement. Dwelling III, at the north end of the group, is the best preserved and can be viewed from a wooden platform. It is a roughly oval house measuring internally some 5·5 m in length and up to 6·1 m in width. The inside wallface has the characteristically scalloped plan formed by a series of irregular, wedge-shaped stone piers projecting into the interior. These were no doubt the supports on which rested the beams of a conical roof which met over the centre of the hut. A courtyard house is probably a primitive form of wheelhouse and is unlikely to have had its central 'courtyard' open to the sky as the name suggests. The main entrance has been from the south, next to Dwelling IV, and a large stone trough quern for grinding grain, complete with the rubber, is on the floor just inside. A heap of charred grain, probably bere (barley), was found on the floor of one of the chambers during excavation. That cattle were kept inside some of these houses is shown by the adjacent Dwelling II in which the paved floor of the innermost transverse chamber is slightly dished to collect manure: a whalebone tether ring was found inserted into its wall. There is a sump for the liquid to drain into under the hearth which was built later—or presumably when the function of the house changed.

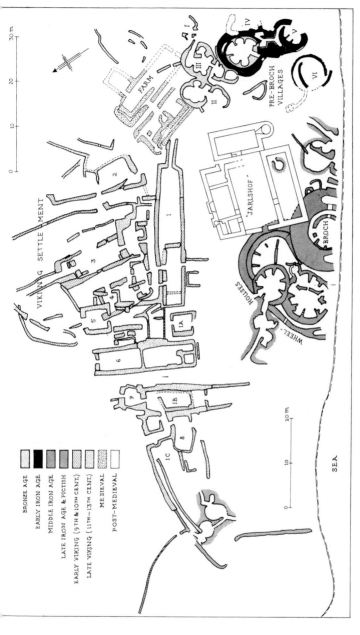

Fig. 36. Plan of Jarlshof, Shetland, showing structures of eight successive periods. The broch is at the bottom centre, the wheelhouses next to it, the pre-broch villages on the right and the Viking settlement along the top half. The Viking house no. I described in the text is immediately N of the broch. Scale. 1:700.

BRONZE AGE

EARLY IRON AGE

MIDDLE IRON AGE

LATE IRON AGE & PICTISH

EARLY VIKING (9TH & 10TH CENT.)

LATE VIKING (11TH–13TH CENT.)

MEDIEVAL

POST-MEDIEVAL

VIKING SETTLEMENT

FARM

PRE-BROCH VILLAGES

'JARLSHOF'

BROCH

WHEEL-HOUSES

SEA

The finds from this early village included trough querns—attesting grain cultivation—many stone-cutting and chopping tools and a variety of bone implements for cutting and piercing. The pottery consisted of hard, red-brown, barrel-shaped vessels. There are only two clues to the age of this settlement. The first is provided by the village of round-houses—shortly to be described—which lies on top of the courtyard house. The iron slag and the Early Iron Age pottery associated with them suggests a date for that settlement in the 5th century B.C. The courtyard houses are thus older and their stone tools could indicate a very much earlier date. However after Dwelling III had ceased to be occupied a bronze-smith set up his workshop in it: many fragments of clay moulds for Late Bronze Age tools and weapons were found on top of an accumulation of blown sand on the floor. The old door at the south end was blocked up and a new one broken through into the transverse chamber from the west.

This discovery is the only direct evidence for a bronze-using period in Shetland (apart from an Early Bronze Age dagger with a horn handle from Wasbister, now in Glasgow University). It has been suggested that the bronze-smith—who was probably from Ireland—went to Shetland after the spread of iron had made his skills redundant on the mainland. It is much more probable, since he produced the formidable new leaf-shaped slashing swords, that he arrived in the train of a conquering Late Bronze Age chief and his war band, perhaps in the 8th or 7th century B.C.

The second *pre-broch village* was established on top of the courtyard houses, apparently by new settlers who had an iron-smith with them and who made shouldered Early Iron Age pottery akin to that of southern England and Wales. The stone houses are circular, with radial stone piers projecting into the interior. The one built on top of Dwelling IV has one such pier preserved but the floor has been removed to expose the filled-in ruins of the courtyard house underneath. Dwelling V, to the south of this, is half preserved and has two radial, roof-supporting piers but Dwelling VI, to the west again, has none and presumably had internal wooden posts to hold up the roof.

The equipment of these new villages did not include the stone- and bone-cutting and chopping tools of the earlier period so they evidently possessed a range of iron implements. They also had stone beads and bracelets for ornamentation. Their round huts are technically simple wheelhouses, comparable to those of the post-broch era (below), yet it is doubtful if this tradition contributed anything to the later wheelhouses. The site was abandoned and covered by a thick layer of blown sand before the broch-builders arrived: the tower-fort was built over this layer.

The *broch complex* was the next phase of settlement on the site. Two-fifths of the broch tower itself, and half of the outer courtyard wall which was attached to it, had been destroyed by the sea before the site was discovered but enough remains to show that the broch was solid-based with an overall diameter of 19·5 m and a wall 5·5 m thick. Half of a mural cell, which may have been a guard cell flanking the entrance passage, is preserved on the west side and another, with one side of its door to the central court, is opposite this. The latter was probably the entrance to the mural stair. It is difficult to see much of the inside face of the broch wall because of the secondary wheelhouse which has been added but the scarcement ledge can be distinguished in places. A well or water tank is sunk into the floor and is reached by a flight of steps. A heap of charred grain was found on these steps during excavation.

The outer wall of the broch is of a rare design, being attached to the tower at two points, very much in the manner of a Norman motte

Plate 47. Iron Age wheelhouses at Jarlshof, Shetland: view showing the aisled wheelhouse in the foreground, the two wheelhouses beyond and the Viking settlement in the background.

and bailey of a millennium later. This courtyard wall is best preserved next to the shore where half the cell which flanked the
vanished outer gate is preserved. The thickening of the wall at this
point, and the flanking cell, recall the design of the Shetland 'blockhouse' forts like Ness of Burgi (p. 269 below). From general con-
siderations the broch seems likely to have been built early in the 1st
century A.D. (p. 28): only a few finds could be clearly associated
with its occupants, namely a scatter of potsherds on the sand floor
of the courtyard.

The *wheelhouse*-building phase followed after the broch had
ceased to be needed as a fort: the date of this important change of
function of the site has to be estimated but it might have been about
A.D. 200. The first *round-house* to be built inside the broch courtyard was probably the biggest but it has been largely destroyed by
the later buildings; it is best seen from the platform up on the
'laird's house' (Pl. 47). The house had an internal diameter of about
27 m and originally had a ring of internal, wooden roof-supporting
posts. The strata against the stump of the outer wall on the north
side showed that this section of it had been largely pulled down
before the round-house was built—hence the inference that the site
had ceased to be primarily a fortified refuge. Later the free-standing
stone piers were added inside and the dwelling became an *aisled
wheelhouse*. Its primary, pier-less state is shown by the scarcement
ledge on the interior wallface which must have supported a raised
wooden floor as in the brochs: such a floor could not conveniently
be combined with the lower roof indicated by the piers and the piers
themselves would have got in the way. Later still some of the piers
were changed by blocking the 'aisle' between pier and wall with
masonry, doubtless because, when free-standing, they were liable to
outward thrust from the roof beams resting on them. The structure
thus became a true wheelhouse.

Presumably the vanished half of the courtyard was filled with
similar wheelhouses, improving architecturally all the time. The last
two of the series survive—magnificent, compact, drystone dwellings
with immensely tall radial piers bonded to the outer wall; they ex-
pand as they rise to permit the roofing of the bays between them
with stone flags. *Wheelhouse 2*, on the west, was built first and caused
the taking down of a part of the aisled wheelhouse. The part of the
latter that remained was still used and a new paved hearth was built
which was later overridden by the second wheelhouse, the last to
be built. A fine, large paved hearth is in *Wheelhouse 3* which, like

Wheelhouse 2, was a free-standing, above-ground structure. Its west wall is braced against the old broch outer wall with a row of lintels which thus create a covered passage.

It is quite possible that the wheelhouse type of dwelling was actually invented at Jarlshof and taken from there to other parts of Shetland and to the Outer Hebrides (p. 172). The sequence from round-house, to aisled wheelhouse to compact true wheelhouse is clear and would doubtless be more complete if the structures in the other half of the courtyard had survived.

The material culture found with the first post-broch dwelling—the aisled wheelhouse—is interesting in that it includes many stone cutting and chopping implements with no apparent evidence of iron-working; this is in sharp contrast to conditions in the much older second pre-broch village (p. 264). Yet the pottery—large situlate jars occasionally burnished black—could be descended from that of the earlier village. It may be that the craft of ironsmithing had died out for a while in southern Shetland at the time the broch was built. In the wheelhouse phase iron was used again and the pottery is slightly different—its hard, red fabric suggesting a resurgence of the old courtyard house wares.

A complex of dug-out storage rooms and byres, contemporary with the wheelhouse settlement, lies immediately east of the broch and north-west of the wheelhouses. It is described as a *passage house* and is one of the latest of the Iron Age buildings. About 40 m from the broch outer wall, back along the path to the site entrance, is part of the field wall which enclosed the whole post-broch settlement; there are some huts associated with it 25 m north of the shore. In one of these huts was found a slate incised with a cross with expanded terminals and probably of 8th-century date: the later wheelhouses themselves may still have been occupied at this time. East of the huts the field wall continues for a distance, until obscured by the Norse houses, and it runs beside the remains of a similar and much earlier enclosure wall to the south of it which evidently belonged to the courtyard house village.

The *Norse settlement* seems to have begun early in the 9th century and is represented by the extensive cluster of long, stone rectangular dwellings along the north side of the site. This is the largest and most complete Norse settlement discovered in Britain and it illustrates the other side of the story of the Viking expansion—the emigration of farmers looking for land as opposed to raiders searching for loot.

The earliest Norse house is number 1, immediately north of

'Jarlshof' and was built at the beginning of the 9th century. It was much altered in later times and its visible masonry reflects three main phases of use. Originally it was a two-roomed house about 21 m long and the west or kitchen end is preserved with an oven and fireplace built against it. The long side walls were typically bow-shaped and part of that on the south can still be seen. The entrance is on the north, with a bar-hole in the wall and also on this side is the raised dais on which tables and beds were placed. There was a rect-angular stone hearth in the middle of the floor, now mostly destroyed, and the roof was held up on a long central row of posts. The east gable was wooden and the post-holes for this were found about 6 m west of the present gable. Finds from this early Viking house suggest that the settlers who built it came from the Møre-Trondelag districts of Norway, on latitude 63°N and some 300 km nearer the Arctic circle than southern Shetland. They imported fine composite bone combs from the mainland and the few more exotic objects found were doubtless obtained from Norse raiders returning from forays to Ireland and Scotland.

The house remained relatively unaltered until the early 11th century when a stone byre was added on to the east end, with a curved, paved passage through which the cattle entered. Part of a pile of burnt stones thrown out earlier from the hearth, and on which the byre was built, can be seen in the north-east corner. The west end of the house was also extended at this time and a partition wall was built across the floor of the living area. A new, larger fireplace replaced the old one but only a few of its stones remain.

In its final phase the large house was abandoned and a small rect-angular dwelling was built, the east gable of which is the partition wall just referred to. The north wall is new and inside the old one, and a new side door was made, west of the original one. A partition wall divides the interior into two halves. The associated finds suggest that this small dwelling was used in the 12th and 13th centuries.

The entire settlement can be divided into an early and a late phase in a similar manner to House 1 and the plan (Fig. 36) shows which buildings are of what period. Other features of interest include the probable bath-house contemporary with the first phase of House 1 and immediately beyond its west end. There is a fine rectangular stone hearth in the centre of the floor. Other out-houses attached to the main farm building are to the north of the latter, beyond an alleyway parallel to the main wall. Houses 2, 3 and 4 were the next farms to be established on the site in the 9th and early 10th centuries. Most of these buildings are overlain by later ones and the details of the history of the site can be found in the official guide-booklet.

The *Medieval farm* is partly preserved immediately east of House 1 of the Viking settlement but a large part of the buildings was removed to expose the Late Bronze Age village underneath. The farm was evidently established in the 13th century and consisted originally of a rectangular dwelling on the north-east side, originally over 20 m long, and a large outhouse parallel to this, also partly removed. This outhouse has a circular kiln built into its north-west corner. The farm continued in occupation, much altered, until the 16th century judging from the finds.

Across the Voe west of Jarlshof is a long, narrow peninsula on which stands an interesting *Iron Age fort*, on *Ness of Burgi**+ (HU/388084: Fig. 37). Just south of the airport a minor road leads south from the main road, at the point where the latter turns east to Jarlshof. A walk of nearly 1 km is required south of the end of this

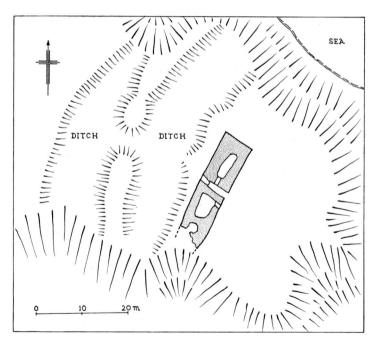

Fig. 37. Plan of the Ness of Burgi promontory fort, Shetland. Scale 1:785.

road to the fort. The defences run across the neck of a short, grass-covered rocky promontory on the east side of the main peninsula and consist of two outer ditches separated by a massive wall which now has the appearance of a rampart. The wall was about 6·4 m thick and still stands 2·1 m above the base of the ditches. Within the inner ditch is a remarkable rectangular drystone building, sometimes known as a 'blockhouse', which is from 5·6 m to 6·4 m thick and equipped with an entrance passage and two large mural cells: the cell on the east communicates with the entrance, the other with the interior. The entrance has checks for a door with a bar-hole in the wall behind these, and there are some lintels in position both over the main passage and over the doorways to the two cells.

The south-west end of the 'blockhouse' evidently continued on to the edge of the cliff, down which the end of it has fallen: there are traces of another cell here. The opposite end is however a carefully built wall, and seems to leave the north-east third of the promontory unguarded. It seems likely that there was an extra length of wall here which was either not completed or has been demolished. At the comparable 'blockhouse' fort in Loch of Huxter on Whalsay island, a complete circuit of wall is attached to the thicker, rectangular entrance section. There are only three such forts known, the third being at Clickhimin (p. 275 below), and they were probably a local Shetland development. Clickhimin shows that they were evolved before the broch period and Ness of Burgi was doubtless established during the hiatus in the occupation of the Jarlshof site across the bay—between the Early Iron Age village and the broch there. As noted earlier (p. 266) the design of the outer gateway of the Jarlshof broch reflects the influence of the indigenous blockhouse fort architecture. Excavations in Ness of Burgi in 1935 failed to produce any evidence of date, or indeed many finds at all except some sherds and, in the south-west cell, two hearths.

Travelling N up the A970 to Lerwick it is worth making a detour to see the site of the Early Christian church which produced a remarkable hoard of silver in 1958. *St. Ninian's chapel* is at the west end of the narrow isthmus which connects St. Ninian's isle with the mainland (HU/369208). It is reached by taking the B9122 to Mewhouse, turning W there down the minor road to Bigton and walking W for 0·9 km. Though there is now nothing to be seen of the Early Christian remains at the site the circumstances of the finding of this unique hoard—now in the National Museum in Edinburgh—must be briefly recounted.

From 1955 to 1958 a party from Aberdeen University excavated at the site to recover details of an Early Medieval church which was known to have existed there until quite recently: the link with St. Ninian was an added incentive. The foundations of a 12th-century church were indeed found and the turfed wallheads of this are now exposed on the site. This church consisted of a rectangular nave, 7 m long internally with walls about 1 m thick, and a narrower chancel with a semicircular end. Stylistically this church has been dated to about 1150.

The foundations of an earlier wall 1 m thick, made of rectangular blocks and plastered on its inner surface, were found lower down. This older wall runs along under most of the south wall of the Medieval nave and is part of a pre-Norse church, presumably disused when the first pagan Scandinavians settled in Shetland. Just south of the chancel an early grave was found—the 'founder's tomb'—in which were six stones inscribed with Pictish symbols. Within the area of the Medieval nave, and within that of the earlier church, a hoard of silver was found on 4 July 1958: it had been buried in a box of larch wood, apparently in a hurry as the objects were tumbled about. Above it was a thin stone slab marked with a cross.

The silver hoard is dated to about A.D. 800 and included 12 penannular brooches, eight bowls (including one hanging bowl), two chapes, a communion spoon and knife, one pommel and three cone-shaped objects. It has been persuasively argued—not without dissension—that the whole hoard is ecclesiastical and represents the only known collection of plate of the early Celtic Church. Certainly its situation would seem to support this theory. One may suppose that the appearance of a Viking raider off west Shetland early in the 9th century caused the speedy burial of the silver and that its non-recovery means that the clergy of this little church did not survive the raid, or were carried off. The hoard provides a rare and fascinating glimpse of the wealth of the Early Christian churches which their physical remains hardly hint at.

Continuing N and rejoining the main road, the *broch of Mousa*[*+] will be seen on the island of that name off Sandwich (HU/457237). A boat can be hired at that village for the short journey across Mousa Sound. This broch is the best preserved of its class, still standing to a height of 13.3 m, and its magnificent architecture is hard to describe adequately (Pl. 48; Fig. 38). Brochs themselves may be said to represent the summit of prehistoric British drystone architecture and Mousa is certainly the best conceived and most skilfully built

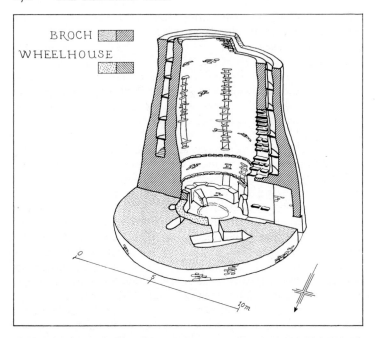

BROCH

WHEELHOUSE

0
5
10m

Fig. 38. Isometric drawing showing the plan and elevation of the broch of Mousa, Shetland. Scale 1:210.

Plate 48. Broch of Mousa, Shetland.

example: it ranks among the major archaeological monuments of Europe. The dimensions and main structural features can be quickly described. The tower has an external diameter at base of 15·25 m and an average internal one of 5·5 m. The massive wallbase, which is solid up to a height of 3·8 m, thus occupies no less than 64 per cent of the overall diameter and this proportion (the highest in any known broch), together with the small, compact ground plan, doubtless explains how the great height of the structure was achieved. The entrance passage is equipped with the usual door-checks and bar-hole but the original low roof of lintels has been broken away in antiquity, so that the passage has been enlarged upwards. Presumably this was done at a stage when several feet of debris had accumulated in the interior, thus blocking the old doorway.

Opening off the central court are three large corbelled mural cells up to 3·7 m high but with low doorways. Inside these cells are small aumbries or wall cupboards and there are three larger and deeper aumbries outside, in the wall of the court. Two ledges, or scarcements, are preserved on the inside wallface, one at 2·1 m above the floor and the other at 3·4 m. The lower ledge probably supported a raised wooden floor and the broch roof doubtless rested on the other. Mousa is the only broch in which the roof was so low but such a position perhaps 12 m below the wallhead, would have protected it from gales and made for easy access for repairs. Also in the inside wallface are several towering series of openings, or voids, which in effect continue the sides of doorways high up the wall. These probably served the double purpose of lighting the galleries behind and reducing the weight of stone in the upper parts of the tower.

The sill of the door to the stairway in the wall is raised about 2·1 m above the floor, at the height of the lower scarcement. The vanished wooden floor on this ledge, and the stair door, must therefore have been reached by a movable ladder. The stair rises clockwise inside the wall to the summit of the tower in a long sweep, broken by two landings. It breaks through the floors of six mural galleries and one can walk from it out on to the wallhead. These galleries are most unusual in that they are all, even the topmost ones, wide enough to walk along quite easily and are well built with few projecting stones. Even so their function was primarily structural, to allow a thick wall to be built with a hollow centre and thus achieve height with lightness and strength. There is no suggestion that they were ever lived in. The broch wall has sagged slightly and some of the rows of lintels, which brace the two halves of the wall apart and create the galleries, are tilted downwards and outwards. Each of the parallel tiers of gallery runs the whole way round the tower, finishing blind behind the stair at one end and stopping short in front of it at the other.

A secondary wheelhouse has been built inside the broch, composed of an added facing of wall and one projecting pier: two other piers have disappeared since they were first exposed in 1861. There is a flat circular platform 0·46 m thick below this and resting on the primary floor. The inner edge of this platform is faced with slabs on edge and seems to have coincided with the inner ends of the radial piers. In the lowest, central floor area is a hearth and a tank; part of the latter is over-ridden by the wheelhouse pier. Platform, pier and secondary wall probably all belong to the wheelhouse phase.

Whatever the reasons for building the brochs (p. 159) the one on Mousa was the masterpiece of its age, blending together normal broch architectural features in unique and perfect form. It is easy to believe that the master builder who probably designed it was the greatest of his class and that the chief for whom Mousa was doubtless built was correspondingly paramount.

The broch was still impregnable in the 12th century. The *Orkneyinga Saga* describes how one Erlend, fleeing from Orkney with Margaret, the mother of Earl Harold Maddadson, whom he had abducted, landed on Mousa in 1153 and took refuge in the broch, which he had previously filled with stores. Margaret's son pursued the eloping pair but found the broch an 'unhandy place to get at'. A reconciliation followed. There were 2·7 m of debris inside the tower when it was cleared in 1861 so it is quite possible that the Norse inhabitants found it almost as full and had to enlarge the main entrance upwards.

Continuing N along the main road, stop about 1 km north of the last road back to Sandwich and the Mousa ferry. Here close to the road are the remarkable *Cunningsburgh steatite quarries* and also two *Viking long-houses* (HU/425272). The outcrops of soft soapstone are along the north bank of the Catpund burn, west of the road, and numerous hollows can be seen from which stone vessels have been carved. Steatite vessels were used as a substitute for pottery in prehistoric and later times; pieces of them were found for example at Jarlshof in the Iron Age and Viking settlements (p. 261 above). The foundations of two Viking long-houses are visible close by.

The loch of Brindister is passed on the left about 12 km further north and there is an island in it with a broch.

Immediately after the loch the farmroad to Brindister turns off to the right and from the farm one can walk 1 km to the SE to see the *broch of Burland*★ (HU/446360). The site, though unexcavated, is well worth a visit because of its spectacular situation—on a high, narrow cliff promontory—and because of the massive outer defences which protect it. The outer defences of the Shetland brochs are the most massive known. In this case they consist of—from the outside—a shallow ditch, a massive stone wall or rampart 5·5 m thick with an entrance through it in the centre, two more shallow ditches separated by a rampart and, finally, an inner wall. The entrance causeway appears to run through the middle of all these defences.

The outer wallface of the broch is well preserved on the seaward side, still standing to about 3 m in height, and an upper gallery is visible in places. The entrance passage faces the west cliff and is very close to it: though half full of debris the passage is intact and all the lintels seem to be in position. The door-checks can be seen and a guard cell is apparent on the right. The broch of Burland is one of the strongest sites of its kind.

Lerwick

Just before reaching the town one can visit the famous site of *Clickhimin*★+ 1 km to the west: it is now on a promontory on the south side of the loch (Fig. 39) (HU/404132). Extensively excavated between 1953 and 1957 by Mr J. R. C. Hamilton on behalf of the then Ministry of Works Clickhimin has, as a result, become one of the most important prehistoric sites in Britain, both because of its remarkable sequence of stone structures and because of the wealth of finds made. Like Jarlshof (p. 261) the site was inhabited over a long period, starting in the Late Bronze Age and continuing on into the Dark Age. The main structures now visible are the outer wall enclosing the whole complex, with a landing stage in front of its entrance, the 'blockhouse' behind the gateway through this, the broch behind that, the remains of a wheelhouse inside the broch and various subsidiary structures within the outer court including a courtyard house. The history of the site as given here is based on the author's research and differs at various points from that expounded by the excavator which is available in several books (p. 292). The site is particularly important in that it is the only one so far known where an Iron Age fort has been found which is earlier than a broch on the same site and which has thus produced vital evidence about the origin of the towers.

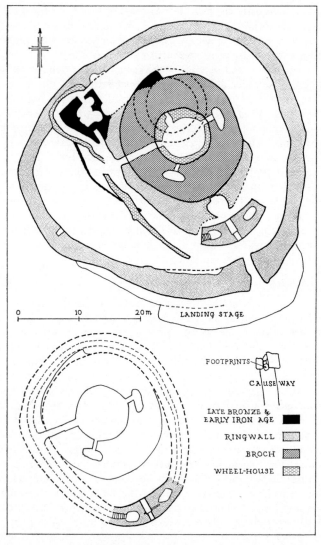

0   10   20m   LANDING STAGE

FOOTPRINTS

CAUSEWAY

LATE BRONZE &
EARLY IRON AGE

RINGWALL

BROCH

WHEEL-HOUSE

Fig. 39. Plans of the Clickhimin site, Shetland. The top shows the structures of four successive periods according to the excavator. Scale 1:590. The bottom drawing shows an alternative interpretation of the second (pre-broch) fort devised by the author.

The earliest settlement on the site seems to have been a *courtyard house* : this is on the north-west side of the broch and well preserved. Artefacts and pottery similar to those found in the first village at Jarlshof were recovered and a date in the 8th or 7th century B.C. seems likely. This house was also used by Early Iron Age people with the same shouldered pottery as that used in the second village at Jarlshof but no unambiguous traces of a round-house were located at Clickhimin. Up to this point the site seems to have been undefended and Shetland was evidently inhabited by scattered, peaceful settlements of farmers. However the next phase in the history of the site marks a sharp change when a massive *stone ring-wall* was built on the end of the promontory; it now forms the present outer wall of the site. This wall is 3·1–3·7 m thick at its base and encloses a pear-shaped area 42 m east–west by 38 m north–south. It still stands 2·6 m high on the west but the top courses were probably rebuilt between 1908 and 1910. The date that these fort-builders arrived is not too clear—it could be almost any time between the 5th and 2nd centuries B.C.—but they brought with them a new kind of pottery which may have come ultimately from western France. There were ranges of timber buildings along the inside of the wall at this stage—some evidently being cattle stalls— and thick deposits of refuse both inside and outside the fort suggest a long period of occupation. In the author's opinion there were no other stone buildings inside the fort at this time except the court-yard house.

Probably early in the 1st century B.C. the construction of an entirely new kind of fort was begun. Some time after the establishment of the first ring-wall the local 'blockhouse' forts had been developed in Shetland and two were built elsewhere (p. 269). The *second ring-fort* at Clickhimin was built within the area enclosed by the first wall and was architecturally much more sophisticated, being a hybrid form in which the design of the local blockhouses was combined with that of the new hollow-walled semibrochs which were being built in the Western Isles in the 2nd and 1st centuries B.C. (p. 166). The major remaining feature of this second hybrid fort is the 'blockhouse' behind the outer gate (Pl. 49) which is architecturally far more sophisticated than the entrance of the old ring-fort (this is the primary reason for the author's belief that it is later than the latter, the main difference between the views expressed here and those in the official report). The blockhouse is a curved, free-standing section of wall containing a well-preserved' lintelled entrance passage 4·1 m long and equipped with door-checks and a bar-hole. Above it is a void—a typical feature of broch architecture—and a short length of upper gallery and there are two large, isolated mural cells in the wall on either side. A stair leads up from the west end.

The 'blockhouse' is a typical Atlantic Iron Age defended entrance passage and clearly makes no sense standing by itself. In fact the inner half of its west end can be seen to be connected with a ruined wall which runs north-west to the later broch (Pl. 49: the plan in the report wrongly shows a gap in the masonry at this point). There the doorway in this early wall can be clearly seen, forming the outer end of the broch entrance the masonry of which overrides it at a straight joint. This early wall is reasonably explained as the inner half (with doorway to the interior) of a galleried fort wall of which the block-house was once the main entrance, the whole being a similar structure to that on Whalsay island but with the addition of numerous structural features derived from the Hebridean semibrochs. The curious 'spur' of masonry projecting from the broch wall on the north side could well be further remains of this early, galleried wall (Fig. 39).

If this is the true explanation of the second fort at Clickhimin it is likely to have been completed and subsequently used for some time. The broch which replaced it as the third fort on the site is an advanced, solid-based form which is perhaps unlikely to have been built before the 1st century A.D. Such a hybrid second fort would show well how the fort-building experts of the Hebrides and the far north were in close contact with one another in the last centuries B.C. The sequence of structures, culminating with the broch, also shows well how the most advanced forts of each era were built in succession at this site, strongly suggesting that it was the seat of a powerful dynasty of rulers. The 'Dark Age' footprints, described below, seem to confirm this.

The *broch* which followed and superseded the blockhouse fort probably caused most of the latter to be demolished for building material. It is a massive, solid-based tower some 19·8 m in overall diameter with an internal diameter of 9·2 m. The lintelled entrance passage, on the west, is well preserved, the outer end showing the broch masonry overriding that of the earlier fort as described. Over the inner end is a fine series of voids running up the wall. Most of the lower part of the interior wallface is concealed by a later wheel-house, described below, but access into one of the two mural cells is possible through the wall of the latter, in which an opening was left

Plate 49. Clickhimin, Shetland; view of the blockhouse from the W showing the stair and part of the adjoining galleried wall.

when it was built. The other broch cell, on the south-west, can now be reached only from the void in the broch wall above it.

The door to the mural stair is opposite the main entrance and is raised 2·1 m above the inside floor; it is now reached by wooden steps. Most of the wall is still solid at this height but there are two secondary entrances—a unique feature among the brochs. One of these is a continuation of the door to the stair (and just above the projecting 'spur' outside) and the other is at 9 o'clock. This second one communicates only with a mural gallery which starts at the opening and runs clockwise, descending all the while, to become the first gallery on the wallhead in the south-west half of the tower. A non-horizontal gallery is also a very unusual feature in brochs. The author has a suspicion that several feet of the top of the broch wall, perhaps including these subsidiary entrances, are a modern reconstruction. A photograph taken before 1874, when the loch was drained, shows that the wallhead even then was level and carefully turfed over. It seems quite possible that much reconstruction and consolidation took place after the excavations of 1862.

The finds of the broch period obtained in the recent excavations show fairly clearly that the new tower-fort was built on a site which had been continuously occupied since the construction of the first fort, perhaps several centuries earlier. Yet there were other objects of this period—such as a spiral bronze finger-ring and a long-handled bone weaving comb—which suggested that the contacts between different parts of Atlantic Scotland, illustrated by the hybrid second fort, were intensified in the broch period. Although many aspects of the material culture of the broch-using peoples, particularly the pottery, remained firmly local there is plenty of other evidence of widespread communication throughout the broch province and further afield, even as far as southern England (p. 160 above).

It is difficult to estimate how long the broch was used as a fort but it may well have been as late as A.D. 200. Eventually, however, peaceful conditions returned and the large *wheelhouse* was constructed inside the tower. The radial piers, formed of slabs on edge, were in position when the broch was first cleared of debris in 1861-2 but have since disappeared. The wheelhouse wall is of uneven thickness, 2·3 m on the north side and only about 0·7 m on the east and west. In the thickest part on the north is a cell wholly within the wheel-house wall: the back of this cell is thus not the hidden broch wall as might be supposed: the latter is about 0·7 m further back at its nearest point.

The wheelhouse, like those at Jarlshof, may well have been occupied almost till the 9th century and the coming of the Norsemen. At some stage, however, the level of the loch rose and a *causeway* was constructed from the site, now an island, to the shore. At the same time a *platform,* or *landing stage,* was erected in front of the outer entrance. This flooding episode is usually referred to the pre-broch period but, in the author's view, the evidence is as well if not better explained by supposing that the water rose in late wheel-house times. To this stage belongs the important stone slab carved with a pair of *footprints* which is now on the causeway, in what may be a 19th-century gateway. A single similar footprint can be seen on top of Dunadd, the Dark Age Scottish capital of Dalriada (p. 147), and others are known in Scotland. There is a widespread tradition that such footprints were used in the inauguration ceremonies for new kings, who symbolically placed their feet in the marks to show that they would follow faithfully in the footsteps of their predecessors. A clearer illustration of the importance of Clickhimin in pre-historic and Dark Age times could hardly be hoped for. It is probable, though quite improvable, that the stone was put on the causeway at a late stage when the site had ceased to be important. Its kingly significance would fit far better into the earlier age of the site, when the series of massive Iron Age forts or castles was being built.

While in Lerwick one should not fail to visit the new museum which contains some *Early Christian stones* including one from *Papil* showing a scene in relief with five priests with hooded capes approaching a cross. This may commemorate the arrival of a bishop and his retinue, perhaps in the 8th century, to bring Christianity to Shetland.

The north-west mainland

Travelling N from Lerwick take the A971 to Sandness to view several remote sites. About 8 km west of the head of Weisdale Voe the B9071 turns north to Aith where a minor road leaves it to run along the west side of Aith Voe to Vementry. It may be possible to get a boat there to cross the 200 m wide sound to the uninhabited island of *Vementry* and see the heel-shaped *chambered cairn* (Fig. 40) of that name: it stands on the hill of Muckle Ward at the north end of the island (HU/295611).

The structure consists of a passage grave surrounded by a heel-shaped platform. The circular cairn is about 7·9 m in diameter, with a trefoil-shaped central chamber reached by a passage coming in from the south-east. Around this cairn is the lower platform, the inner part of the 'heel' being formed by an impressive, slightly concave façade of boulders which runs continuously across in front of the cairn passage and conceals it. This façade is 11 m across and traces of dry walling are visible in places on top of the foundation blocks. Three lintels remain over the inner end of the cairn passage, the outer end of which is destroyed. The chamber is like a clover-leaf in plan, with three recesses, and measures some 2·7 m long with a maximum width of 3·2 m.

Vementry is a good, if simple, example of a Neolithic chambered grave with a sequence of construction which doubtless reflects a succession of social and ritual events. The central cairn must have been built first and the fact that the heel-shaped platform seals the entrance passage strongly implies that this was added at the end of the use of the tomb in order to block it up permanently. The heel-shaped façade seems to illustrate the adoption of a widespread style of horned cairn which must also surely reflect the arrival of some profound though so far unidentified religious belief.

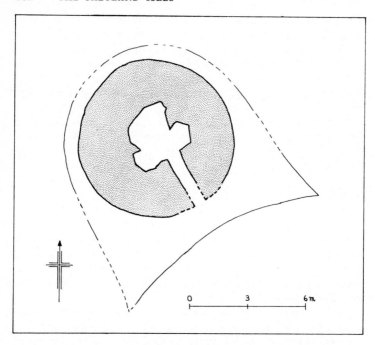

Fig. 40. Plan of the Vementry heel-shaped cairn, Shetland, showing the two successive phases of masonry. Scale 1:185.

At a point some 10 km after passing round the sharp turn at the head of Weisdale Voe take the B9071 S to Culswick, a detour of about 12 km. From the end of the road one must walk 2·4 km slightly S of due W, passing three lochs, to the *broch of Culswick*★ (HU/253448). The site can be seen from far off, as a mass of stone-work standing on a green hillock near the coastal cliffs. The walls of this unexcavated broch still stand up to 4·5 m in height and an upper mural gallery is visible. The outer end of the entrance is partly clear and the outermost lintel is a massive triangular stone, an effective device to divert the weight of the wall above on to the sides of the passage. The situation is wild and lonely.

Two kilometres before the end of this B road one can turn N again towards Bridge of Walls on the main road and visit the so-called 'Neolithic temple' at *Stanydale*★+ (HU/285503: signposted). Other-wise, if not visiting Culswick, turn S off the main road 1·2 km after the B road mentioned above. A walk of 0·5 km N from the road is required. The building is roughly oval or horseshoe-shaped with the east end squared off like the local heel-shaped Neolithic cairns (above) and containing the entrance. The wall is on average 3·8 m thick at the base and is characteristically faced with large, rough stone blocks. The best and flattest blocks have been chosen for the inner face where a few courses remain in places on top of them. The plan of the interior is effectively in two parts. The east part, inside the doorway, is approximately semicircular in plan with a maximum width of 6·5 m. The other, innermost part is larger, some 8·8 m wide and 7·9 m long. The total length of the chamber is 11·9 m. The wall of the west part is divided into six wide recesses which are formed by five short projecting masonry piers, some 1·2 m in length and each having at its inner end a massive boulder. In the beaten earth floor are two large stone-lined post-holes, on the east–west axis of the chamber and 2·1 m apart. These doubtless held the massive wooden uprights for the timber and thatch ridge roof which once spanned the interior. The excavator thought that the masonry of the projecting piers originally rose up 3 m or more and was corbelled laterally so that each bay was roofed with stone. This is possible but it is equally likely that the stone wall was never more than 2 m high and that the piers served as the foundations for the sloping roof beams which must have been attached to the ridge pole. The analogy with the courtyard houses at Jarlshof (p. 262) is close and the Stanydale structure seems likely to be an exceptionally large Neolithic house— a palace perhaps, or a temple. The heel-shaped east end suggests close links with the heel-shaped Neolithic cairns in Shetland (below) but the resemblances to the Neolithic stone temples in Malta are probably fortuitous. Had the local courtyard houses not existed the Maltese parallel might have been more acceptable.

The Stanydale 'temple' was excavated in 1949 and the finds included a beaker sherd, some local Late Neolithic pottery, fragments of Bronze Age urns and what appears to be a piece of the base of an Iron Age pot. A long period of use for the structure seems indicated. The other finds were all stone implements of various kinds, including a whetstone. The lump of plastic yellow clay found seems to confirm that the site was a domestic one at some stage.

There are several *standing stones* near by, forming a rough arc on the south from 12 m to 35 m from the building. They may be associated with the 'temple' and the whole complex could well originate at the time of the great astronomical activity at the beginning of the 2nd millennium B.C. and witnessed by the stone circles and standing stones.

Northmavine

Following the A970 from Lerwick one eventually crosses the narrow isthmus between Sullom Voe and St. Magnus Bay to enter the parish of Northmavine. At 3·2 km north of the isthmus a farmroad turns left to Mangaster. About 400 m along this strike off due W over the hill for 700 m to the *Pund water chambered cairn* (HU/324713). The heel-shaped cairn stands on a low knoll in a wild stretch of moorland among lochs and rocky outcrops. In this case there appears to be no round central cairn: the burial chamber is contained within the heel-shaped structure and the passage leads out to the centre of the façade which measures over 15 m across. It is edged with massive stone walling and boulders lie in front of it, and indeed in front of the edge of the cairn throughout its perimeter. Whether this is due to modern interference or prehistoric activity is not clear.

The trefoil-shaped central chamber is well preserved: the walls still stand 1·5 m high and it has the usual three recesses. The chamber was cleared out in 1930 but no artefacts were found.

If continuing NW to Esha Ness—where the coastal scenery is spectacular in places—one can visit the *broch* at *Loch of Houlland*★ (HU/213793). Take the B9078 just before reaching Hillswick for 6 km and then the side road to the N to its end. The Loch of Houlland is about 1 km south-west of this point and the broch, which is un-excavated, stands on a short promontory on the west shore. An outer wall bars the neck of the promontory with two lines of stones on edge in front of this. The broch mound still stands 4·6 m high and an upper mural gallery is apparent on the north side. The main entrance, on the west-south-west, appears to be still lintelled at its inner end and a tall, domed guard cell stands next to this.

Conversion Tables

1. *Kilometres to miles* (1 mile = 1·609 km)

km	miles	km	miles	km	miles	km	miles
0·1	0·06	1·0	0·62	10·0	6·21	20·0	12·43
0·2	0·12	2·0	1·24	11·0	6·84	30·0	18·64
0·3	0·18	3·0	1·86	12·0	7·46	40·0	24·85
0·4	0·25	4·0	2·49	13·0	8·08	50·0	31·07
0·5	0·3	5·0	3·11	14·0	8·7	60·0	37·28
0·6	0·37	6·0	3·73	15·0	9·32	70·0	43·5
0·7	0·42	7·0	4·35	16·0	9·94	80·0	49·71
0·8	0·5	8·0	4·97	17·0	10·56	90·0	55·92
0·9	0·56	9·0	5·59	18·0	11·18	100·0	62·14
				19·0	11·81		

2. *Metres to yards, feet and inches* (1 foot = 0·305 m)
   For all approximate measurements metres may be read as yards.

m	ft	in	m	ft	in	m	ft	in	m	ft	in
0·05	0	2	1·0	3	3½	10·0	32	10	20·0	65	7
0·1	0	4	2·0	6	7	11·0	36	1	30·0	98	5
0·2	0	8	3·0	9	10	12·0	39	4½	40·0	131	3
0·3	1	0	4·0	13	1½	13·0	42	8	50·0	164	2
0·4	1	4	5·0	16	5	14·0	45	11	60·0	196	6
0·5	1	7½	6·0	19	8	15·0	49	2½	70·0	229	7
0·6	1	11½	7·0	22	11½	16·0	52	6	80·0	262	6
0·7	2	3½	8·0	26	3	17·0	55	9	90·0	295	7
0·8	2	7½	9·0	29	6½	18·0	59	1	100·0	328	4
0·9	2	11½				19·0	62	4½			

3. *Megalithic yards and metres*
   (1 my = 2·72 ft   2 my = 5·44 ft   2½ my (1 megalithic rod) = 6·8 ft)

my	m	my	m	my	m	my	m
½	0·415	6	4·95	12	9·95	20	16·58
1	0·829	7	5·8	13	10·78	30	24·87
2	1·66	8	6·63	14	11·61	40	33·26
3	2·49	9	7·46	15	12·44	50	41·45
4	3·32	10	8·29	16	13·26	60	49·54
5	4·15	11	9·12	17	14·09	70	58·03
				18	14·92	80	66·32
				19	15·75	90	74·61
						100	82·9

Bibliography

This bibliography is in two parts, in each of which the works are listed alphabetically under authors' names. In the first part is a list of general works about the archaeology and early history of Scotland and in the second a list of books and sources of regional interest. The second part is divided into eight sections corresponding to the eight descriptive chapters of this book. Starred entries are booklets.

Part 1: **General**

Alexander, Michael, *The Earliest English Poems,* Penguin Books, Harmondsworth, 1966.

Allen, J. Romilly, *The Early Christian Monuments of Scotland,* Society of Antiquaries of Scotland, Edinburgh, 1903, 2 vols.

Charlesworth, M. P. (*et al.*), *The Heritage of Early Britain,* Bell, London, 1952.

Childe, V. G., *The Prehistory of Scotland,* Kegan Paul, London, 1935.
Scotland before the Scots, Methuen, London, 1946.

Clark, J. G. D., *World Prehistory,* Cambridge University Press, Cambridge, 1969.
Prehistoric Europe: the economic basis, Methuen, London, 1952.

Collingwood, R. G., *Roman Britain,* Clarendon Press, Oxford, 1932.

Collingwood, R. G., and Myres, J. N. L., *Roman Britain and the English Settlements,* 2nd edn., Clarendon Press, Oxford, 1937.

Collingwood, R. G., and Richmond, Ian, *The Archaeology of Roman Britain,* 2nd edn., Methuen, London, 1969.

Corcoran, J. X. W. P., *The Antiquities of the Scottish Countryside,* Methuen, London, 1975 (forthcoming).

Coulton, G. G., *Scottish Abbeys and Social Life,* Cambridge University Press, Cambridge, 1933.

*Cruden, Stewart, *The Early Christian and Pictish Monuments of Scotland*, HMSO, Edinburgh, 1964.

Scottish Abbeys, HMSO, Edinburgh, 1960.

De Paor, Maire and Liam, *Early Christian Ireland*, Thames & Hudson, London, 1968.

Dickinson, William Croft, *A New History of Scotland*, Nelson, London, 1963.

Dillon, Myles, and Chadwick, Nora, *The Celtic Realms*, Weidenfeld & Nicolson, London, 1967.

Feachem, Richard, *A Guide to Prehistoric Scotland*, Batsford, London, 1963.

'Mons Craupius = Duncrub?', *Antiquity*, xliv, 1970, pp. 120–4.

Henderson, Isabel, *The Picts*, Thames & Hudson, London, 1967.

Henshall, Audrey S., *The Chambered Tombs of Scotland*, Edinburgh University Press, Edinburgh, 1963 and 1969, 2 vols.

Lacaille, A. D., *The Stone Age in Scotland*, Oxford University Press for the Wellcome Historical Medical Museum, London, 1954.

MacGibbon, David, and Ross, Thomas, *The Castellated and Domestic Architecture of Scotland*, David Douglas, Edinburgh, 1887–92, 5 vols.

The Ecclesiastical Architecture of Scotland, David Douglas, Edinburgh, 1896–7, 3 vols.

MacKie, E. W., 'The Brochs of Scotland', *Recent Work in Rural Archaeology* (ed. P. J. Fowler), Adams & Dart, Bath, 1975.

'The Vitrified Forts of Scotland', *Hillforts* (ed. D. W. Harding), Seminar Press, London, 1975.

Mackie, J. D., *A History of Scotland*, Penguin Books, Harmondsworth, 1964.

Marsh, Henry, *Dark Age Britain: some sources of history*, David & Charles, Newton Abbot, 1970.

Menzies, Gordon (ed.), *Who are the Scots?*, BBC, London, 1971.

Ogilvie, R. M., and Richmond, Sir Ian (eds.), *'De Vita Agricolae' Cornelii Taciti*, Clarendon Press, Oxford, 1967.

*Ordnance Survey, *Place Names on Maps of Scotland and Wales*, Southampton, 1969.

Piggott, Stuart, *Ancient Europe*, Edinburgh University Press, Edinburgh, 1965.

(ed.), *The Prehistoric Peoples of Scotland*, Routledge & Kegan Paul, London, 1962.

and Henderson, Keith, *Scotland before History*, Nelson, London, 1958.

and Simpson, W. Douglas, *Illustrated Guide to Ancient Monuments: VI – Scotland*, HMSO, Edinburgh, 1970.

Ritchie, R. L. Graeme, *The Normans in Scotland*, Edinburgh University Press, Edinburgh, 1954.

Rivet, A. L. F. (ed.), *The Iron Age in Northern Britain*, Edinburgh University Press, Edinburgh, 1966.

Simpson, W. D., *The Ancient Stones of Scotland*, Hale, London, 1965.

The Historical St. Columba, 3rd edn., Oliver & Boyd, Edinburgh, 1965.

St. Ninian and the Origin of the Christian Church in Scotland, Oliver & Boyd, Edinburgh, 1940.

*Scottish Castles, HMSO, Edinburgh, 1959.

Thom, Alexander, *Megalithic Sites in Britain*, Oxford University Press, London, 1967.

Megalithic Lunar Observatories, Clarendon Press, Oxford, 1971.

Thomas, Charles, *Britain and Ireland in Early Christian Times: A.D. 400–800*, Thames & Hudson, London, 1971.

The Early Christian Archaeology of North Britain, Oxford University Press, London. 1971.

Wainwright, F. T. (ed.), *The Problem of the Picts*, Nelson, Edinburgh, 1955.

Archaeology and Place Names and History, Routledge & Kegan Paul, London, 1962.

Part 2: **Regional**

1. *South-west Scotland:*

*O'Neil, B. H. St. J., *Caerlaverock Castle*, HMSO, Edinburgh, 1952.

*Radford, C. A. R., and Donaldson, Gordon, *Whithorn and Kirkmadrine*, HMSO, Edinburgh, 1953.

*Richardson, James S., *Sweetheart Abbey . . . Kirkcudbright*, HMSO, Edinburgh, 1951.

Royal Commission on the Ancient and Historical Monuments of Scotland, *Fourth Report and Inventory of Monuments . . . in Galloway: I – Wigtown*, HMSO, Edinburgh, 1912.

Fourth Report and Inventory of Monuments . . . in Galloway: II – Kirkcudbright, HMSO, Edinburgh, 1914.

Seventh Report with Inventory of Monuments . . . in Dumfries, HMSO, Edinburgh, 1920.

Scott, Jack G., *South-West Scotland*, Heinemann, London 1966.
19

2. *South-east Scotland*:

Curle, James, *A Roman Frontier Post and its People* (Newstead), Maclehose, Glasgow, 1911, 2 vols.

*Richardson, James S., *The Abbey and Palace of Holyroodhouse*, HMSO, Edinburgh, 1950.

* *Dirleton Castle, East Lothian*, HMSO, Edinburgh, 1950.

* and Wood, Marguerite, *Dryburgh Abbey, Berwickshire*, HMSO, Edinburgh, 1948.

* *Melrose Abbey, Roxburghshire*, HMSO, Edinburgh, 1949.

Ritchie, Graham and Anna, *South-East Scotland*, Heinemann, London, 1972.

Royal Commission on the Ancient and Historical Monuments of Scotland, *First Report and Inventory of Monuments . . . in Berwick*, HMSO, Edinburgh, 1909.
An Inventory of Peebles-shire, HMSO, Edinburgh, 1967.
An Inventory of the Ancient Monuments . . . of Roxburghshire, HMSO, Edinburgh, 1956.
An Inventory of the Ancient Monuments . . . of Selkirkshire, HMSO, Edinburgh, 1957.
Eighth Report with Inventory of Monuments . . . in East Lothian, HMSO, Edinburgh, 1924.
Tenth Report with Inventory of Monuments . . . in Midlothian and West Lothian, HMSO, Edinburgh, 1929.

3. *Central Scotland*:

*Breeze, David J., *The Antonine Wall*, HMSO, Edinburgh, 1973.

*Cruden, Stewart, *St. Andrew's Cathedral*, HMSO, Edinburgh, 1950.

*Mackie, R. L., and Cruden, Stewart, *Arbroath Abbey*, HMSO, Edinburgh, 1954.

*Paterson, J. W., *Inchcolm Abbey*, HMSO, Edinburgh, 1950.

*Radford, C. A. R., *The Cluniac Abbey of Crossraguel*, HMSO, Edinburgh, 1970.

* *Glasgow Cathedral*, HMSO, Edinburgh, 1970.

*Robertson, Anne S., *The Antonine Wall*, Glasgow Archaeological Society, Glasgow, 1972.

Royal Commission on the Ancient and Historical Monuments of Scotland, *Eleventh Report with Inventory of Monuments . . . in Fife, Kinross and Clackmannan*, HMSO, Edinburgh, 1933.
Stirlingshire: An Inventory of the Ancient Monuments, HMSO, Edinburgh, 1963, 2 vols.

*Simpson, W. D., *Bothwell Castle, Lanarkshire*, HMSO, Edinburgh, 1958.

4. *Western Scotland:*
Beveridge, Erskine, *Coll and Tiree: their prehistoric forts and ecclesiastical antiquities*, privately published, Edinburgh, 1903.
  North Uist: its archaeology and topography, privately published, Edinburgh, 1911.
Balfour, J. A., *The Book of Arran: vol. 1 Archaeology*, Arran Society of Glasgow, Glasgow, 1910.
Lamont, W. D., *Ancient and Medieval Sculptured Stones of Islay*, Oliver & Boyd, Edinburgh, 1968.
MacKie, Euan W., *Dun Mor Vaul: an Iron Age broch on Tiree*, University of Glasgow Press, Glasgow, 1974.
Reece, Richard, *Iona*, Iona Community Publishing Dept., Glasgow, n.d.
Royal Commission on the Ancient and Historical Monuments of Scotland, *Argyll: An Inventory of the Ancient Monuments: I – Kintyre*, HMSO, Edinburgh, 1971.
  Ninth Report with Inventory of Monuments . . . in the Outer Hebrides, Skye and the Small Isles, HMSO, Edinburgh, 1928.

5. *North-east Scotland:*
Coutts, Herbert, *Ancient Monuments of Tayside*, Dundee Museum and Art Gallery, Dundee, 1970.
*Root, Margaret E., *Dunkeld Cathedral, Perthshire*, HMSO, Edinburgh, 1965.
*Simpson, W. D., *Huntly Castle*, HMSO, Edinburgh, 1954.
*   *Kildrummy and Glenbuchat Castles*, HMSO, Edinburgh, 1968.
*   *Restenneth and Aberlemno*, HMSO, Edinburgh, 1969.
*   *Urquhart Castle*, HMSO, Edinburgh, 1964.
Wainright, F. T., *The Souterrains of Southern Pictland*, Routledge & Kegan Paul, London, 1963.

6. *Northern Scotland:*
Laing, Samuel, *Prehistoric Remains of Caithness*, Williams & Norgate, London and Edinburgh, 1866.
Royal Commission on the Ancient and Historical Monuments of Scotland, *Second Report and Inventory of Monuments . . . in Sutherland*, HMSO, Edinburgh, 1911.
  Third Report and Inventory of Monuments . . . in Caithness, HMSO, Edinburgh, 1911.

7. *The Orkney Isles:*

*Childe, V. G., *Ancient Dwellings at Skara Brae*, HMSO, Edinburgh, 1950.

Cruden, Stewart, 'Excavations at Birsay, Orkney', *The Fourth Viking Congress* (ed. Alan Small), Oliver & Boyd, Edinburgh, 1965.

*Marwick, Hugh, *Ancient Monuments in Orkney*, HMSO, Edinburgh, 1952.

*Radford, C. A. R., *The Early Christian and Norse Settlements at Birsay, Orkney*, HMSO, Edinburgh, 1959.

Royal Commission on the Ancient and Historical Monuments of Scotland, *Twelfth Report with Inventory of the Ancient Monuments of Orkney and Shetland*, HMSO, Edinburgh, 1946, 3 vols.

*Simpson, W. D., *The Bishop's Palace and the Earl's Palace, Kirkwall, Orkney*, HMSO, Edinburgh, 1965.

8. *The Shetland Isles:*

*Cruden, Stewart, *The Brochs of Mousa and Clickhimin, Shetland*, HMSO, Edinburgh, 1951.

Hamilton, J. R. C., *Excavations at Jarlshof, Shetland*, HMSO, Edinburgh, 1956.

Excavations at Clickhimin, Shetland, HMSO, Edinburgh, 1968.

*   *Jarlshof, Shetland*, HMSO, Edinburgh, 1953.

O'Dell, Andrew C., 'St. Ninian's Isle Treasure', *Aberdeen University Studies*, 141, Oliver & Boyd, Edinburgh, 1960.

Royal Commission on the Ancient and Historical Monuments of Scotland, *Twelfth Report with Inventory of the Ancient Monuments of Orkney and Shetland*, HMSO, Edinburgh, 1946, 3 vols.

Small, A., Thomas, C. and Wilson, D.M. *St. Ninian's Isle and its treasure*. 2 vols. Oxford University Press 1973.

Wainright, F. T. (ed.), *The Northern Isles*, Nelson, London, 1962.

Glossary

aisle internal subdivision of a church formed by an arcade separating it from the main part of the nave or chancel.

ambulatory a place for walking in; an arcade, covered way or cloister.

Angles people originating in north Germany who settled in north-east England and south-east Scotland from the 6th century A.D. onwards.

apse a semicircular polygonal roofed recess at the end of the choir, aisles or nave of a church.

ashlar masonry with rubble core faced with dressed stone blocks.

aumbry small cupboard or recess in a wall.

azimuth horizontal direction, or bearing, in degrees in relation to 0° at true north.

bailey open space or court within a castle enclosure.

barmkin defensive enclosure, usually attached to a tower house.

bastion a projecting angle in a wall to allow missiles to be directed along the wallface.

batter inward slope on the face of a wall or bank.

beaker characteristic reddish pottery made by intrusive people— perhaps the first Indo-Europeans—who came to Britain at the beginning of the Bronze Age, c. 2200 B.C.

ballista long-range, stone-throwing catapult used by the Roman army.

berm area of level ground between a bank and a ditch.

Britons the original P-Celtic-speaking inhabitants of Iron Age Britain; the Welsh are among their modern descendants.

broch cylindrical drystone tower-fort built with a hollow, galleried wall and dating to the Middle Iron Age (Fig. 38).

Bronze Age period during which bronze was the only or primary metal used for tools and weapons; in Britain it lasted from about 2200–500 B.C.

bronze a metal, an alloy of 90 per cent copper and 10 per cent tin.

buttress extra thickness of masonry against a wall designed to resist outward thrust.

cairn an artificial mound of stones.

calefactory the warming house in a monastery.

camp in archaeology now used only for temporary defensive earthworks built by the Roman army, designed for the protection of a legion on the march for one night.

canon a clergyman living celibate with others in a monastery and ordering his life according to church rules. This *canonica vita*, or canons' life, began in the 6th century and was reformed in the 11th by adoption of the rule of no private property, a practice mentioned by St. Augustine. Those following this strict rule were the *canons regular* or *Austin* (Augustinian) *canons*; the rest were secular canons. From the Augustinians were derived the even stricter *Premonstratensian canons*, following the example of Norbert of Premontré. From the colour of their habit they were sometimes known as the black canons; the Augustinians were the white canons for the same reason.

catapulta a long range, arrow-shooting engine used by the Roman army.

cell usually a small room within the thickness of a wall and without windows.

Celts Iron Age tribes inhabitating the zone east, north and west of the Alps from the 7th century B.C. onwards. Also used to describe people speaking a Celtic dialect.

chancel the part of the church east of the nave and crossing, reserved for those performing the services and usually screened off.

check see **door-check**.

Chi-Rho symbol formed by combining the Greek letters Chi and Rho—the first two letters of Christ.

choir (or **quire**) part of the church in which the choir sits, usually east of the nave and crossing.

cinerary urn type of vessel used in the Middle Bronze Age as a receptacle for the cremated bones of the dead; usually found upside down in unmarked graves.

circles, stone type of ceremonial site, related to *henges*, formed of standing stones set in a ring; mostly dated to the Late Neolithic and Early Bronze Age, *c.* 2200–1600 B.C. For types of circles see under **egg-shape, ellipse** and **flattened circle.**

cist a grave, either a box made of stone slabs or a pit cut in the ground. Short cists, for crouched burials, were in use in the Early Bronze Age; long cists, for extended burials, mainly in the Iron and Dark Ages.

clerestorey (pron. 'clear storey') the highest part of the wall of a church, above the aisle roof.

cloister open square space in the centre of a monastery where the monks walked and read.

corbel a block of stone (or timber) projecting from a wall to support a higher feature.

courtyard house a type of Iron Age settlement in Cornwall in which a number of stone cells, forming a continuous building, are grouped around an open central space, or courtyard.

crossing the part of the church where transepts, nave and choir meet, formed by four massive pillars which support the tower above.

Culdees monks and priests of the old Celtic church.

cup- and ring-markings carvings on rock done in the Early Bronze Age with the pecking technique and usually consisting of a central cup surrounded by one or more concentric rings.

Dalriada the first kingdom of the Irish Scots settlers in Argyll, formed in the 5th century A.D.

Dark Age the period between the collapse of Roman Britain in the mid 5th century and the start of the Middle Ages in the 11th century.

declination (δ) the astronomical latitude of a point in the sky. The sky is imagined as a sphere, seen from the inside, spinning on the same axis as the Earth's. Declinations are visualised as parallel circles on this sphere equivalent to terrestrial latitudes projected outwards from the Earth's centre and thus defined by their angular distances above ($+$) and below ($-$) the equatorial plane. The celestial equator is at $\delta 0°$, the north celestial pole at $\delta + 90°$ and so on.

door-check projection from the wall of an entrance passage against which the door shut.

dorter the monks' dormitory in a monastery.

dun small Iron Age drystone fortlet or castle lacking the special high, hollow, galleried wall of the brochs.

Early English the first phase of the Gothic or pointed-arched architectural period (followed by the Decorated and the Perpendicular) and dated to the 13th century.

egg-shaped stone circle According to Thom there are two geometrical constructions which give egg-shapes. In Type I the lower half is a semicircle and the upper half consists of two arcs of larger circles which are joined at the tip by an arc of a much smaller one (see Fig. 9). The three centre points from which the subsidiary arcs are drawn define two opposed Pythagorean triangles the bases of which are on the diameter of the semi-circle.

In the Type II egg-shape the two triangles have a common hypotenuse and the main part of the figure is about two-thirds of a true circle, with its centre at one end of the hypotenuse. The tip of the egg is part of a smaller circle with its centre at the other end, and the two arcs are joined by straight lines.

ellipse the geometrical figure—seen in some stone circles and in two brochs—which is drawn round two fixed centre points, or foci, so that the sum of the distances between each of these foci and any single point on the circumference is always the same. On the ground an ellipse would be drawn with a loop of cord round two pegs.

enceinte an enclosure.

fibula a bow-shaped safety pin or brooch, usually of bronze and of Iron Age or Roman date.

flake a fragment of flint or stone struck from a nodule with a directed blow.

food vessel a type of Early Bronze Age decorated pottery often found in the short cist graves of the time.

forecourt partly or wholly enclosed unroofed space immediately in front of entrance to a building.

fort normally applied to a defended post garrisoned by a professional army but also in archaeology to the strongholds of the Iron Age and later tribes.

frater the dining-room of a monastery.

flattened circle a geometrical figure which was, according to Thom, used in the laying out of a number of stone circles. There are two types: in Type A about two-thirds of the ring is a circle while the flattened part is an arc of a much larger circle the centre point of which is on the opposite part of the circumference of the first circle. Arcs of smaller circles form the 'corners'.

In Type B only half the ring is formed from the main circle and the flattened part and larger 'corners' are formed as before.

Gallo-Brittonic the hypothetical P-Celtic language which was the common ancestor of the Gaulish and British languages.

garderobe a Medieval latrine.

Gaul Celtic France: the same word as 'Gael'.

glacial of an Ice Age.

Gothic the pointed-arched architectural style which succeeded the Romanesque in the late 12th century in Britain.

grooved ware a pottery style ornamented with grooved lines found mainly in Late Neolithic contexts, c. 2200–1800 B.C.

ground-galleried broch type of broch in which the hollow, galleried wall is built directly on the ground: probably the earlier, more primitive form.

henge a circular, probably ceremonial enclosure of Middle or Late Neolithic date defined by a bank with an internal ditch. Class I henges have one entrance and Class II have two opposed entrances.

hillfort defended hilltop settlement, usually of Iron Age date.

Iron Age the period from when iron came into common use—in about the 6th and 5th centuries B.C. in Britain—until the Roman invasions (later in highland Scotland).

Indo-European the hypothetical prehistoric language ancestral to most modern European languages and also to Sanskrit in India. It has been suggested that the original homeland of the Indo-European peoples—before their dispersal—was in south Russia in the 3rd millennium B.C.

jamb the side of a door or window.

lancet a slender window with a pointed-arched head.

la Tène Iron Age lakeside site on Lake Neuchatel, Switzerland, which gave its name to the European Iron Age culture from c. 450–100 B.C. which was noted for its fine, decorated metalwork and its rich chariot burials.

lilia plural of Latin *lilium*, a defensive pit containing a sharp, upright stake.

lug a solid handle, usually on a pot.

Medieval as applied to buildings in Britain the term usually means belonging to the period between the Norman conquest and the end of the 15th century.

megalithic made from massive, usually undressed stones. Sometimes wrongly used instead of Neolithic.

megalithic yard (abbreviated to my) a unit of length equivalent to 2·72 ft or 0·829 m—inferred mathematically to have been used in the setting out of stone circles in the Early Bronze Age.

Mesolithic Middle Stone Age, the period between the end of the last Ice Age in the 9th millennium b.c. and the arrival of the first Neolithic farmers. Mesolithic peoples lived entirely by hunting and gathering.

microlith very small implement of flint or chert; microliths are often thought to have been used as weapon barbs.

moat ditch dug round a fort or castle and filled with water.

motte the earthen mound of a Norman timber castle.

mould negative impression of an object, usually in fired clay in ancient times, designed to make a new metal casting of that object.

multivallate having three or more lines of defence.

nave the part of the church west of the chancel in which sits the congregation.

Neolithic New Stone Age; the period, between about 4200 and 2200 B.C. in Britain, when farming was practised but metal was unknown.

ogham a system of writing, developed in Ireland and brought to Scotland by the Scots probably in the 5th century A.D. (Fig. 26). The letters are indicated by vertical and diagonal strokes on a straight line.

oppidum the Latin word for 'town', applied to exceptionally large Iron Age hillforts which may reasonably be regarded as permanently inhabited small towns, albeit without stone buildings.

oratory a small chapel or shrine.

orthostat a large standing stone incorporated in a structure.

P-Celtic one of two branches of the Celtic languages in which 'p' is used instead of 'q'; modern Welsh, Breton and Cornish are P-Celtic languages as were the tongues of the Iron Age Britons and Gauls.

passage grave type of Early Neolithic round cairn in which a circular, vaulted chamber is at the centre and linked to the outside by a straight entrance passage. Passage graves are widely distributed in Atlantic Europe and the earliest seem to be in Brittany.

peel a fortification, originally timber, the word being derived from the Latin *palus*, a stake.

pend a covered passage (Scots).

peristalith a kerb of upright stones around a prehistoric cairn.

Picts the Dark Age inhabitants of north-east Scotland, north of the river Forth and of Argyll.

piscina a basin in which the Eucharistic vessels are washed, usually set in a niche or recess south of the altar and provided with a drain through the wall.

plinth the projecting base of a column or wall.

pommel the knob terminal of a sword or dagger hilt.

presbytery the part of the church reserved for the clergy; the east part of the chancel beyond the choir.

putlog holes sockets left in the face of a wall for scaffolding.

Q-Celtic the second, and probably more archaic, of the two major divisions of the Celtic languages and in which the 'q' has been retained. Compare *Ap* (son of) in the P-Celtic Welsh with the equivalent word *Mac* (originally Maq) in the Q-Celtic Scottish Gaelic.

ravelin an outwork of a fort beyond the main ditch, consisting of two faces forming a salient angle.

rebate recess to receive a door-frame or to act as a stop.

reredorter the latrine block of a monastery.

Romanesque the round-arched architectural style brought to Britain by the Normans and directly descended from Roman buildings.

rood the cross as a symbol of Christian faith.

rotary quern hand-mill composed of a circular upper stone with a central hole rotating on a lower stone.

runes the first written script developed in the Scandinavian countries, probably based on the Roman alphabet, and used by the Vikings.

saddle quern hand-mill for grinding grain in which a rubbing stone is pushed back and forth on a dish-shaped lower stone.

scarcement a narrow ledge formed where a wall is set back.

scarp the inner slope of a ditch of a fortified place.

Scots the Q-Celtic speaking inhabitants of north-east Ireland who settled in Argyll from the 5th century A.D. onwards.

semibroch a form of small drystone Iron Age fort in which the high hollow wall of the brochs is used but which are open-sided in plan and built next to a natural cliff or precipice.

soffit the under surface of a lintel, arch or vault or the horizontal under face of an architrave or overhanging cornice.

solid-based broch the more evolved form of broch in which the hollow, galleried wall is built on a ring of solid masonry containing only the entrance passage and usually one or more mural cells.

souterrain an underground, drystone structure usually consisting of a passage leading to a lintelled, not corbelled, chamber.

transept the parts of a church east and west of the crossing and usually projecting from the line of the nave and chancel outwards.

Transitional name given to the architectural style in which the round-arched Romanesque gave way to the pointed-arched Gothic, early in the 13th century in Britain.

traverse a short fortification in front of an entrance through the main defences of a fort and protecting it from a frontal attack.

triforium the arcaded corridor in a church wall, on top of the main pillars of the nave and below the clerestorey; it corresponds to the vertical distance occupied by the aisle roof.

undercroft a vaulted under-building or cellar.

univallate having a single line of defences.

vallum (Latin) a fortification consisting of a palisade mounted on a rampart (*vallus*, a stake).

vault a self-supporting arched stone roof.

vitrified fort a fort with a drystone wall which originally had a timber framework within the rubble core of the wall; the burning of this framework generated great heat and fused part of the rubble core.

wheelhouse circular Iron Age drystone dwelling in which the internal roof-supporting posts have been replaced by radial stone piers.

Index

Geographical localities are not included in this index. Page numbers in italics refer to the descriptions of sites or to actual examples of objects mentioned.